The Penguin

HISTORICAL ATLAS of ANCIENT CIVILIZATIONS

John Haywood

PENGUIN BOOKS

Published by the Penguin Group

Penguin Books Ltd, 80 Strand, London WC2R 0RL, England

Penguin Group (USA) Inc., 375 Hudson Street, New York, New York 10014, USA

Penguin Group (Canada), 90 Eglinton Avenue East, Suite 700, Toronto, Ontario, Canada M4P 2Y3
  (a division of Pearson Penguin Canada Inc.)

Penguin Ireland, 25 St Stephen's Green, Dublin 2, Ireland
  (a division of Penguin Books Ltd)

Penguin Group (Australia), 707 Collins Street, Melbourne, Victoria 3008, Australia
  (a division of Pearson Australia Group Pty Ltd)

Penguin Books India Pvt Ltd, 11 Community Centre,
Panchsheel Park, New Delhi – 110 017, India

Penguin Group (NZ), 67 Apollo Drive, Rosedale, Auckland 0632, New Zealand
  (a division of Pearson New Zealand Ltd)

Penguin Books (South Africa) (Pty) Ltd, Block D, Rosebank Office Park, 181 Jan Smuts Avenue,
Parktown North, Gauteng 2193, South Africa

Penguin Books Ltd, Registered Offices: 80 Strand, London WC2R 0RL, England

www.penguin.com

First published 2005
11

Copyright © Penguin Books, 2005
All rights reserved

Made and printed in Italy by Printer Trento Srl

ISBN 978-0-141-01448-7

Produced for Penguin Books by Haywood & Hall

Preface

It is simply stating the obvious to say that the history of the world's ancient civilizations is fundamental to everything that has followed. No ancient civilizations: no modern civilizations. There is no better reason to study ancient history.

This atlas maps the world's early civilizations chronologically, region by region. The accompanying text discusses issues such as the definition of 'civilization' and the factors that led to the development of the early civilizations, and provides a clear and concise narrative, covering something like 10,000 years of human history.

In every region, the appearance of the first farming societies is taken to mark the first step on the road to the development of urban civilization. Deciding what historical development should mark the end of each chapter has been a little more difficult. In the case of the Near East, North Africa and Europe, the end of ancient history is fairly clearly defined by the rise and spread of the enormously influential Classical civilization of Greece between 500 and 300 BC. For the rest of Asia, a date around 200 BC is taken to allow the unification of China by Qin Shi Huangdi and the near-unification of India by the Mauryan dynasty to be included. Although it has meant going far beyond the end of what most people might regard as 'ancient times', all the pre-Columbian civilizations of the Americas up to the point of European contact around AD 1500 are covered, as any earlier date would have been completely arbitrary. There is also a brief treatment of sub-Saharan Africa and the Pacific up to this time.

The production of an illustrated book such as this is necessarily a team effort involving, as well as the author, editors, designers, picture researchers and cartographers. So, I would like to take this opportunity to thank Fiona Plowman, Simon Hall, Darren Bennett, Veneta Bullen and Tim Aspden for their very considerable contributions to the book.

John Haywood
2005

Contents

What is Civilization?

"The distinctive achievements of civilizations that differentiate them from barbarism are the invention of writing and the elaboration of exact sciences."

Gordon Childe,
What Happened in History (1942)

The world's first civilization – the Sumerian – developed in Mesopotamia, on the flood plain of the Tigris and Euphrates rivers in Iraq, some 5500 years ago. Within a few hundred years the Sumerian civilization had been joined by others in Egypt and the Indus valley. Later still, civilizations began to develop in Europe, the Far East and the Americas. Historians and archaeologists are agreed that the emergence of the first civilizations is one of the most important events in human history but what do we really mean by 'civilization'? The word itself is derived from *civitas*, the Latin for 'city', and through much of history it has been city life that the 'civilized' have seen as what separated them more than anything else from the 'barbarians'.

Definitions of Civilization

As used in everyday conversation, the word civilization implies 'civility' and 'civilized' values. Many of us, if asked to define civilization, would stress the moral qualities shown by a society, a compassionate attitude towards the sick and elderly, for example, or respect for human rights. Such an approach might seem to be no more than common sense, but such definitions are often nothing more than ethnocentric value judgements. What is considered civilized behaviour in one culture may be judged barbaric and anti-social in another. The limitations of value-based definitions of civilization are seen at their starkest in times of war: 'We' are the defenders of civilisation, 'They', the enemy, are barbarians who will inflict a new dark age on the world. Less obvious, but more insidious, is the way that value-based assumptions of cultural superiority affect the judgement of observers. In the 19th century Europeans regarded Africa as a 'Dark Continent' inhabited by savage tribes. Christian missionaries had no doubts that they were spreading civilization as well as the Gospel. In fact pre-colonial Africa was home to many indigenous civilizations which Europeans simply failed to recognize because they were alien to their preconceptions. In reaction to this, some historians, influenced by a concern for political correctness, have begun describing all human societies as civilizations. This is undoubtedly an effective way for formerly colonized peoples to escape pejorative definitions forced on them by outsiders, but it also turns 'civilization' into a synonym for 'culture' and does nothing to help us make objective assessments of the qualitative differences between societies. All human societies have culture – technology, customs, beliefs and so on – but is that all it takes to make a civilization?

Classifying Societies

In order to avoid value judgements, most archaeologists and ancient historians classify societies in terms of the scale and complexity of their social organization. Perhaps the most widely accepted system is a four-fold classification which divides societies into bands, segmentary societies or tribes, chiefdoms and states or civilizations. The band is the typical form of society among hunter-gatherers. Bands are small-scale societies numbering, usually, fewer than 100 people. Most members of a band are related to one another by birth or marriage. Bands do not have formal leadership and there are few disparities of wealth or status between members. Because most hunter-gatherers are seasonally migratory they do not build to last and use only simple and easily portable technologies.

Segmentary societies are larger than bands, numbering up to a few thousand people. Although in a few areas with especially rich wild resources hunter-gatherers have formed this type of society, tribes are usually associated with settled farming peoples. In segmentary societies peoples are usually divided into several communities (hence the name), which are all integrated into the greater

This ivory plaque of a woman's head was found at the Assyrian palace in Nimrud. It is thought to represent the goddess Ishtar. The Assyrian empire was founded around 1800 BC in northern Mesopotamia.

society by kinship ties. People build permanent structures for both practical and ceremonial use and they may live in either dispersed farmsteads or nucleated villages. Segmentary societies have more formal leadership than bands, but leaders usually lack real coercive power. This type of society still survives in the New Guinea Highlands. Segmentary societies are sometimes described as 'tribes', but confusingly this word is also used to describe ethnic groups: segmentary societies can form tribes in this sense, but do not always do so.

Chiefdoms are ranked societies in which there are marked differences of status between individuals. Different lineages or clans (groups claiming descent from a common ancestor) are graded on a scale of prestige. The whole society is governed by a chief, who is the senior member of the senior lineage. Prestige and status depend on how closely an individual is related to the chief. Social ranking is often visible in burial customs, with higher status individuals being buried with precious grave offerings, perhaps with a grave marker, like a tumulus. Chiefs control food surpluses and other commodities and use them to support retainers, such as a warrior class, and specialist craftsmen. Chiefs can also command the labour of the whole society to conduct major building projects, such as ceremonial centres or defences. Chiefdoms have power centres, such as the hillforts of Celtic Europe, with residences for the chief, his retainers and craftsmen. Chiefdoms can vary considerably in size but are generally reckoned to have populations between 5000 and 20,000. The dividing line between a large and powerful chiefdom and the next type of society, the state, is often not a very clear one. Chiefdoms are generally the type of society that ancient authors characteristically described as 'barbarian'.

This Babylonian stone tablet contains a cuneiform inscription (top) and an ancient map of the world. The map relates to a mythological, rather than a geographical, view of the world. The Babylonians had advanced systems of writing, science and mathematics. Most of what we know about ancient Babylonia is from their cuneiform writing.

States are the most complex form of social organization, with considerable specialization of roles and settlement in cities. States are larger societies than chiefdoms and status is no longer defined primarily by lineage. Society has become stratified into different classes, with agricultural workers (by far the largest class in all pre-industrial societies) at the bottom, followed by craftsmen, merchants and an upper class made up of relatives of the ruler. Rulers have true coercive power through the use of a standing army, but this is usually justified by a political or religious ideology and by law-making to regulate society. Subjects have the duty of paying taxes which the ruler uses to support armies, craftsmen and the administrators who are essential to regulate the system. This definition of a state is to all intents and purposes synonymous with civilization.

The Characteristics of Civilization

The British prehistorian Gordon Childe proposed ten characteristics by which a civilization can be recognized. These have been refined by the American archaeologist Charles Redman, who has divided them into primary and secondary characteristics:

Primary characteristics	Secondary characteristics
1. settlement in cities	6. monumental public works
2. full-time specialization of labour	7. long-distance trade
3. concentration of surplus production	8. standardized monumental artwork
4. class structure	9. writing
5. state organization (government)	10. arithmetic, geometry and astronomy

The primary characteristics are all aspects of social organization. The secondary characteristics are aspects of material culture which can be recognized from archaeological remains and which are evidence of the existence of some, or all, of the primary characteristics. Monumental public works and standardized monumental artwork are evidence of a strong central government and state organization. The characteristics of any society can be compared objectively to this list, which is free of value judgements. We would not expect bands or segmentary societies to display more than a couple of these characteristics; a chiefdom might display around half of them, but a civilization should display all, or at least most, of those characteristics. We would then be justified in describing a society as a civilization, no matter how unpleasant we may find its values.

Many theories have been advanced to try to explain the emergence of civilization, some of which can readily be dismissed. Civilization did not arise because of any mental or physical evolutionary changes in humans themselves.

Physically modern humans evolved between 120,000 and 100,000 years ago and such changes as have occurred since are superficial adaptations to climate or are the result of changes in nutrition and lifestyle – and are potentially reversible. Early farming peoples around the world were always much shorter and less robust than their hunter-gatherer forebears. This was the result of arrested growth during childhood, resulting from malnutrition during periodic harvest failures. Improved diet in modern industrialized countries reversed this shrinking tendency, and in the 20th century each generation was taller than the last.

Mentally fully modern humans probably evolved between 50,000 and 40,000 years ago, when art, body ornaments and other material evidence of symbolic thought begin to appear in the archaeological record. The immense scientific and technological accomplishments of the present day are not, however, evidence that human mental capacities have gone on evolving. Present day hunter-gatherers or people who live in surviving stone-age farming societies, for example in the New Guinea Highlands, are not less intelligent than people who live in industrialized, high technology societies. In fact, there is some evidence that the reverse may be true: modern industrialized societies promote the development of narrowly specialized skills above general intelligence.

Excavations of Jericho, identified as Tell es-Sultan in Palestine, revealed the remains of this round tower which dates to 8000 BC. Jericho is one of the oldest known settlements in the world, dating back more than 10,000 years. Although Jericho is often mentioned in the Bible, archaeological evidence does not support the biblical chronology of events.

Perhaps surprisingly, technological innovation does not seem to have been a critical factor in the emergence of civilization. Most of the technology on which the Old World civilizations depended had been developed hundreds, or even thousands, of years earlier. Even advanced techniques, such as the lost-wax method of bronze-casting, iron-working and shipbuilding, were not the exclusive preserve of civilized societies. The civilization of ancient Egypt illustrates this point very clearly. The pyramids of the Old Kingdom Period (2649–2150 BC) were built without knowledge of pulleys or the wheel, using stone tools and soft copper chisels. Egypt's was essentially a stone-age civilization, dependent on technology that was no more advanced than that used by the contemporary small-scale farming societies of northwest Europe. Most of the early civilizations of the Americas were based on simpler technology still, as they lacked metal tools of any kind.

The Transition to Farming

The critical factor in the emergence of the first civilizations was the transition from hunting and gathering to the farming way of life, which allowed population increases and the accumulation of surpluses ('wealth'). The numbers of hunter-gatherers are limited by the productive capacity of the natural environment, and they need large territories to support them. Except in very rich environments, the Pacific coast of North America for example, settled life is impossible. As a rule, hunter-gatherer populations are dispersed and of low density. Estimates suggest that the maximum global population that could be supported by hunting and gathering might be less than ten million. Farming began to free humans from the constraints imposed by the natural environment, allowing populations to grow. As there is a direct relationship between yields and the amount of labour put in, rising populations were generally a good thing as they led to increased productivity. New lands could be brought into cultivation, allowing yet more population growth. Farming permitted permanent settlement and stimulated the advent of new technologies, such as pottery, polished stone tools, ploughs and breakthroughs like the wheel and metalworking. Farming also set in train social changes leading to the emergence of hierarchical forms of society.

One of the disadvantages of farming was that crop failures were inevitable: in most parts of the world this would happen on average every five to eight years. Fortunately, in most years farmers could grow more than they needed to feed themselves and their families. This surplus food, the first form of wealth, could be stored (most hunter-gatherers could not store food because they were migratory) and used in bad years or exchanged for other commodities or services. Surpluses could also be used to gain power over others. A loan of food in a bad year might have to be paid back with interest: failure to pay back a loan might result in a poor farmer becoming a dependent or even a slave of the lender. In this way divisions of wealth and poverty, and of status, emerged in farming societies. However, farming did not of itself make civilization inevitable.

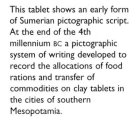

This tablet shows an early form of Sumerian pictographic script. At the end of the 4th millennium BC a pictographic system of writing developed to record the allocations of food rations and transfer of commodities on clay tablets in the cities of southern Mesopotamia.

The Role of Domestication

Farming was only able to develop in areas where there were plants and animals suitable for domestication, the process of selective breeding by which wild animals and plants are made more useful to humans, including cereals or root crops. It is no coincidence that farming first developed in the Middle East, because this region had the widest range of plants and animals suitable for domestication. The relatively late development of civilizations in the New World can be explained mainly in terms of the difficulty of domesticating teosinte, the wild predecessor of maize. Cereals make ideal staples as they can easily be stored for very long periods. In some areas, like the Arctic, farming was never going to develop because the climate is too hostile. In other areas, where the climate was favourable but potential domesticates were rare or absent, such as northern Europe, North America or Australia, farming could begin only when suitable crops and livestock were introduced from outside. In Australia this did not happen until the arrival of Europeans at the end of the 18th century.

The simple methods used by early farmers were not productive enough to support the large numbers of non-agricultural workers associated with civilizations: this required the intensification of farming. The development of the plough and irrigation were two of the most important ways by which intensification was achieved, but there were other ways. Introducing new crops which could be grown on land that was previously unsuited to agriculture was one. In the Mediterranean, for example, growing olives and vines on rough hillsides that were unsuitable for cultivating cereals increased productivity. The productivity of animals could be intensified by selective breeding. Sheep were first domesticated for their meat but were later bred to give better milk yields and fleeces.

In some areas, intensification was not possible because of environmental constraints. Many rainforest soils are too quickly exhausted for intensive agriculture to be sustainable. In semi-arid areas over-cultivation or over-grazing by domestic animals can lead to soil erosion and desertification, with similarly fatal consequences for intensive agriculture. Where intensive agriculture is not possible, civilizations cannot arise.

The Lion Gate was one of the monumental stone gates leading into the city of Hattusas, the capital of the Hittite empire. The Hittites ruled most of Anatolia between 1650 and 1200 BC. The image of a lion, intended to ward off evil spirits, was a recurring theme in Hittite and Mesopotamian architecture.

If intensive agriculture is a key prerequisite for the development of civilizations, it is probably not the only factor. Historians noted long ago that the earliest civilizations of the Old World – in Mesopotamia, Egypt and the Indus valley – all developed on the flood plains of great rivers. Although the soils in these areas were extremely fertile alluvium, there was so little rainfall that farming was possible only with the aid of irrigation. This gave rise to the 'hydraulic theory' of the emergence of civilization. Large-scale irrigation required not just plentiful labour but also advanced organizational skills to build, maintain and regulate it. These could only be supplied by a central body which acquired power by its control of the water supply and used this to establish its authority over other aspects of life. Irrigation made possible huge increases in agricultural productivity that enabled the central authority to support large numbers of specialist craft workers and the administrators needed to supervise the collection and redistribution of food surpluses.

Population Growth

Some theories emphasise the population growth that farming made possible as the major factor in the emergence of civilizations. As populations grew, the kinship links which formed the basis of social bonds in segmentary societies and chiefdoms became too attenuated to hold large communities together, so forcing the development of more complex social structures. In areas of dense population, where it was not possible for communities to expand, they would be forced to compete with one another for resources. In these circumstances communities would tend to get larger, to be able to defend themselves against attack or improve their chances of success when attacking others. In this way segmentary societies would amalgamate into chiefdoms and chiefdoms would amalgamate into states. Good leadership is essential for success in war. Leaders who enjoyed success in battle would have gained prestige that perhaps gave them wider authority, and so established themselves as a ruling class. At the same time, conquered populations might have been absorbed by the victors as a lower class. In this way the hierarchical class structure associated with states and civilizations would emerge. Even where it had originated in response to external aggression, once a military class was established it had the means to maintain its authority within its own community, by force if need be.

Marxist historians see class conflict as a major agent of historical change. As the distinctions of wealth and poverty that had first developed in early farming societies gradually became wider, the rich sought to institutionalize their dominant social position, using coercion if necessary, in order to deny the poorer classes equal access to resources. Therefore, in Marxist theory, the civilized state was developed by the wealthy ruling class to maintain their position.

Another factor that has been seen as playing a central part in the growth of civilizations is trade. In regions like Mesopotamia which lacked any natural resources other than fertile soil, stone, building timber and metals all had to be imported. This may have led to the development of a centralized body to organize the procurement and transport of basic commodities. By controlling the distribution, and therefore use, of imported commodities, this body would have gained great power and been able to extend its authority into other fields of life.

Although all these theories have their merits, it is unlikely that any one of them alone is sufficient to explain the emergence of the first civilizations. It is much more likely that civilizations arose because of a complex interaction of different environmental, economic and social factors. Once a civilization has developed, it begins to exert a strong influence over its pre-civilized neighbours through trade, war and culture exchange, so accelerating their development towards civilization. Civilizations are therefore divided into 'primary' and 'secondary' types. A primary civilization is one which developed independently of any outside influences: these include the Mesopotamian, Egyptian, Indus valley, Chinese, Minoan and Olmec civilizations. A secondary civilization is one which developed under the influence of older civilisations: examples of these include the Classical civilizations of Greece and Rome, and the Aztecs.

Writing

One of the characteristics most closely associated with civilizations is writing. Writing has been invented independently several times in different parts of the world, suggesting that it is a natural result of the human capacity for abstract and symbolic thought. Although all human societies have probably had the potential to invent writing, it was only in complex societies that it actually arose. Writing was, therefore, probably invented as an aid for administration in societies that had grown so large and complex that human memory alone could no longer hold all the information needed for efficient government.

The earliest writing systems, in Mesopotamia, Egypt, Europe, China and the Americas, were based on pictographs, simple drawings of the object the writing symbol was meant to represent. As writing developed, pictographs were modified so that they could stand for phonetic values or ideas, so allowing them accurately to record spoken language. Most early writing systems took years to learn, as up to thousands of symbols had to be learned. As a result writing was a skill that was confined to a small elite who enjoyed high social status.

The Alphabet

In the 16th century BC a simpler writing system, the alphabet, was invented by the Canaanite people of present-day Israel and Lebanon. The proto-Canaanite alphabet consisted of only 28 letters, which stood for syllables that could be combined to spell out a word. By 1000 BC many variants of the proto-Canaanite alphabet had appeared in the Middle East, the most influential of which were the Phoenician and the Aramaic alphabets. After its adoption by the Assyrian empire, the Aramaic alphabet became widespread in the Middle East. A version of the Aramaic alphabet was also adopted in India, becoming the ancestor of modern Indian scripts and of the Indian-derived scripts of Central and Southeast Asia. The Phoenician alphabet was the ancestor of the Hebrew and Greek alphabets. The Greeks refined it by introducing separate letters for consonants and vowels. The Greek alphabet was in turn adapted by the peoples of Anatolia, the Balkans and Italy, including the Etruscans. The Etruscan script was developed by the Romans into the Latin alphabet, now the world's most widely used. Alphabetic writing allowed literacy to become widespread. Writing is vitally important to historians as it is only from written records that we can reconstruct systems of government, political, religious and philosophical beliefs, the true significance of objects and structures, the narrative of historical events and much else besides. Civilization and history, therefore, go hand in hand.

Colossal stone heads, a typical feature of the Olmec civilization, are thought to represent rulers who were probably deified and worshipped as ancestors. The Olmecs are regarded as the 'mother culture' of Mesoamerica. Their civilization flourished between 1300 and 400 BC.

Timeline I: NEAR EAST, AFRICA, EUROPE 10,500–1651 BC

NEAR EAST

c. **10,500** BC Natufian hunter-gatherers harvest wild cereals in Syria and Lebanon.

c. **9000** Incipient agriculture: cultivation of wild cereals and management of wild sheep flocks in the Fertile Crescent.

c. **8000** Wheat and barley are domesticated in the Fertile Crescent.

c. **7000** Earliest use of pottery.

c. **6200** Evidence of copper smelting and textile manufacture at Çatal Höyük (Turkey).

c. **5500** Irrigation agriculture is developed in the foothills of the Zagros Mts.

c. **4500** Invention of the plough.

3800 Arsenical bronze is invented.

c. **3500** City-states develop in Sumeria.

c. **3400** Writing comes into use in Sumeria.

c. **3000** Tin bronze is invented. Development of the cuneiform script.

c. **2350** The earliest known law code is issued by Urukagina of Lagash.
2334–2279 Sargon of Agade conquers Mesopotamia.

c. **2100** The first ziggurats are built in Sumeria.
2004 Sumerian civilization enters its final decline after the sack of Ur.

c. **1813–1781** Assyria becomes a great power under Shamshi-Adad.
1792–1750 Babylon is the dominant Mesopotamian power under Hammurabi.

c. **1700** The horse-drawn war chariot is invented.

AFRICA

c. **7000** Cattle-herding and cereal cultivation are practised in the Sahara.

c. **5000** Farmers begin to settle in the Nile valley in Egypt.

c. **3500** Climate change has turned the Sahara into a desert.
c. **3500** Earliest cities and kingdoms in Egypt.

c. **3100** Narmer unites Upper and Lower Egypt.
c. **3100** Origins of Egyptian hieroglyphic writing.
c. **2920–2649** Early Dynastic Period in Egypt.
2649–2134 Old Kingdom period in Egypt.
c. **2630** Construction of the first pyramid at Saqqara (the 'step pyramid').
c. **2550** The Great Pyramid is built at Giza.

c. **2150** Foundation of Nubian kingdom of Kerma.
2134–2040 First Intermediate Period in Egypt.
2040–1640 Middle Kingdom in Egypt.

EUROPE

c. **6500** Farming begins in Greece and the Balkans.

c. **5400** Linear Pottery Culture marks the spread of farming to central Europe.

c. **4300** The earliest megalithic tombs are built in Brittany.
c. **4000** Farming has spread to most of Europe.
c. **4000** The horse is domesticated on the southwestern steppes.

c. **3100** The Newgrange chamber tomb is built in Ireland.

c. **2500–2000** Beginning of the European Bronze Age.

c. **2000** Emergence of the Minoan palace civilization in Crete. Development of Minoan hieroglyphic script.
c. **2000** The main stage of Stonehenge stone circle is completed.

c. **1700** Knossos becomes the dominant palace on Crete.
c. **1700** Development of Minoan Linear A script.

NEAR EAST, AFRICA, EUROPE 1650–500 BC

NEAR EAST

c. **1600** The Canaanites invent the alphabet.
1595 Babylon is sacked by the Hittites.
1570–1154 Kassite dynasty rules Babylon.

c. **1500** Ironworking is developed, probably in Anatolia.

c. **1220–1100** The Hebrews settle in Canaan.
c. **1200** The Hittite empire is destroyed by unidentified invaders.

c. **1000** Hebrew king David captures Jerusalem.
934–912 Reign of Ashur-dan II: Assyria enters its period of imperial greatness.
928 After the death of Solomon, the Hebrew kingdom splits into Israel and Judah.
c. **900** First use of cavalry.

744–727 Tiglath-pileser III reforms the government of the Assyrian empire.
c. **700** Babylonian astrologers have identified the signs of the zodiac.
c. **700** First metal coinage introduced in the Lydian kingdom (Anatolia).
680–627 Assyrian empire is at its greatest extent under Esarhaddon and Ashurbanipal.
630–553 Life of the Persian prophet Zoroaster, founder of Zoroastrianism.
612 The Assyrian empire is overthrown by the Babylonians and Medes.
c. **600** The books of the Old Testament approach their present form.

559–530 Cyrus the Great founds the Achaemenid empire of Persia.
539 Babylon is conquered by Cyrus the Great.

AFRICA

1640–1550 Second Intermediate Period: Hyksos rule Lower Egypt.

1550–1070 New Kingdom Period.
1504–1492 Tuthmosis III conquers Nubia and the Levant, taking the Egyptian empire to its greatest extent.

1353–1335 Reign of Akhenaten, the 'heretic pharaoh'.
1285 Ramesses II is defeated by the Hittites at the battle of Qadesh.

c. **1180** Ramesses III defeats an invasion of the 'Sea Peoples'.
1070–712 Third Intermediate Period: Egyptian power is in decline.

924 Pharaoh Shoshenq I invades Israel and Judah.

c. **900** Foundation of Nubian kingdom of Kush.
835–783 Dynastic disputes cause Egypt to break up into several rival kingdoms.
814 Traditional date for the foundation of Carthage by Phoenician settlers.

712 Piye, king of Kush, conquers Egypt.

663 Nubians expelled from Egypt by the Assyrians.
651 The Egyptians expel the Assyrians.

c. **600** Iron-working has spread to sub-Saharan Africa.
593 After their capital, Napata, is sacked by the Egyptians, the Nubians move their capital to Meroë.
525 The Persians under Cambyses conquer Egypt.

EUROPE

1628 The Minoan city of Akrotiri is buried by ash from the volcanic eruption of Thera.
c. **1600** Emergence of the Mycenaean civilization in Greece.

c. **1450** The Mycenaeans conquer Crete ending the Minoan civilization.

c. **1200** Mycenaean civilization destroyed by invaders.
1184 Traditional date for the fall of Troy.
c. **1100** The Dorians invade Greece.

c. **1000** Iron is in widespread use in Greece.

c. **800** Greeks adopt the Phoenician alphabet and introduce separate vowel and consonant signs.
c. **800** Emergence of the Etruscan civilization in Italy.
800–500 Main period of Greek overseas colonization.
776 Earliest recorded Olympic Games.
753 Traditional date for the founding of Rome by Romulus.
c. **750** The beginning of the Hallstatt ('Celtic') Iron Age in central Europe.
c. **750** Homer composes the *Iliad* and the *Odyssey*.

c. **600** Coinage is adopted in Greece.

560–510 Rule of the tyrants in Athens.
c. **550** Thespis writes the first Greek dramas.
509–507 Athens adopts democracy.
509 The Romans overthrow their monarchy and found a republic.

Timeline 2: EAST AND SOUTH ASIA 6500–180 BC

SOUTH ASIA

c. 6000 Earliest farming villages develop in the mountains of Baluchistan.
c. 5500 Cotton is domesticated.

c. 4000 Farmers begin to settle on the Indus valley plain.
c. 4000 Copper comes into use in the Indus region.
c. 4000 The Asian ox (or zebu) is domesticated.
c. 3500 The potter's wheel is in use in the Indus region.

c. 3000 Beginning of urban development on the Indus plain.

c. 2600 Emergence of the Indus civilization.

c. 2350 Sumerian records of trade in copper and other commodities with the Indus civilization.

c. 2000 Bronze comes into use in the Indus region.

c. 1900 The river Saraswati begins to dry up.

c. 1800 The Indus civilization goes into decline and its cities are gradually abandoned.

c. 1500 Vedic Aryans migrate to India from central Asia.

c. 1100 Iron-working is introduced on the Ganges plain.

c. 1000 A megalithic tomb culture develops in southern India.
c. 1000 Vedic Aryan settlers begin rice farming on the Ganges plain.
c. 1000–600 Formative period of early Hinduism.

c. 900 Earliest kingdoms and tribal republics form on the Ganges plain.

c. 700–300 Age of the *mahajanapadas* ('great realms') on the Ganges plain.

c. 563–483 Life of Siddhartha Gautama, the Buddha.
c. 540–490 Magadha becomes the leading *mahajanapada* under King Bimbisara.
518 The Persians under Darius I conquer the Indus valley.
c. 483 Vijaya founds the kingdom in Sri Lanka.

327–325 Alexander the Great conquers the Indus valley.
321 Chandragupta Maurya seizes power in Magadha, founding the Mauryan empire.
268–233 Reign of Ashoka: the Mauryan empire is at its peak.
c. 260 Ashoka converts to Buddhism and sends missionaries to Sri Lanka and central Asia.

184 Deposition of the last Mauryan emperor.

EAST ASIA

c. 6500 Rice farming begins in the Yangtze valley.

c. 5800–5500 Millet farming begins in the Yellow River valley.

c. 5000–3200 Yangshao Neolithic culture flourishes in the Yellow River valley.
c. 4500 Water buffaloes domesticated in southern China.

c. 3200–1800 Longshan Neolithic culture sees the emergence of hierarchical socities in northern China.

2205 Traditional date for the foundation of the legendary Xia dynasty.

c. 1800–1650 Erlitou early Bronze Age culture in the Yellow River valley.
1766 Traditional date for the foundation of China's first historical dynasty, the Shang, by King Tang.

c. 1500 Origins of Chinese pictographic writing.
c. 1400–1100 Shang royal burials at Anyang include human sacrifices.
c. 1350 The war chariot is introduced to China.

1027 King Wu of Zhou overthrows the Shang dynasty.

770 Barbarian raids force the Zhou dynasty to move its capital from Hao to Luoyang.
770–481 Springs and Autumns Period: rivalries of feudal lords undermine royal authority.

c. 600 Earliest use of iron in China.
551–479 Life of the sage Confucius.

480–221 Warring States Period: China breaks up into independent kingdoms.
361–338 Qin becomes the leading Chinese state under King Xiao.

256 Qin overthrows the last king of the Zhou dynasty.
230–221 King Zheng of Qin unifies China and takes the title Shi Huangdi ('First Emperor').
210 Death of Shihuangdi: his lavish burial offerings includes the terracotta army.
209–202 Civil war: the Qin dynasty is overthrown and the Han dynasty (202 BC-AD 220) is established.

Timeline 3: THE AMERICAS 3500 BC– AD 1550

SOUTH AMERICA

c. 3500 Earliest pottery using cultures develop in Colombia.
3000–2500 Domestication of quinoa, potatoes, alpacas and llamas in the Peruvian highlands.
c. 2600 Monumental ceremonial centres of the Aspero tradition are built on the Peruvian coast.

c. 1800–1500 Intensive agriculture using irrigation begins on the Peruvian coast: pottery comes into use and U-shaped ceremonial centres are built.
c. 1440 Earliest metalworking in the Americas: tools and ornaments of beaten gold made at Waywaka, Peru.

c. 850 Foundation of Chavín de Huántar.

c. 400 Influence of Chavín art styles at their peak.
200 BC–AD 600 The Nazca lines, huge ground drawings, are completed.
200 BC–AD 700 The Moche culture flourishes in the coastal lowlands of Peru.

c. AD 100 The Tiwanaku state is founded on Lake Titicaca.

c. 600 Tiwanaku and Wari empires at their peak.

c. 850 Foundation of the Chimú empire.

c. 1000 Collapse of Tiwanaku and Wari empires.

c. 1200–1230 Manco Capac founds the Inca state.

1470 The Incas conquer the Chimú empire.
1493–1525 Reign of Huayna Capac: the Inca empire is at its height.

1532–36 Spanish conquest of the Inca empire.

MESOAMERICA

c. 2700 Domestication of maize under way.
c. 2300 Permanent farming villages develop and pottery comes into use.

c. 1200 Earliest Olmec ceremonial centre is built at Tres Zapotes.

c. 800 Origins of the Zapotec hieroglyphic script.
c. 600 Earliest Maya temple pyramids are built.
c. 400 The Olmec civilization is in decline.
c. 200 Foundation of Teotihuacán in the Valley of Mexico.

31 BC The 'long count' calendar is devised, probably by the Olmecs.
AD 36 Earliest Maya calendrical inscriptions.
c. 150 The Pyramid of the Sun, the largest building of the pre-Columbian Americas, is completed at Teotihuacán.
300–800 The Classic Period of Maya civilization.

c. 700 Teotihuacán is sacked and abandoned.

c. 900 Chichén Itzá becomes the main centre of Maya civilization.
c. 900 Foundation of the Toltec state at Tula.
987 A Toltec dynasty takes power at Chichén Itzá.

1168 The Toltec state collapses after Tula is destroyed.

1325 Foundation of the Aztec state at Tenochtitlán.

1492 Columbus reaches the West Indies.
1502–20 Aztec empire at its peak under Moctezuma II.
1519–21 Spanish conquest of the Aztecs.

NORTH AMERICA

c. 1300 Ceremonial earthworks built at Poverty Point, Louisiana.

500–100 Adena culture burial mound builders in the eastern woodlands.

c. AD 1 The 390-metre long Great Serpent Mound is built in Ohio.

c. 300 Maize farming becomes an important source of food in the South-western deserts.
700–1500 Anasazi (Ancestral Pueblo) maize farming culture flourishes in the Southwestern deserts.
c. 800 Maize farming becomes an important source of food in the eastern woodlands.
800–1700 Mississippian temple mound building cultures in the eastern woodlands.

c. 1000 Norse explorers become the first Europeans to reach the Americas.
1000–1150 Chaco Canyon, New Mexico, is the major centre of the Anasazi culture.
c. 1200 Cahokia, Missouri, is the largest city in Precolumbian North America.
c. 1300 Prolonged drought causes the decline of the Anasazi culture.

c. 1450 Depopulation causes the decline of the Mississippian culture.

Part 1: The Ancient Near East

For over 3000 years the Near Eastern civilizations were the most advanced in the world, providing impetus and inspiration for younger neighbouring civilizations, which later overshadowed them.

The Near East is a region defined by archaeologists as that part of southwest Asia extending from Iran to the Mediterranean Sea. The Near East is therefore more or less identical to the region most people nowadays call the Middle East. However, the term Middle East has only been current since World War I (1914–18) and archaeologists, who are accustomed to thinking in terms of millennia rather than years, see no reason to adopt the newfangled terminology.

The Near East is an arid region but its landscape was not always as barren as it is today. This is especially true of the area known as the Fertile Crescent, which stretches in an arc from Israel, through Lebanon, Syria, and southern Turkey to the foothills of the Zagros Mountains in Iraq. This was the area where the farming way of life first became established around 10,000 years ago. The name Fertile Crescent is misleading as it suggests that farming became established here because its soils were outstandingly fertile, which was not the case even 10,000 years ago. The advantages of this area were twofold. Firstly it had enough rainfall to allow dry farming, that is farming without irrigation. Secondly, the area was more richly supplied with wild animals and plants suitable for domestication than any other on Earth. The transition from hunting and gathering to settled farming took around 2000 years to complete.

Mesopotamia

Far more fertile than the soils in the Fertile Crescent were those on the flood plain of the Tigris and Euphrates rivers in modern Iraq. In antiquity this region was known as Mesopotamia, meaning 'the land between the rivers'. The Tigris and the Euphrates were often violent rivers, flooding in the spring as the snows melted on the surrounding mountains and spreading rich alluvium across the countryside. However, early farmers could not exploit these rich soils because the region has very low rainfall. It was only after *c.* 6000 BC, when farmers in the foothills of the Zagros Mountains learned the technique of building irrigation channels to divert water from rivers to fields, that the huge productive capacity of the Mesopotamian plain could be unlocked.

Irrigating the Mesopotamian plains required a great deal of labour but it was not technically difficult. Like other great rivers, the Tigris and Euphrates have built up high levees so that the river beds are actually higher than the surrounding plains which means that no special technology was required to lift water from the river: canals dug from the river into the surrounding countryside were simply fed by gravity. If building the canals was not challenging, then maintenance was. Irrigation canals needed frequent digging out as they silted up quickly, flood damage had to be repaired and if, as often happened, the rivers changed course, completely new canals had to be dug. It was in the need for a central body to organize these vital tasks that many historians have identified the beginning of state formation in Mesopotamia. Not only had labour to be marshalled for the tasks, the workers had to be fed and this required the collection of food supplies and their efficient redistribution as rations. The effort was worth it. Irrigation, allied to the

This gold helmet, dating to around 2500 BC, was found at the Royal Cemetery of Ur. It belonged to the Sumerian king Meskalamdug and was carefully engraved to reproduce the curls of his hair and the bun at the back of his head.

development of heat tolerant strains of wheat and barley and the invention of the plough, enabled Mesopotamian farmers to produce large surpluses and the population grew rapidly. By 5300 BC the whole plain was densely settled.

Although the recent discovery of early urban centres at Tell Brak and Tell Hamoukar in the far north of Mesopotamia may be about to force a reappraisal, the established view is that the largest communities developed in southern Mesopotamia in the region known as Sumeria. The Ubaid period (5900–4300 BC) saw the growth of many small towns, which, characteristically, were centred on temple precincts. The rulers of these communities probably combined secular and religious authority, as was common in the ancient world: the clear division between religious and secular fields is a relatively modern development. The farmers of the plains were always vulnerable to floods and unpredictable changes in the course of the rivers on whose waters they relied. They must have felt they were at the mercy of capricious gods: the most famous of the Mesopotamian myths is that of the flood which the gods sent to drown humanity because they had tired of their constant chattering. This was the prototype for the biblical story of Noah. Under such circumstances a ruler who was believed to have the ability to intercede with the gods on behalf of his subjects would have enjoyed considerable authority. In historical times, Mesopotamian rulers had personally to participate in a calendar of ceremonies, the correct performance of which were believed to be essential to the welfare of the people.

The Invention of Writing

The breakthrough to urban civilization took place during the Uruk period (4300–3100 BC), which was named after the first city to develop in Sumeria. All the major Sumerian cities grew up from earlier settlements of the Ubaid period and kept the same basic layout, having temple complexes at their centres. These complexes were administrative, economic and religious centres. Food surpluses were stored at the temple, either to be reserved for famine years, traded for raw materials such as metals or timber, or redistributed as rations to specialized craftworkers. To manage this system efficiently writing was invented. The earliest examples of writing come from Uruk and date to around 3300 BC but the system must have originated earlier as it was already a complete system with over 700 symbols. This early writing was based on pictographs: the symbol for barley, for example, was a simplified picture of an ear of barley. More complex ideas were expressed by combining symbols: a head symbol combined with a bowl symbol meant 'to eat'. Symbols were inscribed on wet clay tablets, which were dried and stored in archives. As the system developed the symbols became more abstract and were inscribed with a rectangular-ended reed stylus that left wedge-shaped impressions from which the script gets its name, cuneiform. The script was also refined so that it could represent phonetic values, allowing all aspects of spoken language to be recorded.

The needs of administration also led to the first developments of advanced mathematics and the measurement of time. The Sumerian civilization was also responsible for a major technological breakthrough, the invention of bronze. The earliest bronze was made by alloying copper with arsenic but by 3000 BC a better quality bronze was being made using copper and tin. Copper (and also gold and silver) had been used for thousands of years for ornaments and small tools but it was too soft to replace stone in general use. Bronze was tougher and kept an edge better, was easier to re-sharpen than stone tools and, although expensive, could be melted down and recast when worn out. It was in Sumeria that the Stone Age truly began to come to an end. The Sumerians were also the first people known to have made extensive use of wheeled vehicles.

The main political unit among the Sumerians was the city-state, that is each city and its surrounding villages and fields was an independent kingdom. As

This alabaster statue is of Ebih-II, superintendent of the important Mesopotamian city of Mari. The role of 'superintendent' was probably rather like that of a Minister of Finance. Ebih-II is portrayed wearing *kaunakes*, the fur skirt made from sheep or goat's hair worn by Mesopotamian men.

settlement on the Mesopotamian plain became increasingly dense, conflict between the cities became more common. In the 3rd millennium BC the cities built defensive walls. Weapons production increased and slaves appeared for the first time, many of them probably prisoners of war. Rulers also began to issue law codes as a way of reinforcing their authority. New urban civilizations began to develop under Sumerian influence in northern Mesopotamia and by 2350 BC these were beginning to overtake Sumeria.

The age of the city-states was brought to an end *c.* 2334 BC by Sargon, king of the northern city of Agade, the first great empire builder of history. Sargon conquered a vast swathe of territory stretching from the Mediterranean to Sumeria and the Persian Gulf. Sargon's empire lasted only four generations before it fell apart but it established a tradition of militaristic kingship that endured throughout the history of the ancient Near East. United under the Third Dynasty of Ur (2112–2004 BC), Sumeria made a brief revival but thereafter the centre of the Mesopotamian civilization shifted permanently north to Babylon and Assyria, whose rivalry is a dominant theme of the next 1500 years of the region's history. In this period too civilizations developed in other areas of the Near East – in the Levant, Anatolia and Iran. Although the Levant remained a land of city-states and small territorial kingdoms, powerful empires would arise in Anatolia and Iran that would challenge the dominance of Mesopotamia.

The Importance of Strong Kings

The histories of the Mesopotamian empires display the same compelling pattern of expansion under strong warrior kings, like Sargon of Agade or Hammurabi of Babylon, and decline under weak kings. The Mesopotamians recognized this pattern, believing that the gods permitted one dynasty to achieve dominance for a time only to cast it down and replace it with another when they tired of it. The success of a Mesopotamian kingdom was closely linked to the abilities of its ruler because their administrative structures were inherently weak. Without the king's constant attention government could easily break down as inefficiency and corruption took over.

Military skill counted for much. Successful warrior kings could expect to form alliances with other rulers who were ready to accept vassal status in return for protection or a share of the spoils of war after a successful campaign. In this way a good soldier could build an empire quickly through a mixture of diplomacy and conquest. However, it was not easy for a conqueror to consolidate his gains. Conquered cities might be garrisoned in the short term but states did not have professional standing armies which could be kept in the field indefinitely, so direct rule was rarely imposed. Instead governors were recruited from the local elite to collect taxes on behalf of the imperial power. The native governor might well have an imperial agent appointed to 'advise' him but there was no question of imposing an alien administration. Rebellion was discouraged by the threat of savage reprisals. The bloodthirsty friezes of Assyrian palaces, which show rebels being impaled, flayed alive and so on, were meant to ensure that the message got across. This system worked fine while the imperial power was strong enough to deter, or crush, rebellion. In times of weakness or dynastic instability, the native governors could withhold the taxes they collected, appeal to traditional local loyalties and declare themselves independent. The imperial power would also find itself deserted by its vassals, who now had little to gain from the alliance.

All rulers faced the problem that Mesopotamia lacked defensible frontiers and so was always vulnerable to invasion by the nomads, such as the Aramaeans and Chaldaeans, of the Syrian desert to the west, and hill tribes, such as the Gutians and Kassites, from the Zagros Mountains to the east. These invaders

This terracotta bull is in the Ubaid style. Clay was the most abundant material in the ancient Near East and was used in pottery and sculpture as well as for making the bricks used for buildings. Bulls were associated with many of the gods and kings of ancient Sumeria.

wanted to share in the prosperity and fertility of the plains and so, while they might topple dynasties, they were not hostile to Mesopotamian civilization itself. Those who settled in Mesopotamia soon became integrated into the local population.

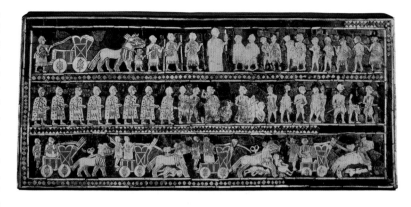

In the 8th and 9th centuries BC the Assyrian empire developed stronger institutions of government that allowed it to impose direct rule on conquered states. Provincial governorships were given to eunuchs to prevent them from becoming hereditary posts. Travelling inspectors were appointed to check on the conduct of local officials and a postal system was introduced. A professional standing army and an intelligence service were created. Troublesome populations were deported and resettled in Mesopotamia, where they could be supervised, with the aim of undermining local identities and loyalties. These innovations allowed the Assyrians to achieve an unprecedented regional dominance but they eventually over-reached themselves and their monarchy was overthrown by the Babylonians in 612. However, the Assyrians had established a strong tradition of imperial rule and the Babylonians were able to rule in much the same way. Under King Nebuchadnezzar II, Babylon was rebuilt in a lavish imperial style that made it a byword for luxury and decadent excess but this was to be the final flourish of ancient Mesopotamian civilization.

The Royal Standard of Ur consists of two rectangular panels decorated with scenes made from a mosaic of white shell, red limestone and blue lapis lazuli. This side, known as the 'war' side, shows 'war wagons' running over fallen enemies and warriors seizing prisoners who are then being paraded before a king figure. As city-states in the ancient Near East developed, the principal concern of kings became the waging of war.

The Persian Empire

In 539 Cyrus the Great, ruler of Persia, conquered the Babylonian empire. Cyrus faced little resistance. The centuries of imperial government had weakened local identities and accustomed people to rule by outsiders to such an extent that they regarded the conquest as little more than the accession of a new dynasty. It is likely that economic factors were at play. Agriculture in Mesopotamia depended on irrigation but in such a hot dry climate this led over thousands of years to a decline in fertility: as irrigation water from the silt-laden rivers evaporated it left salts in the soil, which could not be leached away by rainfall because there was none. The development of salt-resistant crops, and an increased reliance on date palms, helped but agricultural productivity gradually declined while it was increasing in neighbouring areas. After its conquest by Persia, Mesopotamia never regained its independence and its cities went into decline and were mostly abandoned by the Christian era. Built mainly of mud brick, they have not left impressive ruins.

The Persian empire created by Cyrus united the entire Near East into a single state for the first time. The empire's vast size, huge armies and great wealth gave it an aura of invincibility but these were not the advantages they seemed. The empire's size led to delays in communications and in gathering armies, most of whose soldiers were poorly equipped conscripts. Although they were tolerant of local customs and religions, and did not make unreasonable tax demands on their subjects, the Persians never won their true loyalty. When Alexander the Great of Macedon invaded in 334 he met no popular resistance and took the empire in just eight years. By his conquest, Alexander extended the influence of Greek civilization across the region and into central and south Asia, so effectively bringing the history of the ancient Near Eastern civilizations to an end.

The First Farmers

The first farming societies developed in the 'Fertile Crescent', a broad arc of territory extending from Israel in the south-west, through Lebanon, Syria and southern Turkey and then south-east across the foothills of Iraq's Zagros Mountains almost to the Persian Gulf.

"Sustenance is in a plough."

Sumerian farmer's almanac *c.* 2000 BC

The term 'Fertile Crescent' is in fact something of a misnomer, its soils are not outstandingly fertile, at least not today after 10,000 years of intensive agriculture. The real advantages of the area were that it had sufficient rainfall to support dry farming and a wide range of plants and animals that were suitable for domestication. Chief among these were wild strains of emmer and einkorn wheat, barley, peas and lentils and wild sheep, cattle and pigs. Around the end of the Ice Age, *c.* 10,500 years ago, these rich, natural food sources allowed local hunter-gatherers, like the Natufians, to live in permanent villages, instead of migrating with the seasons. The Natufians began the transition to a farming way of life in the 9th millennium BC when they began to cultivate wild cereals. Climatic changes accompanying the end of the Ice Age meant that the natural range of wild cereals was shrinking, so this was probably an attempt by the Natufians to secure their food supply. These proto-farmers learned to selectively breed wild cereals for desirable characteristics that increased the yield and made them easier to harvest. By 8000 BC fully domesticated strains of wheat and barley had been developed.

Domesticating animals

At around the same time other groups, as at Zawi Chemi in the Zagros Mountains, had begun intensively managing flocks of wild sheep. By keeping animals in pens and controlling their breeding, selecting for characteristics such as docility, which made them easier to manage, proto-farmers produced domesticated sheep, goats, pigs and cattle.

The transition from hunting and gathering to farming took over 2000 years. Even after domesticated crops had developed, people continued to take food from the wild. At Jericho, a large settlement of proto-farmers that grew up by a spring around 8000 BC, domesticated cereals, pulses and figs were grown but the inhabitants hunted wild gazelle, sheep and goats for their meat. The abundance of food in proto-farming communities led to a steady rise in population. By 7500 BC communities in many parts of the Fertile Crescent had come to depend almost totally on farming for their food.

As is still the case in much of the Middle East today, the main building material used by early

This skull was among a cache of human skulls found at Jericho. They are thought to have been part of a cult involving the preservation of skulls with the facial features reconstructed from clay and lime plaster.

Mediterranean
Sea

Haci

Nile

N

| 0 | 300 km |
| 0 | 200 mil |

farmers was sun-dried mud brick. Although not as durable as baked bricks, mud bricks are cheap and easy to make and build with. When a house fell into disrepair it was simply levelled and replaced by a new one. In time successive rebuilding on the same site produced mounds of debris, elevating the settlements high above the surrounding countryside. Known as a *tell* in Arabic, *höyük* in Turkish and *tepe* in Persian, these settlement mounds are the most characteristic archaeological sites of the region.

The newly settled farmers did not have access to as broad a range of resources as their more mobile hunter-gatherer ancestors and in the 8th millennium long-distance trade in commodities such as obsidian – a volcanic glass which makes excellent tools – developed.

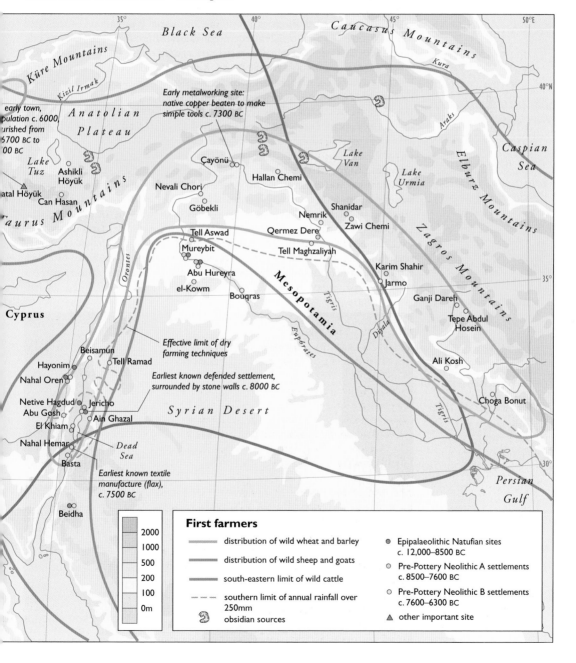

First farmers

— distribution of wild wheat and barley

— distribution of wild sheep and goats

— south-eastern limit of wild cattle

- - - southern limit of annual rainfall over 250mm

🦪 obsidian sources

● Epipalaeolithic Natufian sites c. 12,000–8500 BC

○ Pre-Pottery Neolithic A settlements c. 8500–7600 BC

○ Pre-Pottery Neolithic B settlements c. 7600–6300 BC

△ other important site

2000 / 1000 / 500 / 200 / 100 / 0m

The First Towns

Mesopotamia was the first part of the world to see the widespread and sustainable growth of towns and cities. Meaning the 'land between the rivers,' Mesopotamia was situated on the flood plain of the Euphrates and Tigris rivers. Although it was blessed with rich alluvial soils, Mesopotamia had a low rainfall. Its settlement only became possible with the development of irrigation around 5500 BC.

The spread of farming across Mesopotamia is marked by a succession of cultures, each of which is defined by its distinctive style of decorated pottery. These cultures laid the technological, economic and social foundations of the later Mesopotamian civilizations. The earliest of these cultures was the Hassuna culture 6500–6000 BC), which was restricted mainly to northern Mesopotamia where there was sufficient rainfall for dry farming. The Hassuna people were the first to produce painted pottery, which they fired in purpose-built kilns (most early potters simply fired their pots in bonfires). They were also the earliest to use stamp seals as marks of ownership – a practice which became widespread in Mesopotamia – and were among the first to smelt lead and copper, which they used to make simple tools and ornaments.

"After the kingship had descended from heaven, Eridu was the first to become the seat of kingship. In Eridu Alulim reigned for 28,800 years, then Alalgar reigned for 36,000 years — these two kings reigned for 64,800 years. Then Eridu was abandoned and its kingship was carried off to Badtibira."

The Sumerian King List, *c.* 2000 BC

Growing Signs of Wealth

The Hassuna was typical of early farming cultures in having a simple social structure with little evidence of great differences of wealth and status. The succeeding Halafian and Samarran cultures both show signs of greater social complexity. The Halafians were still largely confined to the dry farming area but excavations of a storehouse at Arpachiyeh, which contained high quality pottery and stone tools, jewellery and sculpture, suggests that they were ruled by chiefs who became wealthy by controlling their communities' trade. The Samarrans were the first to develop canal building techniques needed for large-scale irri-

This limestone tripod bowl is an example of early stoneware from one of the oldest Mesopotamian cultures, the Halafian. The bowl, found in a grave at Tell Halaf in north-east Syria, is carved with a hunting scene and may have been an incense burner.

gation. These communal works are evidence of a well-organized society with strong leadership. Using these techniques, developed first to boost yields in the dry farming area, the Samarrans became the first farmers to settle the arid flood plain of central Mesopotamia. The farming settlement of southern Mesopotamia was completed by the Ubaid culture, which arose around 5900 BC.

Irrigation allowed farmers to exploit the productive capacity of the rich alluvial soils and population density on the flood plains rose rapidly. Productivity grew even higher after the invention of the plough around 4500 BC. Other innovations made by the Ubaid people included the potter's wheel and, probably, the sail. Many new villages were founded by the Ubaid people and several of these grew quickly into small towns with populations of several thousand people. The best known, and probably also the earliest, of these was Eridu in southern Mesopotamia. Eridu was centred on a temple complex which already had many of the architectural features typical of later Mesopotamian temples. Apart from its rich soils, southern Mesopotamia is lacking in basic natural resources, such as stone for tool making and building, timber and metal ores, so trade links were vital for the Ubaid people: they also helped spread the influence of the Ubaid culture more widely than any earlier Near Eastern culture. By around 5400 BC it had replaced the Halafian culture in northern Mesopotamia and Ubaid influence extended far south along the shores of the Persian Gulf as far as Bahrein.

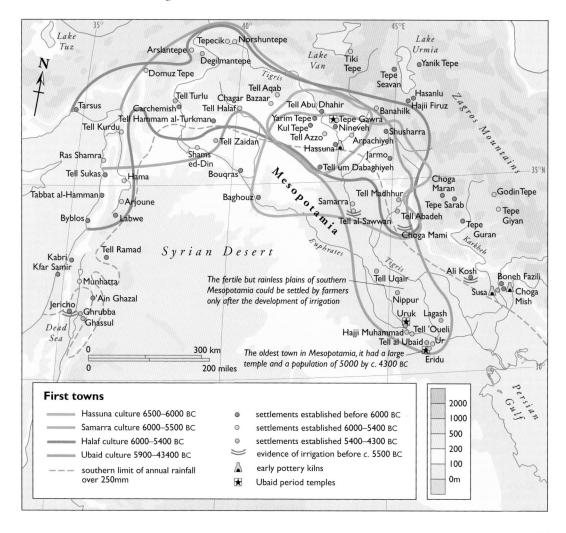

The fertile but rainless plains of southern Mesopotamia could be settled by farmers only after the development of irrigation

The oldest town in Mesopotamia, it had a large temple and a population of 5000 by c. 4300 BC

First towns

——— Hassuna culture 6500–6000 BC	● settlements established before 6000 BC
——— Samarra culture 6000–5500 BC	○ settlements established 6000–5400 BC
——— Halaf culture 6000–5400 BC	◎ settlements established 5400–4300 BC
——— Ubaid culture 5900–43400 BC	≋ evidence of irrigation before c. 5500 BC
– – – southern limit of annual rainfall over 250mm	▲ early pottery kilns
	★ Ubaid period temples

2000
1000
500
200
100
0m

The Sumerians

The Sumerian civilization was the earliest of the world's urban civilizations. The civilization is named after Sumer or Sumeria, the ancient name for the area of southern Mesopotamia where it developed around the middle of the 4th millennium BC.

"In Uruk Gilgamesh built walls, a great rampart…. Look at it still today … touch the ancient threshold. Climb upon the wall of Uruk and walk along it. Look at the foundation terrace and examine the masonry; is it not burnt brick and good?"

The Epic of Gilgamesh, *c.* 2200 BC

Votive statues like this one from Uruk were placed in temples to offer prayers to a god or goddess on behalf of the donor.

The Sumerian civilization emerged during what is known as the Uruk Period (4300–3100 BC), the culture period which followed the Ubaid. The rapid population growth of Ubaid times continued during the Uruk Period and many of Sumeria's towns developed into city-states, ruled by kings and literate administrators. Uruk, the city for which the period is named, was the earliest of these city-states and by some way the largest with a population of around 50,000 people by 2700 BC.

Emerging Governments

The challenge of ruling such large communities provided the impetus for the development of governments, the annual food surpluses produced by Sumerian farmers provided the resources to maintain large numbers of people in specialist occupations, not just administrators but craftsmen of all sorts too, including metalworkers. The invention of bronze (probably in Iran) and of the lost wax method of metal casting led to metal tools and weapons coming into widespread use for the first time. Temples were the focal points of Sumerian cities. These became centres where surplus food and craft products, offered in the name of the city gods, could be stored and later redistributed as rations to specialist workers or traded for raw materials that were not available locally.

Pictographs

It was probably to keep track of these stores that writing first developed *c.* 3400 BC from a clay token system used widely in Mesopotamia in early Uruk times. The first writing system was based on pictographs and was used only for record keeping. It was only after the development of the more sophisticated cuneiform system *c.* 2900 BC that a more wide ranging literature was produced.

By the beginning of the Early Dynastic Period (2900–2334 BC) kingship was firmly established as the central institution of city government. Kings had religious as well as secular functions and it was their conduct which would determine whether the city enjoyed the

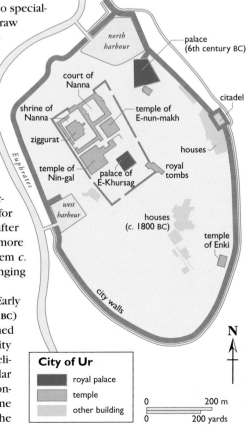

City of Ur
- royal palace
- temple
- other building

0   200 m
0   200 yards

N

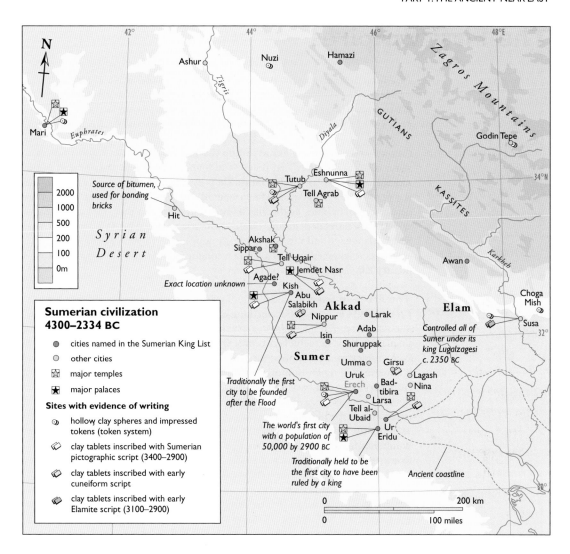

Sumerian civilization
4300–2334 BC

- ● cities named in the Sumerian King List
- ○ other cities
- ▦ major temples
- ★ major palaces

Sites with evidence of writing

- ◎ hollow clay spheres and impressed tokens (token system)
- ✎ clay tablets inscribed with Sumerian pictographic script (3400–2900)
- ✎ clay tablets inscribed with early cuneiform script
- ✎ clay tablets inscribed with early Elamite script (3100–2900)

favour of the gods. For all its prosperity, there was always an element of insecurity in the lives of ordinary Sumerians because of the threat of crop failure through disease or flooding. The king's claim to be close to the gods bolstered his authority and so kings built their palaces next to the temples to emphasize this point. Law codes issued by kings such as Urukagina of Lagash were not intended solely for their people; they were also ways to demonstrate their commitment to good government to the city gods.

Competing City-states

The Early Dynastic Period was a time of intense competition between the city-states. Population was now so dense in Sumeria that if one city was to expand it could only do so at the expense of its neighbours. Cities were defended by circuits of walls and martial display became an important part of kingship. In the Early Dynastic Period Kish, Uruk and Ur vied with one another for dominance. By around 2500 BC King Mesilim of Kish had made himself the nominal overlord of Sumeria. About 100 years later the hegemony of Kish was overthrown by King Eannatum of Lagash. The era of the independent city-states was finally brought to an end by King Lugalzagesi of Umma around 2350 BC when he conquered all of Sumeria.

Periods in Sumerian History

Uruk Period 4300–3100 BC

Jemdet Nasr Period 3100–2900 BC

Early Dynastic Period 2900–2334 BC

27

The First Empires

In 2334 BC Sumeria was eclipsed by Akkad as the main centre of Mesopotamian civilization. Akkad was the region of central Mesopotamia around the city of Agade, whose ruler Sargon (r. 2334–2279 BC) founded the first great empire of the Near East.

"To Sargon, the king of Agade, Enlil (the god of kingship) allowed no rival and gave him the entire territory from the upper sea to the lower sea. The sons of Agade held the governorships everywhere ... the men of Mari and the men of Elam served Sargon as their master."

Inscription of
Sargon of Agade

City-states developed in Akkad during the Early Dynastic Period for much the same reasons that they had done so in Sumeria. Although the Sumerians and Akkadians shared the same culture they were of different ethnic origins and spoke different languages. The origin of the Sumerians is unknown; they described themselves as the 'black-headed people' and they spoke a language which was unrelated to any other known language. The Akkadians spoke a Semitic language and this was gradually adopted by the Sumerians, whose own language became extinct as a spoken tongue around 1650 BC: it survived as a literary language until the 1st century BC.

The Story of Sargon

Around 2334 BC Sargon became king of the northern Sumerian city of Kish. Sargon was the son of a date grower who made a career as a royal servant: it is more than likely that he achieved power by a coup as his name means 'legitimate king'. Later legends supplied Sargon with a suitable royal pedigree. Sargon was really the illegitimate son of a royal priestess who cast her baby adrift on the river Euphrates in a basket to avoid being publicly shamed. The baby was saved by the royal gardener of Kish who brought him up as his own son and secured employment for him in the royal household he would one day take over after winning the love of Ishtar, the Mesopotamian goddess of sex and war. Ishtar would not have been disappointed by her lover's military abilities. Sargon overthrew Lugalzagesi of Umma and took over Sumeria before going on to conquer a vast swathe of territory stretching from the Persian Gulf to the Mediterranean. Sargon celebrated his achievement by founding the new city of Agade as his capital: its site has never been located. Sargon's grandson Naram-Sin extended the empire still further but it then went into decline. Mesopotamia lacks defendable frontiers so Akkad's rulers struggled to repel invasions of desert nomads and hill tribes from the Zagros Mountains, attracted by the region's wealth. Weakened, the empire fell apart around 2193 BC when the Mesopotamian cities reasserted their independence.

The Rise of Ur

The struggle to be the successor to Agade lasted about 80 years. The winner was Ur-Nammu (r. 2112–2095), the first king of the Third Dynasty of the Sumerian city of Ur, who built a new empire encompassing most of Mesopotamia and Elam. Ur-Nammu's reign saw the construction of the first ziggurats, high temple platforms that are as distinctive to ancient Mesopotamia as pyramids are to ancient Egypt. Ur-Nammu's successors had to contend with the same problems the empire of Agade faced. The empire of the Third Dynasty collapsed in 2004 BC when Ur itself was captured by the Elamites. This marked the end of Sumerian cultural and political pre-eminence in Mesopotamia. The main beneficiaries of Ur's demise were the Amorites, Semitic-speaking desert nomads who were able to infiltrate and settle in Mesopotamia during the long period of political disorder which followed.

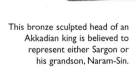

This bronze sculpted head of an Akkadian king is believed to represent either Sargon or his grandson, Naram-Sin.

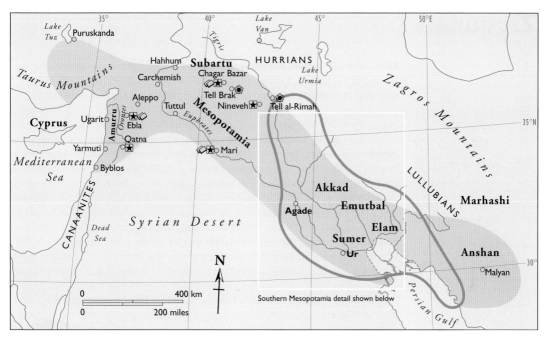

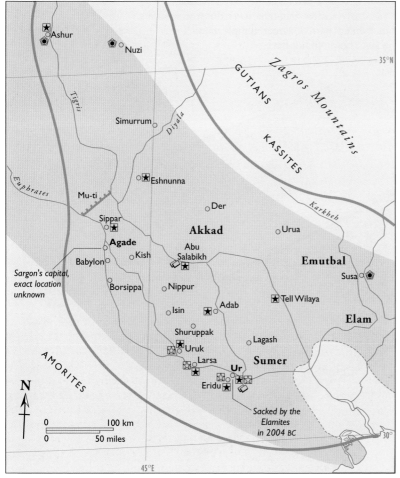

First empires

- empire of Sargon the Great of Agade c. 2279 BC
- empire of the Third Dynasty of Ur, 2112–2004 BC
- ancient coastline
- ○ cities
- ★ royal palaces
- preserved palace archives of clay tablets
- Akkadian garrison under Sargon
- ziggurats built by the Ur III dynasty
- Ur / Agade } capitals of empire
- defensive wall built by King Naram-Sin of Ur (2037–2029 BC) to defend Sumer and Akkad from attack

Kings of Agade

Sargon 2334–2279 BC
Rimush 2278–2270
Manishtushu 2269–2255
Naram-Sin 2037–2029
Shar-Kali-Shari 2217–2193

Ziggurats

The most distinctive architectural monuments of the ancient Near East are ziggurats (from ancient Akkadian ziqqurratu*), imposing stepped pyramids built of brick with temples on their summits.*

"In the middle of the sacred precinct there is a tower of solid brick, one furlong (220 yards) square, on which is built a second tower, and on that a third and so on up to eight.... On the top ... there is a great temple."

Herodotus, *Histories*

Ziggurats developed from the Sumerian practice of building temples on platforms to raise them above the ground. There are various theories about their symbolic meaning, the most likely being that they represented stairways to heaven to allow priests to get closer to the gods. The oldest known ziggurats, at Ur, Eridu, Nippur and Uruk in Sumeria, date from the reign of Ur-Nammu (2112–2095) of the Third Dynasty of Ur. However, they may not have been the first to be built as representations of stepped buildings are known in Sumerian art from around 2500 BC. In Sumeria and Babylonia ziggurats were free-standing structures; access to the summit shrine was by either a triple external stairway or a spiral ramp. The most famous ziggurat was that of the god Marduk at Babylon. Known to the Babylonians as Etemenanki ('the house that is the foundation of Heaven and Earth') it has been immortalized in Judaeo-Christian mythology as the Tower of Babel. The Babylonians believed that Marduk actually slept at night on a couch in the temple on Etemananki's summit, accompanied by a human priestess whom it was believed he had taken in sacred marriage.

In Assyria, most ziggurats were not free standing but formed part of larger temple complexes. These did not have

This drawing shows a reconstruction of the Etemenanki ziggurat at Babylon. Ziggurats contained no internal chambers and were not used for burials like Egyptian pyramids.

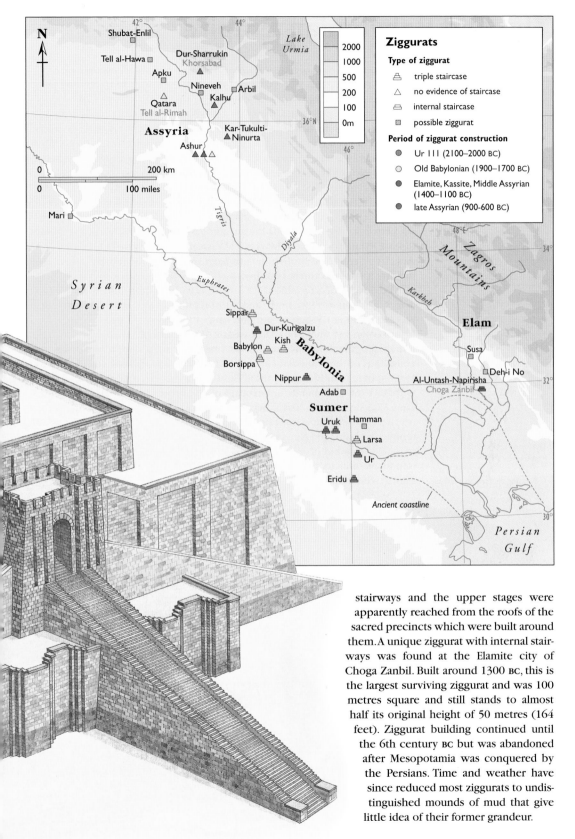

Ziggurats

Type of ziggurat

- △ triple staircase
- △ no evidence of staircase
- △ internal staircase
- ☐ possible ziggurat

Period of ziggurat construction

- ● Ur III (2100–2000 BC)
- ○ Old Babylonian (1900–1700 BC)
- ● Elamite, Kassite, Middle Assyrian (1400–1100 BC)
- ● late Assyrian (900-600 BC)

N

Shubat-Enlil
Tell al-Hawa
Dur-Sharrukin
Khorsabad
Apku
Nineveh   Arbil
Qatara   Kalhu
Tell al-Rimah
Assyria   Kar-Tukulti-
Ashur   Ninurta

Lake Urmia

0   200 km
0   100 miles

Mari

Syrian Desert

Euphrates

Tigris

Diyala

Sippar
Dur-Kurigalzu
Babylon   Kish
Borsippa   **Babylonia**
Nippur
Adab
Sumer
Uruk   Hamman
Larsa
Ur
Eridu

Ancient coastline

Zagros Mountains

Karkheh

Elam
Susa
Deh-i No
Al-Untash-Napirisha
Choga Zanbil

Persian Gulf

stairways and the upper stages were apparently reached from the roofs of the sacred precincts which were built around them. A unique ziggurat with internal stairways was found at the Elamite city of Choga Zanbil. Built around 1300 BC, this is the largest surviving ziggurat and was 100 metres square and still stands to almost half its original height of 50 metres (164 feet). Ziggurat building continued until the 6th century BC but was abandoned after Mesopotamia was conquered by the Persians. Time and weather have since reduced most ziggurats to undistinguished mounds of mud that give little idea of their former grandeur.

The Old Babylonian Empire

The 200 years following the fall of Ur saw the rise to prominence of the two states that were to dominate Mesopotamia until the 6th century BC – Babylon and Assyria.

> *"[The gods] Anum and Enlil chose me to promote the welfare of the people, me, Hammurabi, the devout god-fearing king, to cause justice to prevail in the land. "*
>
> Law Code of Hammurabi (r. 1792–1750 BC)

The stone stele of the Code of Hammurabi shows the sun god and god of justice Shamash dictating his laws to the king.

Babylon and Assyria had both been established in the Early Dynastic Period but neither had been first rank powers. Assyria, famously militaristic in later times, was primarily a trading power while Babylon lived in the shadow of Agade. In the 19th century BC both came under the control of Amorite dynasties, Babylon in 1894, Assyria in 1813. Under its first Amorite king, Shamshi-Adad (r. 1813–1781 BC), Assyria conquered all of northern Mesopotamia but the achievement was short-lived. On his death Shamshi-Adad's kingdom was divided between his sons, Ishme-Dagan and Yasmah-Addu. An archive of letters discovered in the palace at Mari reveal Yasmah-Addu to have been an immature and lazy ruler and his brother to have been an overconfident one. Neither could hold their father's empire together.

The decline of Shamshi-Adad's Assyria was the opportunity for Babylon to assert itself under its sixth and most famous Amorite king, Hammurabi (r. 1792–1750 BC). When he became king of Babylon in 1792 Hammurabi was probably one of Shamshi-Adad's vassals. While Shamshi-Adad was alive Hammurabi confined himself mainly to building canals and temples; his only conquests, of the Sumerian cities of Isin and Uruk, were well outside his overlord's sphere of influence. By the 1760s Babylon had become a power to reckon with. In 1761 Hammurabi annexed all of Sumeria after defeating its dominant king, Rim-Sin of Larsa. Then, between 1757 and 1755, he conquered most of northern Mesopotamia and imposed vassal status on Assyria, where he restored temples in Ashur and Nineveh. In Mesopotamian tradition this was not an act of reconciliation but a way to demonstrate overlordship. Hammurabi's most impressive military achievement was his conquest of the northern city of Eshnunna, which he forced to surrender by diverting its water supply.

Hammurabi's Law Code

Under Hammurabi Babylon emerged as Mesopotamia's leading cultural centre. Hammurabi is probably best known for his law code, one of the most complete (although not the earliest) to survive from the ancient world. It is most notable for its reliance on brutal punishments. Hammurabi's code is divided into 282 sections dealing with family, property and commercial law and with slavery, professional fees, prices and wages. The code presents an idealized picture of Babylonian society. The king was the head of society and below him were three classes: the *awilum* or property-owning freemen, the *mushkennum* or non-property owning dependents of the state and the *wardum* or slaves. This society was not static. Slaves could accumulate wealth or property and buy their freedom, while a freeman might find himself enslaved because of unpaid debts. Women and children were treated as the property of their husbands and fathers, while all people were considered to be slaves in their relationships with the king.

Although the code advises plaintiffs to consult it, it is likely that the stele on which it was written was actually set in a temple, primarily for the benefit of the gods, that

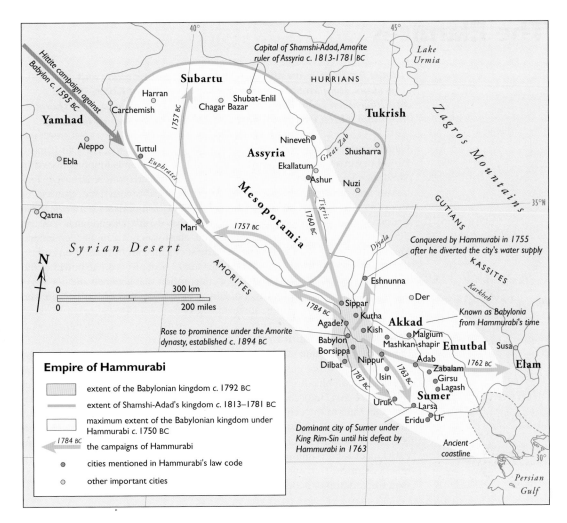

Capital of Shamshi-Adad, Amorite ruler of Assyria c. 1813–1781 BC

Empire of Hammurabi

	extent of the Babylonian kingdom c. 1792 BC
	extent of Shamshi-Adad's kingdom c. 1813–1781 BC
	maximum extent of the Babylonian kingdom under Hammurabi c. 1750 BC
1784 BC	the campaigns of Hammurabi
●	cities mentioned in Hammurabi's law code
○	other important cities

Conquered by Hammurabi in 1755 after he diverted the city's water supply

Known as Babylonia from Hammurabi's time

Rose to prominence under the Amorite dynasty, established c. 1894 BC

Dominant city of Sumer under King Rim-Sin until his defeat by Hammurabi in 1763

they might see what a just king Hammurabi was. Following Hammurabi's death Babylonian power gradually declined under his less able successors. The rise of new powers in Anatolia, the Hurrians and the Hittites, increasingly threatened Babylon from the north. In 1595 Babylon was sacked by the Hittite King Mursilis. The Amorite dynasty was overthrown and for 200 years Babylon lapsed back into obscurity.

Short-lived empires

The most striking characteristic of these early Mesopotamian empires is their lack of staying power. Empires rose rapidly under able warrior kings like Sargon, Ur-Nammu, Shamshi-Adad and Hammurabi because weaker rulers would readily accept vassal status in return for protection and a share of the spoils of war. However, conquered states were not subjected to the direct rule of the conqueror because the administrative structures of Mesopotamian states were too weak, they were essentially city councils and they required the constant attention of the king if they were to work effectively.

Conquered states had to be left under the rule of a local governor who was appointed the responsibility of tax collection. This system worked well enough while the imperial power was strong and could deter rebellion but under a weak and ineffective ruler like Yasmah-Addu allies deserted and subject states easily reasserted their independence.

The Elamites

Known for their wars with the Sumerians, Babylonians and Assyrians, the Elamites were a powerful people of Khuzestan in south-western Iran. Their ethnic origins are obscure as they spoke a language which was quite unrelated to any other known language.

"When hard times came to Elam and famine filled the land, I sent king Urtaki grain to keep his people alive. I supported him.... In my heart I should never have expected an attack from the Elamite, never have suspected he hated me."

Inscription of Ashurbanipal *c.* 665 BC

Elamite history is conventionally divided into three periods. The Old Elamite Period began around 2700 BC when the Elamite kingdom is first mentioned in Mesopotamian records. Elam comprised fertile lowlands, where intensive agriculture was practiced, and part of the Zagros Mountains with their resources of stone, metals, timber and pastures. Exchange of commodities between these regions spurred the development of towns in the late 4th millennium BC and the development of the Elamite kingdom itself. Elam was not a highly centralized kingdom. The king ruled from Susa, the largest city in Elam, but exercised authority over most of his kingdom indirectly through vassal princes. The power of the monarchy was also circumscribed by a constitution that generally did not allow a king to be succeeded by his son. Direct hereditary succession became the norm in later Elamite periods, however.

Conflict with Mesopotamia

From the beginning there were hostilities between the Elamite and Mesopotamian kingdoms. In the 23rd century BC Elam briefly became a vassal to Naram-Sin of Akkad. Over a century later King Shulgi of the Third Dynasty of Ur (r. 2094–2047 BC) conquered Susa but the highland areas remained independent. Later in the century the Elamites regained control of their capital and in 2004 BC King Kindattu captured and sacked Ur, a disaster from which Sumerian civilization never recovered. In 1764 BC the Elamites were conquered by the Babylonian King Hammurabi. However, their subjection did not last long; they rebelled against Hammurabi's less able son Samsuiluna (r. 1749–1712 BC) and won back their independence.

Periods of Elamite History

Old Elamite Period
2700–1300 BC

Middle Elamite Period
1300–750 BC

Neo-Elamite Period
750–644 BC

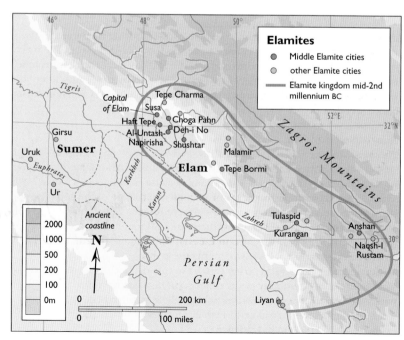

34

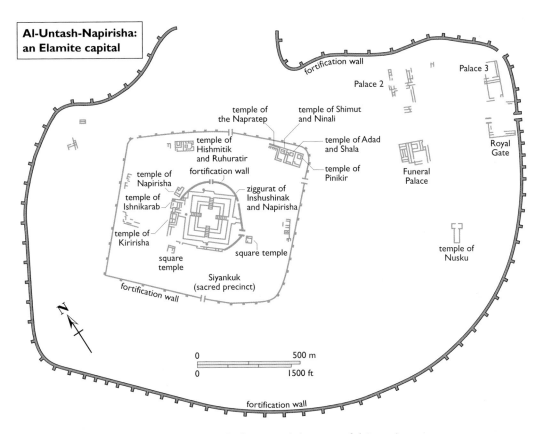

Al-Untash-Napirisha: an Elamite capital

fortification wall

Palace 2

Palace 3

temple of the Napratep

temple of Shimut and Ninali

temple of Hishmitik and Ruhuratir

temple of Adad and Shala

Royal Gate

temple of Napirisha

fortification wall

temple of Pinikir

Funeral Palace

temple of Ishnikarab

ziggurat of Inshushinak and Napirisha

temple of Kiririsha

square temple

temple of Nusku

square temple

Siyankuk (sacred precinct)

fortification wall

N

0   500 m

0   1500 ft

fortification wall

The Middle Elamite Period begins with the rise of the powerful Anzanite dynasty towards 1300 BC. The fifth king of this dynasty, Untash-Napirisha, founded a new capital city (named after himself) at Choga Zanbil but it was never completed and abandoned after his death. The rise of the Middle Elamite kingdom coincided with the rise of the Middle Assyrian empire and the two states were rivals for control over Babylon. The period of internal strife in Assyria following the death of Tukulti-Ninurta I in 1207 (see page 39) gave the Elamites the opportunity to become a major power in Mesopotamia and in 1154 they overthrew the Kassite dynasty of Babylon. Babylon soon recovered under a new dynasty and when King Nebuchadnezzar I (r. 1125–1104) launched a devastating surprise attack in the heat of midsummer, Elam collapsed. Little is known about Elam for the next 300 years.

A recovery, marking the beginning of the Neo-Elamite Period, began in the mid-8th century. The Elamites tried to exert influence in Mesopotamia by supporting Babylonian rebellions against Assyria. The Assyrians took terrible revenge for this in 647–6 BC when Ashurbanipal destroyed Susa, a blow from which Elam did not recover. The last Elamite king, Humban-Haltash III, held out for a few years in the mountains until he was betrayed to the Assyrians in 644 BC: he is last heard of towing Ashurbanipal's chariot at the celebration of the spring New Year festival. After the fall of the Assyrian empire in 612 BC, Elam passed under Babylonian control and then, in 539 BC, to the Persian empire. Elamite culture and language finally died out early in the Christian era.

This 7th-century carved stone relief is from King Ashurbanipal's palace in Nineveh in modern Iraq. It depicts the Elamites being led into captivity by the Assyrians in 653 BC.

The Hittite Empire

The greatest power of the Near East region in the middle of the 2nd millennium was the Hittite empire of Anatolia. The Hittites take their name from the land of Hatti, in central Anatolia, which they conquered when they migrated into the region from Thrace around 2000 BC.

"Afterwards Hattusilis became king.... And wherever he marched into battle, he subdued the lands of his enemies by might. "

Edict of King
Telipinus, c.1500 BC

The earliest references to the Hittites are recorded in Assyrian texts dating to around 1900–1750 BC, at which time they were probably still a tribal people. The first historical Hittite king was Hattusilis I (r. c.1650–1620) who established Hattusas (modern Boghazköy) as his capital.

History in Clay Tablets

Extensive archives of clay tablets discovered in archaeological excavations of the ancient city of Hattusas have provided the majority of our knowledge of Hittite history. The Hittite people spoke three related Indo-European languages and wrote using a mixture of Mesopotamian cuneiform and their own unique hieroglyphic script. Under Hattusilis and later his son Mursilis the Hittite kingdom expanded rapidly south into northern Mesopotamia and in 1595 Mursilis conducted a daring raid down the Euphrates river to Babylon, which was sacked. Mursilis' glory, however, was short-lived for he was assassinated around 1590 and the Hittite kingdom subsequently collapsed.

For more than 100 years the Hittites were divided and they even lost their capital to the Kaskas, a tribe from northern Anatolia. Most of the southern conquests of Hattusilis and Mursilis fell to the Hurrian kingdom of Mitanni, which comprised most of modern Syria. The Hittites had recovered their unity by 1400 and under King Suppiluliumas (r. 1344–1322 BC) they once again became a mighty power. Suppiluliumas recaptured Hattusas, which was rebuilt and fortified, and took advantage of a dynastic dispute to invade Mitanni and destroy its capital at Washukanni.

Into the Levant

A period of political weakness in Egypt after the death of Akhenaten in 1335 BC provided the Hittites with the opportunity to extend their empire into the Levant. In 1285 the pharaoh Ramesses II attempted to restore Egyptian dominance in the area and fought an important battle against the Hittite king Muwattalis II at Qadesh in Syria. Both sides claimed victory but as the Hittites subsequently extended their border south to Damascus it is clear

Processional Way
to Yazilikaya (5 km)
Hittite rock-cut
sanctuary

Büyükkaya

N

Assyrian
trading quarter
(Karum)
gate

north
gate

gate

Great
temple I

bridge

Halentuua
house

**lower
city**

Büyükkaya
(citadel & palace)

gate

gate

citadel

southern
citadel

Nisantepe

Sarikale

**upper
city**

Yenicekale

Lion
gate

temple VI

King's
gate

temple V

temple IV   temple II

temple III

0   250 m
0   250 yards

Sphinx gate

Hattusas: the Hittite capital

⌐ surviving city walls

⌐ reconstructed city wall

⋈ postern gates

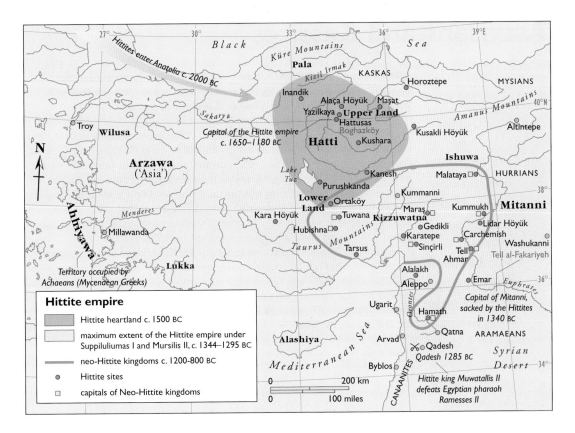

Hittite empire

	Hittite heartland c. 1500 BC
	maximum extent of the Hittite empire under Suppiluliumas I and Mursilis II, c. 1344–1295 BC
	neo-Hittite kingdoms c. 1200-800 BC
●	Hittite sites
□	capitals of Neo-Hittite kingdoms

who really had the best of the fight. Possibly because both kingdoms felt threatened by the rising power of Assyria, the Hittites and Egyptians settled their differences in 1258 with a peace treaty whose terms were recorded on tablets of silver. Although these have not survived, copies of the text have been discovered both at Hattusas and in Egypt. Terms of the treaty included provisions for the extradition of suspects and mutual military support if either kingdom was attacked by a third party. The Hittites also allied themselves with Babylon, Assyria's chief rival in Mesopotamia.

A Hittite king is depicted striking down his enemies with a bow and arrow from his chariot in this Neo-Hittite stone relief from Carchemish in Turkey.

Decline of an Empire

After 1205 Hittite inscriptions suddenly cease and excavations have revealed that Hattusas was sacked and abandoned about this time. The culprits were probably the Phrygians, another Indo-European speaking people who had crossed into Anatolia from Thrace.

Many other cities of the Hittite empire, such as Carchemish and Aleppo, were also sacked at this time, probably by the Sea Peoples (see page 40). The Hittite empire disintegrated under these successive assaults. The old Hittite heartland in Anatolia was settled by the Phrygians but in the south provincial cities such as Carchemish survived as city-states under independent 'neo-Hittite' dynasties. Although frequently at war with the neighbouring Aramaean city-states, the neo-Hittites maintained their independence until the 9th century BC when they were absorbed into the Assyrian empire.

Assyrians and Kassites

After its sack by the Hittites in 1595 BC, Babylon came under the control of the Kassite King Agum. The dynasty he founded would prove to be the most long-lived in Babylonian history.

"*I killed on foot 120 lions with my wild and vigorous assault. In addition I felled 800 lions from my light chariot. I have brought down every kind of wild animal and winged bird of the sky whenever I have shot an arrow.* **"**

Annals of King Tiglath-pileser I (r. 1115-1076 BC)

The Kassites are thought to have originated in the Zagros Mountains or the Iranian plateau. They are first recorded during the reign of Hammurabi's successor Samsuiluna (r. 1749-1712 BC), who defeated them and allowed them to settle under their own kings along the Diyala river, northeast of Babylon. The first 200 years of Kassite rule are very obscure and it is not known how they came to power. In the immediate aftermath of the Hittite attack, Babylon was seized by Sealand, a mysterious dynasty apparently from the far south of Mesopotamia and it was this dynasty that the Kassites expelled, probably around 1570.

Around 1475 King Ulamburiash conquered the Sealand and restored Babylonian control of all of southern Mesopotamia and welded it into a single political entity: under the Kassites the city-state of Babylon became Babylonia, a territorial state. By the 14th century Babylon was again a major power and the Kassite kings maintained close and friendly diplomatic relations with Egypt and the Hittite empire. With their immediate neighbours, Assyria and Elam, the Kas-

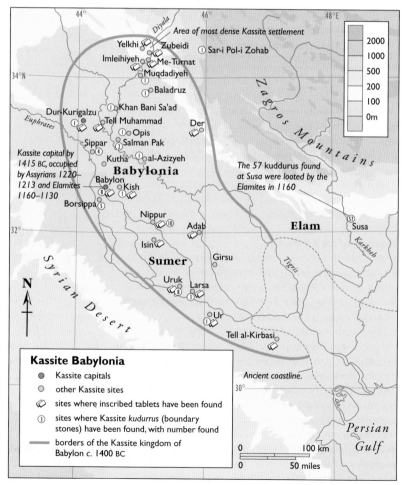

Kassite Babylonia

- ● Kassite capitals
- ○ other Kassite sites
- ⬦ sites where inscribed tablets have been found
- ① sites where Kassite *kudurrus* (boundary stones) have been found, with number found
- ▬ borders of the Kassite kingdom of Babylon c. 1400 BC

Area of most dense Kassite settlement

Kassite capital by 1415 BC, occupied by Assyrians 1220–1213 and Elamites 1160–1130

The 57 kudurrus found at Susa were looted by the Elamites in 1160

Ancient coastline.

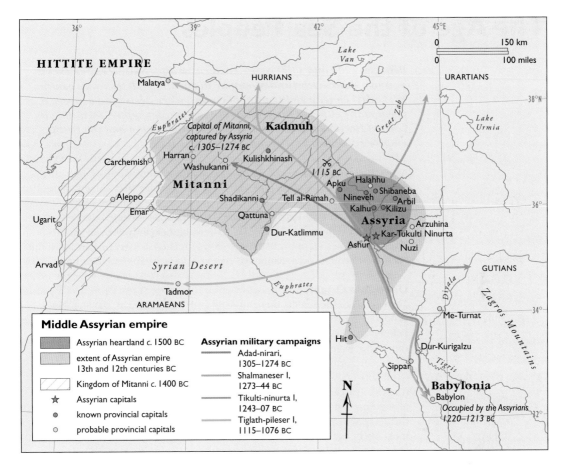

Middle Assyrian empire

▨	Assyrian heartland c. 1500 BC
░	extent of Assyrian empire 13th and 12th centuries BC
▨	Kingdom of Mitanni c. 1400 BC
★	Assyrian capitals
●	known provincial capitals
○	probable provincial capitals

Assyrian military campaigns

——	Adad-nirari, 1305–1274 BC
——	Shalmaneser I, 1273–44 BC
——	Tikulti-ninurta I, 1243–07 BC
——	Tiglath-pileser I, 1115–1076 BC

site kings were often at war. After over 400 years in power, the Kassite dynasty was finally brought down by an Elamite invasion in 1154 but Babylon itself recovered under a native dynasty.

Assyrian Revival

After the fall of Shamshi-Adad, Assyria became a minor power, a vassal to Babylon and, after Babylon was sacked by the Hittites, to the kingdom of Mitanni. Assyrian revival began under Ashur-uballit I (r. 1363–1328), who was the beneficiary of the Hittite King Suppiluliumas' attacks on Mitanni. Ashur-uballit was followed by a number of able kings, the greatest of whom were Shalmaneser I (1273–1244) and Tikulti-ninurta I (1243–1207). Tukulti-ninurta extended the Assyrian empire as far as the western Euphrates and, after he captured Babylon in 1220, as far south as the Persian Gulf. Although Babylon soon regained its independence, it was a sign of the shifting balance of power in Mesopotamia.

The cost of his campaigns made Tikulti-ninurta so unpopular that he was murdered in 1207 and much of his empire fell away under his weak successors. Assyria's rulers showed a return to militaristic form with the accession of Tiglath-pileser I (r. 1115–1076). In one of his campaigns Tiglath-pileser reached the Mediterranean Sea at Arvad and went hunting for whales. Assyrian kings were always passionate about hunting, which, after war, was the most important way for them to demonstrate their strength and martial vigour. Despite Tiglath-pileser's successes, the constant pressure on Assyria's borders by Aramaean nomads proved too much for his successors and by 1000 BC it was reduced to its ancient heartland around Ashur and Nineveh.

Kudurrus, such as this unfinished example, are the artefacts most typically associated with the Kassites. These stones recording donations of land by Kassite kings were displayed in temples.

The Age of the Sea Peoples

Between 1200 and 1150 BC the eastern Mediterranean experienced massive destruction and economic dislocation. All the main centres of the Mycenaean civilization of Greece were destroyed as were a great many cities of the Levant and the Hittite empire, including its capital Hattusas. Both the Mycenaean civilization and the Hittite empire collapsed as a result of these assaults.

Associated with this wave of destruction is a mysterious group of migrating peoples known as the Sea Peoples. The term 'Sea Peoples' was coined in the 19th century and they are not referred to by any collective name in ancient sources. According to ancient Egyptian sources these peoples included the Peleset, Tjeker, Shardana, Denyen, Meshwesh, Lukka, Teresh, Shekelesh, Ekwesh and Weshesh. The Sea Peoples were probably not closely related as Egyptian art shows that each group had its own distinctive styles of dress, weapons and armour.

Uncertain Origins

The origins of the Sea Peoples can really only be guessed at. The Shardana were probably from Sardinia, the Shekelesh from Sicily, the Meshwesh from Libya, the Peleset and Ekwesh from the Greek Aegean and the Lukka from western Anatolia: the Teresh may have been Etruscans. What caused the Sea Peoples to migrate is also extremely unclear as no single factor is likely to explain the motives of such a diverse group. Some, at least, may have been refugees from the Phrygians, whose invasion of Anatolia is the most likely cause of the fall of the Hittite empire. Similarly, the Peleset and Ekwesh may have been refugees created by the collapse of the Mycenaean civilization (see page 101).

Whatever their origins, the Sea Peoples moved around the eastern Mediterranean, attacking the coast of Anatolia, Cyprus, Syria and Canaan, before invading Egypt in the 1180s when they were eventually defeated in a naval battle in the Nile delta by the pharaoh Ramesses III. Many of the survivors were settled in Egypt, where they were soon assimilated to the native population, but the Tjeker, Shardana and Peleset withdrew and settled in Canaanite territory.

The Peleset, better known from the Bible as Philistines, maintained their identity the longest, giving their name to Palestine. Philistine settlements are recognized by their distinctive pottery which is derived from Mycenaean pottery styles. Philistine settlements were often built on unoccupied land but excavations have revealed that some were built on the sites of destroyed Canaanite settlements. Despite frequent wars with the Hebrew kingdoms, the Philistines survived until the 7th century BC when they were finally conquered by the Assyrians and subjected to resettlement in Mesopotamia.

> *"The foreigners made a conspiracy in their islands. All at once the lands were shattered in the fray. No land could stand before their arms, Hatti, Kode, Carchemish, Arzawa and Alashiya were destroyed one after the other. On they came towards Egypt ... Their confederation was the Peleset, Tjeker, Shekelesh, Denyen and Meshwesh. "*
>
> Inscription from Ramesses III's mortuary temple *c.* 1186 BC

Although less spectacular, other migrations in this period with far-reaching consequences were those of the Hebrews, Chaldaeans and Aramaeans, all Semitic-speaking desert nomads. The most numerous of these were the Aramaeans who settled on Hittite lands in Syria and Canaanite lands in Palestine. The Aramaeans kept the Assyrian empire under constant pressure. Tiglath-pileser I (r. 1115–1076) successfully kept the Aramaeans at bay but under his less able successors they reduced the empire to its heartland around Ashur and Nineveh.

Aramaic

In the following centuries the Aramaeans were subjugated by the Assyrians, who deported and resettled rebellious tribes, spreading them even more widely in the Near East. As a result the Aramaic language had become the 'lingua franca' of the Near East by the 6th century BC and was an official administrative language of the Persian empire. The modern Hebrew, Syriac and Arabic scripts are all derived from the Aramaic alphabet.

The Chaldaeans initially settled around the old Sumerian cities of Ur and Uruk. By the 8th century a Chaldaean dynasty was also in control of Babylon and in 612 it would overthrow the Assyrian empire. Another notable group of migrants were the Urartians, a people of uncertain origin who established a powerful kingdom around Lake Van in Armenia that would briefly challenge Assyria at the end of the 9th century.

This statue is from the Nuraghic civilization of Sardinia. One of the 'Sea Peoples', the Shardana, may have originated in Sardinia.

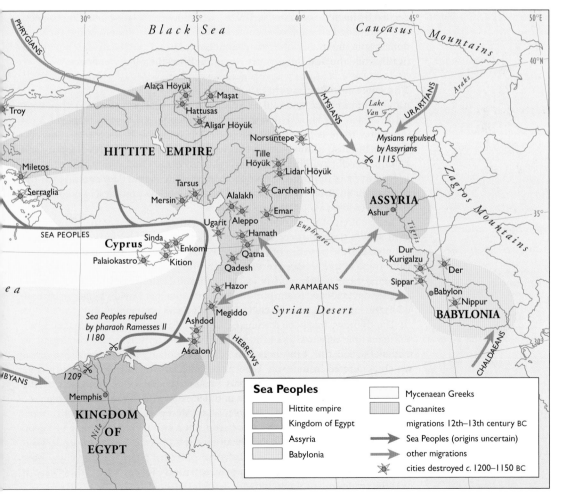

The Kingdoms of the Bible Lands

The kingdoms founded by the Hebrews in the Levant have an importance in world history out of all proportion to their modest size. The period of independent monarchy was the formative period for the Jewish religion, from which both Christianity and Islam are ultimately derived.

"So all the elders of Israel came to the king of Hebron; and king David made a league with them in Hebron before the Lord: and they anointed David king over Israel. "

II Samuel 5:3

The main source for the history of the Hebrew kingdoms has traditionally been the Bible. According to the Bible, the Hebrews or Israelites were a nomadic people who migrated into the land of Canaan sometime around 1200 BC, settling in scattered tribes under chieftains called 'judges'. The need to organize more effectively to resist the Philistines and Canaanites, with whom they were often at war, eventually led the tribes to unite under a monarchy.

The first king Saul (c. 1020–c. 1006) was killed in battle with the Philistines but his successor David (c. 1006–965) consolidated the monarchy and greatly expanded the Hebrew kingdom, defeating the Philistines and conquering the last Canaanite enclaves, including the city of Jerusalem. Jerusalem became David's capital and the main centre for the Hebrews' monotheistic religion. By the time of his death David had conquered a small empire that stretched from the Gulf of Aqaba in the south to the Euphrates river in the north. David was succeeded by his son Solomon (965–928), who undertook lavish building projects and maintained an expensive court life. Economic discontent caused the kingdom to split into the two separate kingdoms of Israel and Judah after Solomon's death, while the non-Hebrew provinces regained their independence.

The Bible and Archaeology

Although most historians still broadly accept the Biblical account, archaeological evidence has shown that it may be inaccurate in several respects. Most important, there is no archaeological evidence for the Hebrew migration into Canaan. Because of this some archaeologists believe that Hebrew identity and culture developed directly from the indigenous Canaanite culture in the uplands west of the Dead Sea. Jericho had been uninhabited for centuries by the time the Bible claims it was captured by the Hebrews and there were no walls to be brought down by Joshua's trumpets.

Archaeology also casts doubt on the monotheistic nature of the Hebrew religion at this time as there is clear evidence of a popular fertility cult in the countryside: the worship of Yahweh may have been originally part of a specifically royal cult. The discovery of an Amorite writing tablet at Dan in 1994 provided the first independent evidence for the existence of King David and his dynasty but evidence to support the Biblical claim that David's kingdom extended to the Euphrates and the Gulf of Aqaba has still not been found.

The Hebrews had been fortunate that their rise to statehood had taken place during a time of weakness in Egypt and Mesopotamia. This was coming to an end by the late 10th century and in 924 the Egyptian pharaoh Shoshenq invaded and imposed tribute on Israel and Judah. In the next century the two kingdoms became rebellious vassals of Assyria. Israel was destroyed by the Assyrians in 722 but Judah survived until 586, when the Babylonians conquered it and deported much of the population to Mesopotamia (see page 48). Many other Jews (as Hebrews were now called, after Judah) fled into exile in Egypt. Although the Persian Cyrus the Great gave Jews permission to return to their homeland after he conquered Babylon in 539 (see page 50), many had built prosperous lives for themselves in exile and chose to stay where they were. It was the beginning of the worldwide Jewish Diaspora.

The seige of Lachish, a Judaean fortress town on the approach to Jerusalem, is depicted on the walls of Sennacherib's palace at Nineveh. This section of the relief shows the Assyrians removing booty from the town.

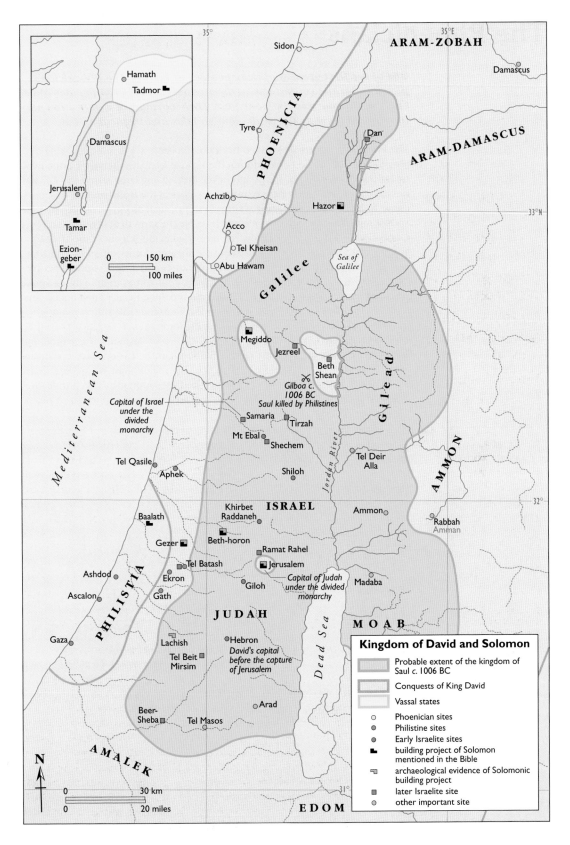

Hamath
Tadmor

Damascus

Jerusalem

Tamar

Ezion-
geber

0   150 km
0   100 miles

Sidon

ARAM-ZOBAH

Damascus

PHOENICIA

Tyre

Dan

ARAM-DAMASCUS

Achzib

Hazor

33°N

Acco

Tel Kheisan

Sea of
Galilee

Abu Hawam

Galilee

Mediterranean Sea

Megiddo

Jezreel

Beth
Shean

Gilboa c.
1006 BC
Saul killed by Philistines

Gilead

Capital of Israel
under the
divided
monarchy

Samaria

Tirzah

Mt Ebal

Shechem

Jordan River

Tel Deir
Alla

AMMON

Tel Qasile

Aphek

Shiloh

Khirbet
Raddaneh

ISRAEL

Ammon

32°

Rabbah
Amman

Baalath

Gezer

Beth-horon

Ramat Rahel

Ashdod

Tel Batash

Jerusalem

Ekron

Giloh

Capital of Judah
under the divided
monarchy

Madaba

Ascalon

Gath

JUDAH

MOAB

Gaza

Lachish

Hebron
David's capital
before the capture
of Jerusalem

Dead Sea

PHILISTIA

Tel Beit
Mirsim

Arad

Beer-
Sheba

Tel Masos

N

AMALEK

0   30 km
0   20 miles

31°

EDOM

Kingdom of David and Solomon

Probable extent of the kingdom of
Saul c. 1006 BC

Conquests of King David

Vassal states

○ Phoenician sites

● Philistine sites

● Early Israelite sites

■ building project of Solomon
mentioned in the Bible

▱ archaeological evidence of Solomonic
building project

■ later Israelite site

○ other important site

The Phoenicians

One of the first great seafaring peoples of history, the Phoenicians pioneered trade routes across the Mediterranean, creating new links between Europe and the Near East. Their voyages of exploration may have taken them as far as the British Isles and tropical Africa.

"The Phoenicians introduced into Greece … writing, an art which was, I think, until then unknown to the Greeks."

Herodotus, *Histories*

The Phoenicians were descended from the Canaanites, a Semitic-speaking people who inhabited the Levant during the Bronze Age. Although they often lived under the domination of Egypt and never formed any large states, the Canaanites have a major place in history as the inventors of the alphabet. As it was much easier to learn than other early writing systems, such as Egyptian hieroglyphic and Mesopotamian cuneiform, it made possible the growth of literacy that is the foundation of western civilization. The term 'Canaanite' fell out of use after 1000 BC, probably because it had ceased to be meaningful as different Canaanite groups had developed their own distinct identities and dialects. Several peoples familiar from the Bible, including the Hebrews, Edomites and Moabites, spoke languages derived from Canaanite, as also did the Phoenicians. The Phoenicians' religious beliefs were also derived from the Canaanites but there were great variations as each city had its own unique customs.

The homeland of the Phoenicians was the coast of modern Lebanon and Syria, where there are the best natural harbours in the eastern Mediterranean. Small ports began to develop here in the 3rd millennium BC, trading cedar wood, ivory and purple dye with Egypt and Mesopotamia. The purple dye, obtained from the murex shellfish, was such an important export that it proba-

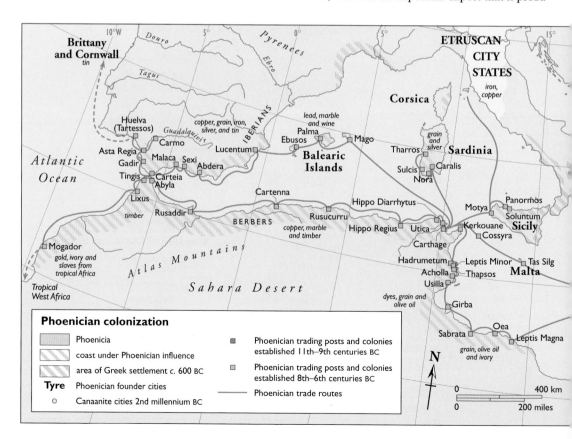

Phoenician colonization

- Phoenicia
- coast under Phoenician influence
- area of Greek settlement *c.* 600 BC
- **Tyre** Phoenician founder cities
- ○ Canaanite cities 2nd millennium BC

- ■ Phoenician trading posts and colonies established 11th–9th centuries BC
- □ Phoenician trading posts and colonies established 8th–6th centuries BC
- —— Phoenician trade routes

0 400 km
0 200 miles

bly gave the Phoenicians their name, from 'phoinix', derived from the Greek word for red. By around 1000 BC the main Phoenician centres (see Main Phoenician Cities list below) had become independent city-states. These cities were ruled by hereditary kings, like Hiram of Tyre who supplied timber and craftsmen for King Solomon's building projects in Israel. But by the 6th century BC monarchs had been replaced by elected magistrates.

Until the end of the 9th century BC Phoenician trading activity was confined largely to the eastern Mediterranean and the Aegean. Through these contacts the Greeks learned of the alphabet, writing there having fallen out of use after the fall of the Mycenaean civilization (see page 100). In the 8th century the growth of the Assyrian empire, and its demands for metals and exotic products, stimulated Phoenicians to travel further afield and by around 700 BC their trade routes extended throughout the western Mediterranean and along the Atlantic coasts of Europe and Africa. Across these new trade routes the Phoenician city-states founded trading posts and colonies, the most important of which was Carthage in Tunisia (see page 68). Through these colonies the peoples of Atlantic Europe first felt the influence of the civilizations of the Near East and the eastern Mediterranean.

Although the Assyrian empire stimulated trade it also curtailed the Phoenicians' independence. From the 9th century on, the Assyrians' exacted tribute from the Phoenician city-states, while Assyrian officials supervised commercial activities. After the fall of the Assyrian empire, Phoenicia passed under first Babylonian and then Persian control before it was conquered by Alexander the Great of Macedon in 332 BC. The Phoenicians gradually lost their distinctive identity and after Alexander's conquest their culture became increasingly Hellenized.

This openwork ivory plaque showing a winged sphinx was found at the Assyrian palace at Nimrud. The style suggests that it was probably carved by a Phoenician craftsman on the coast of the Levant.

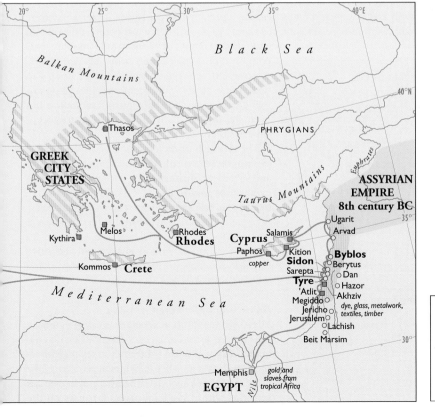

Main Phoenician Cities
Tyre
Sidon
Berytus (Beirut)
Byblos
Arvad
Ugarit

Assyria's Imperial Prime

Military and administrative efficiency made Assyria the dominant power of the ancient Near East in the first half of the 1st millennium BC. Assyrian kings were skilful propagandists who carefully cultivated an image of overwhelming might to cow their opponents into submission.

"I am king, I am lord, I am praiseworthy, I am exalted, I am magnificent, I am the foremost, I am a great warrior, I am a hero, I am a lion, and I am virile; Ashurnasirpal ... king of Assyria. "

Royal Annals
of Ashurnasirpal II

Assyria's period of imperial greatness started in the reign of Ashur-dan II (r. 934–912 BC). By securing Assyria's frontiers and pursuing a policy of agricultural improvement he increased his kingdom's resources and created a strong base for his successor Adad-nirari II (r. 911–891) to reconquer most of the lands held by the Middle Assyrian empire.

Expansion continued steadily for most of the 9th century. In a pattern that had long been typical of Mesopotamian imperialism, conquered rulers became vassals. So long as they were obedient and paid tribute they were secure but if they rebelled they were overthrown, humiliated or killed and replaced by a puppet ruler. If this failed, however, troublesome populations were deported and resettled in Assyria where they could be supervised.

Reforms under Tiglath-pileser III

After the death of Shalmaneser III in 824, Assyria was weakened by internal problems which allowed the kingdom of Urartu, in Armenia, to dominate Anatolia. Most vassal states recovered their independence. The empire was rebuilt by Tiglath-pileser III (r. 744–727 BC), an able administrator whose reforms included setting up a postal service and an intelligence corps. Assyrian government became so effective that vassal rulers could increasingly be dispensed with and conquered lands became directly ruled provinces under governors, who were themselves subject to spot checks by roving inspectors. Deportation and resettlement of conquered peoples was employed on a large scale – some 220,000 people were resettled in Tiglath-pileser's reign alone – to undermine local loyalties and identities. Assyrians had great respect for Babylonian civilization but even the king of Babylon was forced to accept supervision by an Assyrian eunuch governor.

The strength of the empire was displayed after Tiglath-pileser's death. In 722 Tiglath-pileser's son and successor, Shalmaneser V, was overthrown in a civil war by Sargon II (721–705). Rebellions broke out across the empire but they were all easily defeated, except that in Babylon, which, because it was supported by the Elamites, took Sargon 10 years to suppress. Sargon also ended the main threat to Assyria's northern border by destroying the kingdom of Urartu.

Ashurbanipal's Reign

The Assyrian empire reached its greatest extent in the reign of Ashurbanipal (r. 668–c. 627) who conquered Egypt and Elam, the latter in revenge for its support for yet another Babylonian rebellion. Like other Assyrian kings, Ashurbanipal publicized his victories with carved and painted friezes on the

Nineveh
areas excavated by archaeologists

Map labels:
N
moat
Halahhu Gate
Ajileh dam
Adad Gate
Nergal Gate
Shibaniba Gate
Sin Gate
Palace of Ashurbanipal
Nabu temple
Mushlalu Gate
Gate of the Watering Places
Khosr
Kar-Mulissi Gate
Palace of Sennacherib
Ishtar temple
Quay Gate
Sibitti altar
Desert Gate
temple
Shamash Gate
Arsenal Gate
Arsenal of Esarhaddon
Tigris
0   1000 m
0   1000 yards
canal
Halzi Gate
Handuri Gate
moat
Ashur Gate

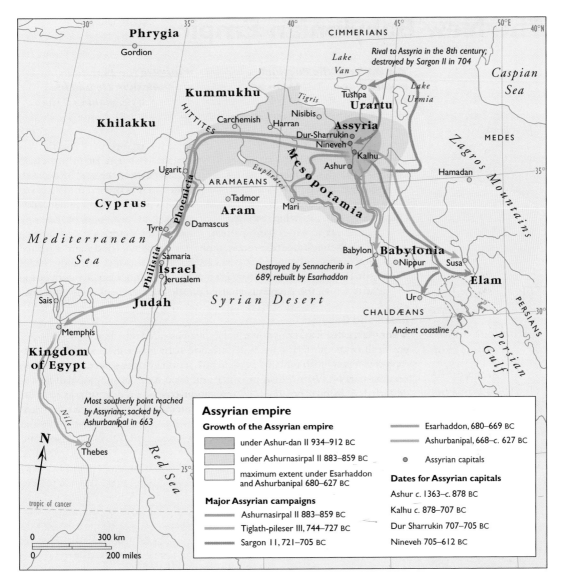

Assyrian empire

Growth of the Assyrian empire

- under Ashur-dan II 934–912 BC
- under Ashurnasirpal II 883–859 BC
- maximum extent under Esarhaddon and Ashurbanipal 680–627 BC

Major Assyrian campaigns

- Ashurnasirpal II 883–859 BC
- Tiglath-pileser III, 744–727 BC
- Sargon II, 721–705 BC
- Esarhaddon, 680–669 BC
- Ashurbanipal, 668–c. 627 BC
- Assyrian capitals

Dates for Assyrian capitals

Ashur c. 1363–c. 878 BC
Kalhu c. 878–707 BC
Dur Sharrukin 707–705 BC
Nineveh 705–612 BC

walls of his palace at Nineveh illustrating the ghastly fate that awaited Assyria's enemies. Ashurbanipal was one of Assyria's most cultured rulers and he built a vast library of cuneiform tablets at Nineveh. Rediscovered in the 19th century, they are the source of much of our knowledge of the history, literature and beliefs of ancient Mesopotamia.

End of Assyrian Dominance

Ashurbanipal's conquests greatly overextended the empire while his oppressive rule led to increasing internal disorder. Egypt had already regained its independence before Ashurbanipal died and no sooner was he dead than Babylon rebelled again, this time successfully. In alliance with the Medes of Iran, the Babylonians went into the offensive and captured Nineveh in 612. The Assyrian empire had become so centralized that this proved to be a knock out blow. The policy of deportation and resettlement had weakened Assyrian identity, while the subject populations had no real loyalty to the state. By 609 the last Assyrian resistance had been crushed and the empire passed virtually intact to Babylon.

Imposing stone beasts, such as this human-headed, winged bull, often supported the doorways of important Assyrian palaces.

The New Babylonian Empire

The leader of the Babylonian revolt that toppled the Assyrian empire was a Chaldaean noble called Nabopolassar. He and his son Nebuchadnezzar rebuilt Babylon in lavish style, making it the most magnificent city of the ancient Near East.

"I slaughtered the land of Assyria, I turned that hostile land into heaps of ruins. The Assyrian, who since ancient times had ruled over all the peoples with a heavy yoke, I turned his feet away from Babylonia, I threw off his yoke. "

Inscription of Nabopolassar

Nabopolassar's main problem in consolidating his victory over Assyria was Egypt. Although nominally an ally of Assyria against Babylon, Egypt had taken control of Palestine, Phoenicia and Syria in the last years of the war. After Assyrian resistance ended in 609, the pharaoh Necho was determined to hold on to these gains. Nabopolassar was equally determined to bring them under Babylonian control and, being too old to campaign in person, sent his son, Nebuchadnezzar, to expel the Egyptians in 605. After victories at Carchemish and Hamath, Nebuchadnezzar received news of his father's death and returned to Babylon for his coronation but was soon back on campaign, pursuing Necho into Egypt. However, Nebuchadnezzar's attempt to conquer Egypt was defeated in 601 after which the Egyptians focused on stirring up rebellions in Palestine.

Judah and Babylon

When Nebuchadnezzar put down an Egyptian-inspired rebellion in Judah in 597 BC, much of the population was deported to Babylonia and its vassal king was replaced. When Judah rebelled again in 587, Jerusalem was sacked, the kingdom became part of a Babylonian province and even more of the population was deported. Babylon's posthumous reputation has suffered greatly as a result because the disgruntled Jews damned Babylon in their influential scriptures as a den of luxurious decadence and unnatural vice, a reputation of which it is no more deserving than any other ancient city.

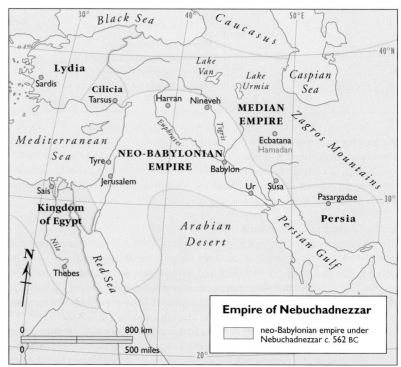

Empire of Nebuchadnezzar

neo-Babylonian empire under Nebuchadnezzar c. 562 BC

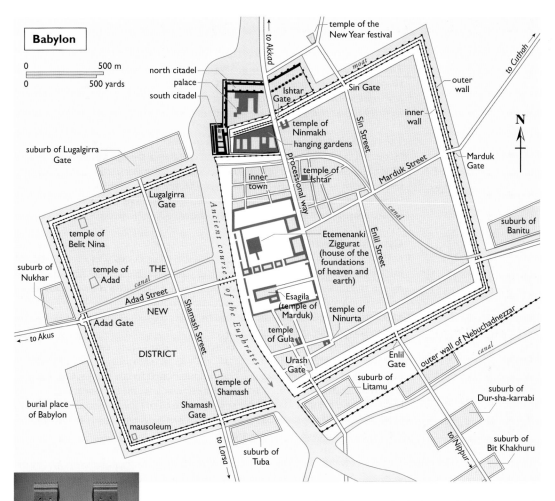

Babylon

| 0 | 500 m |
| 0 | 500 yards |

temple of the New Year festival

north citadel
palace
south citadel

Ishtar Gate

Sin Gate

moat

outer wall

inner wall

to Akkad

to Cuthah

N

temple of Ninmakh
hanging gardens

Sin Street

Marduk Street

Marduk Gate

suburb of Lugalgirra Gate

inner town

temple of Ishtar

Processional way

Lugalgirra Gate

canal

suburb of Banitu

temple of Belit Nina

Ancient course of the Euphrates

Etemenanki Ziggurat (house of the foundations of heaven and earth)

Enlil Street

suburb of Nukhar

temple of Adad

THE

canal

Adad Street

NEW

Shamash Street

Esagila (temple of Marduk)

temple of Ninurta

temple of Gula

Adad Gate

to Akus

outer wall of Nebuchadnezzar

canal

DISTRICT

Urash Gate

Enlil Gate

temple of Shamash

suburb of Litamu

suburb of Dur-sha-karrabi

burial place of Babylon

Shamash Gate

mausoleum

to Larsa

suburb of Tuba

to Nippur

suburb of Bit Khakhuru

Nebuchadnezzar (604–562 BC) built the Ishtar Gate, one of eight gates that led into the inner city of Babylon (see map above). This reconstruction in Baghdad, Iraq reveals the original decoration of the monumental gate. It was covered in blue glazed bricks with reliefs of dragons and bulls.

Nebuchadnezzar's reign saw the rebuilding of Babylon, including the temple of its patron god Marduk at Esagila, the Etemenanki ziggurat and the Hanging Gardens, one of the Seven Wonders of the World. According to legend, the Hanging Gardens, which have not been identified with certainty, were built so that his bride would not miss the mountains of her Median home. Nebuchadnezzar also fortified Babylon's defences with brick walls and monumental gateways.

The period of Babylonian glory proved to be brief. Following Nebuchadnezzar's death in 562 BC the throne passed in quick succession to his son, brother-in-law and grandson, the last murdered in 556 and replaced by Nabonidus. A commoner and a religious man, Nabonidus had an interest in antiquarianism and he conducted excavations of the foundations of ancient Mesopotamian temples to discover their origins. Nabonidus' mother, who was 104 when she died in 547, was a priestess of the Moon god Sin. Nabonidus shared her devotion to Sin but this made him unpopular with the priests of Marduk and he went into self-imposed exile at Taima in Arabia, leaving his son Bel-shar-usur (the Biblical Belshazzar) as regent in Babylon. This made him even more unpopular as the all-important New Year festival could not be celebrated without the king. Absorbed in their religious controversies, the Babylonians had ignored the rising power of Persia under Cyrus the Great. In September 539 Cyrus invaded Babylonia. There was little opposition and on 14th October Babylon fell without a fight, bringing the 2000-year-old Mesopotamian imperial tradition to an anti-climactic end.

The Persian Empire

The greatest and last of the empires of the ancient Near East was the Achaemenid empire of Persia. Extending from the Indus river in the east to the Aegean Sea in the west, this vast realm was created in little more than a decade by Cyrus the Great.

“Oh man, I am Cyrus, who founded the empire of the Persians and was king of Asia. Grudge me not therefore this monument. ”

Epitaph of Cyrus the Great

The Persians were one of two Indo-Iranian nomad peoples, the other being the Medes, who had migrated into Iran from central Asia around the 8th century BC. While the Medes settled on the Iranian plateau, the Persians migrated further south, finally settling between the Zagros Mountains and the Persian Gulf. The Persian kingdom was supposedly founded by Achaemenes, from whom the ruling dynasty takes its name, but it is not known when he lived.

Cyrus the Great

At the time Cyrus came to the throne around 559 BC Persia was a vassal state of the Median empire. Media was a powerful state – the Medes had played a major role in the downfall of the Assyrian empire – but very little is known about its organization or even its extent. Its eastern border probably lay in modern Afghanistan, its western border, agreed by treaty with the kingdom of Lydia, was on the Kizil Irmak river in Anatolia.

In 550 Cyrus rebelled against his Median overlord, King Astyages, who retaliated by invading Persia. Astyages, however, was an unpopular ruler and when he met Cyrus in battle at Pasargadae he was abandoned by his troops. Cyrus quickly seized the Median capital at Ecbatana (Hamadan) and by a nearly bloodless coup became ruler of Media. This success gave Cyrus the resources to conquer Lydia in 546 and the Babylonian empire in 539. Cyrus was finally killed fighting the Scythian nomads in central Asia.

Cyrus the Great's success was due as much to diplomacy as generalship. He was merciful to defeated rulers, he did not burden conquered populations with excessive demands for tribute and he did not interfere with local customs, religions and laws. Cyrus was also aided by the long traditions of imperial rule

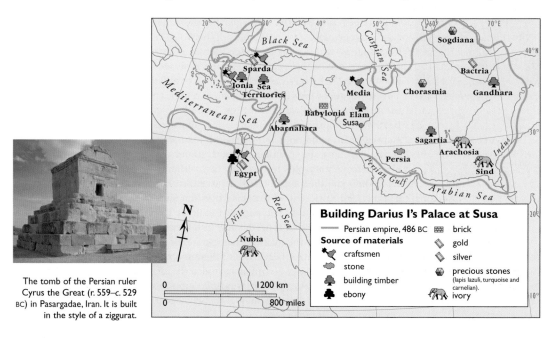

The tomb of the Persian ruler Cyrus the Great (r. 559–c. 529 BC) in Pasargadae, Iran. It is built in the style of a ziggurat.

Building Darius I's Palace at Susa

— Persian empire, 486 BC

Source of materials

- craftsmen
- stone
- building timber
- ebony
- brick
- gold
- silver
- precious stones (lapis lazuli, turquoise and carnelian).
- ivory

0 — 1200 km
0 — 800 miles

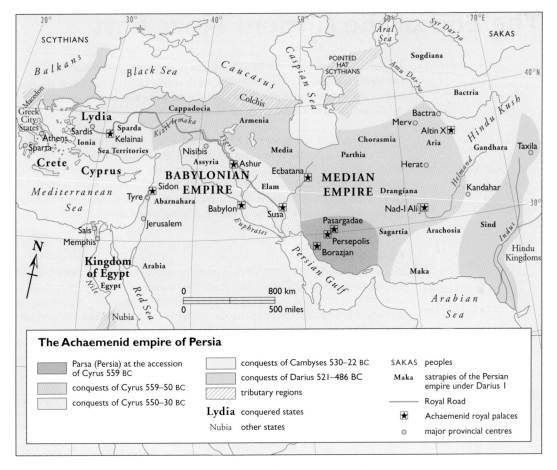

The Achaemenid empire of Persia

Parsa (Persia) at the accession of Cyrus 559 BC

conquests of Cyrus 559–50 BC

conquests of Cyrus 550–30 BC

conquests of Cambyses 530–22 BC

conquests of Darius 521–486 BC

tributary regions

Lydia conquered states

Nubia other states

SAKAS peoples

Maka satrapies of the Persian empire under Darius I

Royal Road

★ Achaemenid royal palaces

○ major provincial centres

in the Near East which, over time, had weakened local identities and accustomed people to foreign rule.

Expansion continued under Cyrus' successors: his son Cambyses (r. 529–522) conquered Egypt and Libya; Darius I (r. 521–486) conquered the Indus valley before turning west and seizing Thrace in southeast Europe in 513. This turned out to be the high point of Persian expansion. In 494 Darius put down a rebellion by the Greek cities on the Aegean coast of Lydia. The rebels had been helped by Athens and other cities on the Greek mainland. Darius sent a punitive expedition in 491 but it was defeated by the Athenians at Marathon. A more concerted effort to conquer Greece by Darius' son Xerxes (r. 485–465) in 480–479 was also crushed (see page 102). While Cyrus had ruled through existing institutions, Darius reorganized the empire into about 20 satrapies (provinces). Tax was assessed at about half the level each satrapy was thought able to pay and the power of governors was limited by separating civil and military authority. The old Assyrian postal system was upgraded and internal communications were speeded by the building of the 2500 km-long (1600 miles) Royal Road linking Susa, the administrative capital, to Sardis on the Aegean Sea.

The Greeks, understandably, regarded Persia as a great tyranny but it was in many ways a tolerant empire and a melting pot of cultures. When Darius built a new palace at Susa he deliberately incorporated materials and styles from across the empire to display its size, wealth and diversity. This diversity was also celebrated in a frieze at the ceremonial capital of Persepolis depicting the empire's different ethnic groups in their distinctive costumes queuing to present exotic gifts to the king.

The End of the Ancient Near East

"Though in other respects his conduct appears to have been moderate and decent, in military matters Darius III was the feeblest ... of men.... His life was an unbroken series of disasters from the moment of his accession to the Persian throne."

Arrian, *The Campaigns of Alexander*

For all its great size, the Persian empire suffered from many of the same weaknesses as its Babylonian and Assyrian predecessors. These led to the rapid collapse of the empire when it was invaded by Alexander the Great, king of Macedon.

For 150 years after the failure of Xerxes' expedition to Greece in 480–479, Persia struggled to maintain an image of might. Fortunately, the Greeks were too divided among themselves to make the most of their victory and by exploiting the rivalry between Athens and Sparta, Persia was able to restore its dominance of the Aegean by 404. In the same year there was a rebellion in Egypt, where the people still had a strong sense of national identity, and it was 60 years before Persian control was restored.

Persia is Weakened

Internally, the Achaemenid family was riven by palace intrigues and in 401 a civil war broke out between Artaxerxes II and his brother Cyrus. Cyrus recruited an army of 13,000 Greek mercenaries and advanced as far as Babylon, where he was killed in a cavalry skirmish. The Greeks, their employer dead, refused to surrender and successfully fought their way home, evading or defeating the Persian forces in their way. Xenophon, one of the Greek commanders, wrote an account of the campaign in which he observed that: 'While the Persian empire was strong in that it covered vast territories with large populations, it was also weak because of the need to travel great distances and the wide dispersal of its forces, making it vulnerable to a swift attack'.

Alexander the Great

That swift attack was started by King Philip II of Macedon (r. 359–336 BC), who, having conquered the Greeks in 338, wanted to bind them in loyalty to him in a common war against the old Persian enemy. Philip sent an army to invade Anatolia but was murdered before he could join it, and it was left to his 20-year-old son Alexander to take command. Alexander, known to history as 'the Great', was a megalomaniac with a genius for war and his father had bequeathed him a highly disciplined, efficient and well-equipped army. Opposing him was Darius III (r. 336–330) who was

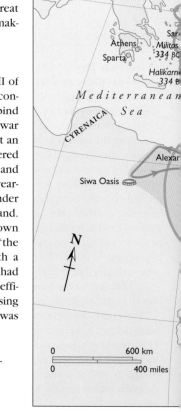

A bronze Hellenistic statue showing Alexander the Great taming a horse. As well as being an excellent military leader, Alexander was an accomplished athlete.

THRA
MACEDON
Athens
Sparta
Sar
Militos
334 BC
Halikarn
334 B
Mediterranean Sea
CYRENAICA
Alexan
Siwa Oasis

N

0	600 km
0	400 miles

conspicuously lacking in military ability. Persia could raise vast armies but they were composed mostly of poorly equipped levies who were no match for the Greek and Macedonian troops. Even their enormous numbers were not the advantage they seemed as they could not be controlled effectively on the battlefield and were difficult to provision. Moreover, as Xenophon had noted, because contingents often had to travel long distances, these armies took time to gather. It took Alexander only eight years of campaigning to conquer the entire Achaemenid empire. Darius, the last of the dynasty, was murdered by one of his courtiers as he fled from Persepolis in 330 BC.

Alexander's Death

Alexander the Great died in 324 BC, aged only 32, and had no chance to consolidate his conquests. Alexander's generals fought one another over his inheritance and the empire broke up into separate kingdoms ruled by Greek and Macedonian dynasties. There were no popular uprisings, the centuries of imperial rule had so diminished local identities that most of the empire's inhabitants did not really care who ruled them so long as they did not make unreasonable demands for tribute. The fall of the Persian empire effectively marks the end of the ancient Near East. Alexander's conquests opened the Near East to the influence of Greek civilization, the region's ancient traditions went into decline and died out around the beginning of the Christian era.

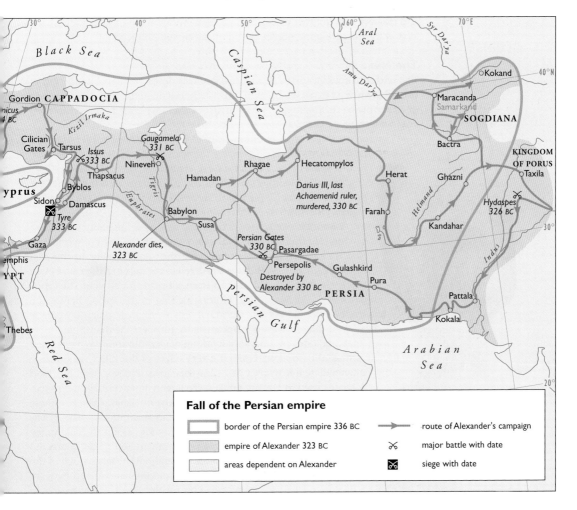

Fall of the Persian empire

- border of the Persian empire 336 BC
- empire of Alexander 323 BC
- areas dependent on Alexander
- route of Alexander's campaign
- major battle with date
- siege with date

Part II: The African Civilizations

*Even as late as the early 20th century Africa was regarded as the
'Dark Continent', a place of savage barbarism that needed to be
civilized from without. Yet the history of civilization in Africa is
as old and diverse as it is on any continent.*

Africa's first, and best known, civilization developed in the valley of the lower
Nile in Egypt around 3100 BC: it survived as an unbroken cultural tradition until
the conversion of the Egyptians to Christianity in the 4th century AD. Perhaps
because of its long interaction with the civilizations of the ancient Near East and
Europe, the 'African-ness' of ancient Egyptian civilization is, if not exactly denied,
at least largely overlooked.

The modern study of ancient Egypt began in 1798 when Napoleon Bona-
parte invaded the country with the intention of using it as a base to threaten the
British empire in India. Napoleon's expedition came to a bad end after Nelson
sank his fleet at Aboukir Bay, however, the team of antiquarians he had taken
with him made astonishing discoveries, including the Rosetta stone, which provided the key to deciphering the ancient Egyptian hieroglyphic writing system.
Unlike the ancient Mesopotamians, who built in friable mud brick, the Egyptians
built in hard stone, so their civilization has left a legacy of awesome architecture
and colossal statuary that has proved perennially fascinating, as has their obses-
sion with preserving the bodies of their dead by mummification.

The Nile

The ancient Greek historian Herodotus famously described Egypt as 'the gift of
the Nile'. Ancient Egypt was indeed totally dependent on the river Nile; the lives
of its people were dominated by its annual cycle and without it their civilization
could never have existed as Egypt has too little rainfall for agriculture. From the
First Cataract, the rapids that traditionally marked the southern border of Egypt,
the Nile flows in a narrow valley for nearly 800 kilometres (500 miles)
until it splits up into a multitude of channels in the Delta before flow-
ing into the Mediterranean Sea. Until it widens into the Delta, the
Nile's flood plain is nowhere more than a few miles wide and in
places it narrows to just a few hundred yards.

Although somewhat confined, this was arguably the most
favourable farming environment anywhere in the ancient world. The
Nile flooded every August, following the summer rains in the East
African highlands. As the river level fell in the autumn, the flood plain
was left moist and fertilized with fresh silt ready for sowing. The crops
grew through the warm dry winter, ripening in the spring before the
next cycle of flooding began. Good harvests were made year after year as
the fertility of the soil was to all intents and purposes inexhaustible.

Canals and ditches and a simple lifting device, the *shadouf*, were used
to help spread the flood waters to the very edges of the valley, maximizing
the cultivable area. However, the complex irrigation systems and flood
defences used in Mesopotamia were largely unnecessary. In comparison to Mesopotamia, where the rivers could change course
violently and unpredictably and the main flood season was
spring, after the beginning of the growing season, the Nile valley
was a stable and predictable environment. But if the floods did
fail, then there would be famine throughout the land. Much of the
authority of Egyptian kings derived from the belief that they were
divine and had the power to control the flood. A succession of

This statue of a
bird deity from
Predynastic Egypt
shows a dancing,
bird-headed girl.
Gods were often
worshipped in the
form of animals in
ancient Egypt.

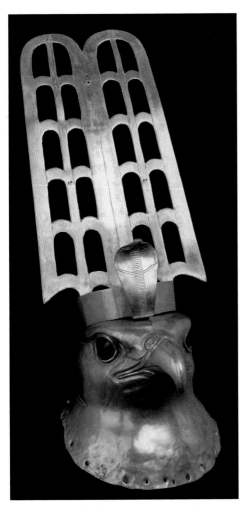

This gold headdress with falcon's head was found at the Temple of Nekhen in Hierakonpolis, Upper Egypt. The god Horus in the shape of a falcon was worshipped there during the Predynastic and Early Dynastic Periods.

failures could undermine royal authority as it would appear that the king had lost the favour of the gods.

The Nile was also Egypt's main highway. The prevailing winds in Egypt blow from north to south, enabling ships to travel upstream using sails and make the return journey downstream with the flow of the river. Few settlements lay far from the Nile so heavy and cumbersome loads of grain or building stone could be transported easily and economically over long distances.

The transition between the lush valley and the deserts on either side of the river was sudden and stark. The deserts were an important source of metal ores, gems and stone for building, sculpture and tool making, and had rough grazing that supported nomadic pastoralists. The deserts were also important because they isolated Egypt from other civilizations and protected it from invasions, helping to preserve its unique character. Egyptian civilization was nearly 1500 years old before it experienced a major invasion.

Farming settlement of the Nile valley started around 5000 BC. The first settlers were probably refugees from the Sahara which was beginning then to dry out and change into desert. The valley had become densely populated by the 4th millennium BC and chiefdoms and towns had started to develop. Competition between chiefdoms in the narrow valley was intense and by *c*. 3100 BC they had been amalgamated into the two kingdoms of Upper (southern) and Lower (northern) Egypt.

Many of the defining, most well-known characteristics of Egyptian civilization had now appeared, including divine kingship, the beginnings of hieroglyphic writing, and mummification of the dead. Around 3100 the two kingdoms were united by King Narmer, who was ruler of the kingdom of Upper Egypt. It is not certain that Narmer's achievement was a permanent one and it was not until *c*. 2900 BC that Egypt had emerged as a stable territorial kingdom.

Periods of Egyptian History

It is conventional to divide Egypt's subsequent history into clearly defined periods. The first, the Early Dynastic Period (2920–2650 BC), is the period of the first two historically documented dynasties of Egypt and saw the consolidation of the kingdom of Egypt. The following Old Kingdom Period (2649–2134 BC), was a period of strong royal government which saw Egypt become a great imperial power. This was also the age during which the Great Pyramids at Giza were built. The First Intermediate Period (2134–2040 BC) saw Egypt break up into two kingdoms again after a period of low Nile floods damaged royal authority. The Middle Kingdom (2040–*c*. 1640 BC) was another era of strong royal government and imperial expansion.

Egypt was again divided in the Second Intermediate Period (1640–1532) when the Hyksos, invaders from the Near East, overran the Delta. The expulsion of the Hyksos ushered in Egypt's last and greatest period as an imperial power, the New Kingdom (1532–1070 BC). This was the period when Egyptian kings began to be known as pharaohs. The Third Intermediate Period (1070–712) saw weak pharaohs struggling to maintain their authority against an increasingly powerful priesthood: it ended in a civil war which split the country into half a

The gold sarcophagus of Tutankhamun from his tomb at Thebes. Despite being a short-lived and relatively unmemorable ruler, Tutankhamun is the most famous of all pharaohs because his splendid tomb treasure survived. He died c. 1325 BC, possibly from a skull injury.

dozen petty kingdoms, which were easily conquered by the Nubian kingdom of Kush. The Nubian conquest began the Late Period (712–332 BC), a period of foreign rule interspersed with native revivals.

After Alexander the Great conquered Egypt in 332 BC, the country was permanently under foreign rule. Egyptian civilization survived, sustained by its religion and the statesmanship of foreign rulers, who found it expedient to adopt the trappings of traditional Egyptian kingship to make themselves more acceptable to their subjects. It was only when Christianity destroyed its religious basis that ancient Egyptian civilization finally died out.

One of the striking characteristics of ancient Egyptian civilization is its lack of technological innovation, a result, probably, of its cultural conservatism – no other civilization in world history has shown the same degree of continuity in its traditions of art, religion and rulership for such a long span of time. It was not until the Second Intermediate Period that bronze tools and wheeled vehicles were used in Egypt, even though they had been used in the Near East for more than 1500 years. This confirms that civilization is first and foremost defined by the complexity of its social organization rather than by its technology. The Great Pyramids of Giza were built with much the same technology that was available to those who, around the same time, erected the trilithon circle at Stonehenge. The difference in scale of the monuments is a measure of the difference in the scale of their social organization.

The Nubians

The Nubians, who conquered Egypt in 712 BC, were the founders of the first civilization of tropical Africa. Nubia, usually called Kush by the Egyptians, stretched for hundreds of miles south from the First Cataract of the Nile: its southern border was undefined. Like the Egyptians, the Nubians were dependent on the Nile. Farming in Nubia began around the same time as it did in Egypt and its early cultures were similar to those of Egypt. However, Nubia's development towards statehood and civilization was held back by frequent Egyptian interventions in the 3rd millennium BC. Nubia was rich in gold deposits and other minerals, which were an irresistible attraction for the Egyptians, who also raided Nubia for slaves and cattle. It was only while Egypt was weak, during the First Intermediate Period, that a native Nubian kingdom emerged. This was suppressed when Egypt regained strength during the Middle Kingdom, only to rise again when Egypt was invaded by the Hyksos in the Second Intermediate Period. In New Kingdom times, Egyptian power was extended further into Nubia than ever before and it was not until Egypt entered its long final decline that a stable Nubian kingdom emerged. Despite its destructive interventions, Nubian rulers saw Egypt's traditions of kingship and government as things to be emulated and Nubian civilization became very Egyptianized in its art, architecture and religion.

Egyptian influence was surprisingly limited in other parts of Africa. Even in North Africa, the main external influences on the development of civilizations were the Phoenicians, from the Lebanon, and the Greeks. The greatest power of North Africa, after Egypt, was the Phoenician city of Carthage, founded in 814 BC. At its height in the 3rd century BC, Carthage challenged Rome for the domination of the western Mediterranean and lost: it was finally overthrown by the Romans in 146 BC.

The civilizations of sub-Saharan Africa do not properly belong to ancient history since none of them originated before 500 BC. For thousands of years the Sahara desert was a near insuperable obstacle to communication between sub-Saharan Africa and the civilizations of the north. The primary routes of communication existed along the Nile valley through Nubia and by sea down the Red Sea from Egypt (as well as across the Red Sea from Arabia).

This bronze votive statue of a soldier comes from the Qustul tombs of Nubia in Sudan. The Nubians, who established the first civilization of tropical Africa, were excellent warriors. Ancient Nubia was a centre of culture and military power in Africa, and had a wealth of natural resources including gold, ebony, copper and ivory.

Although Phoenician mariners probably visited the West African coast in the 7th century BC, regular maritime contacts with the Mediterranean did not develop until the 15th century AD. Mediterranean mariners were discouraged from trying to reach West Africa because the prevailing north-westerly winds made the return journey almost impossible in the ships of the time. Regular caravan routes across the Sahara were opened up only after the introduction of the camel from the Near East early in the Christian era, but knowledge of bronze casting and iron smelting had crossed the desert to West Africa as early as 700 BC. There is still a common tendency to regard sub-Saharan Africa as technologically backward; in fact, however, it would be another 200 years before iron was worked in China.

Environmental Problems

As a result of this isolation, except on the east coast, civilizations in sub-Saharan Africa developed mainly in response to local factors, such as intensification of agriculture and rising population, rather than external influences. By the time Europeans first began to explore sub-Saharan Africa in the late 15th century, it was home to a great diversity of indigenous civilizations: the white man did not bring civilization to Africa.

There were, however, serious environmental constraints on the development of civilizations in sub-Saharan Africa. Civilizations developed on the fertile delta of the river Niger in the Middle Ages but in much of the rest of the rainforest zone of West and Central Africa the soils are too poor and easily leached by the high rainfall to support intensive farming. Much of the rest of Africa is too arid to support intensive cultivation of crops. This caused many African societies to rely on pastoralism but the prevalence in many lowland areas of southern and east Africa of the tsetse fly – which carries serious cattle diseases – limits herding to upland areas. While intensive pastoralism can be a source of great wealth, it is rarely sustainable in semi-arid environments as overgrazing inevitably leads to desertification.

In the Middle Ages a succession of powerful empires flourished in the West African Sahel (the savanna between the Sahara desert and the edge of the tropical forest zone) that were every bit the equal of the greatest kingdoms of medieval Europe. However, overgrazing by the herds on which their agricultural economies were based caused the Sahara to advance south, as it continues to do today. From being the richest region of sub-Saharan Africa, the Sahel is now the poorest.

Predynastic Egypt

Africa's first civilization developed in the narrow but fertile valley of the river Nile in Egypt. Its stable environment and relative isolation behind desert barriers made the Egyptian civilization the most long-lived of the ancient world.

"We see that the beginning of Egypt is the oldest of all kingdoms, so let us record its beginning."

Chronicle of Africanus (AD 220)

Improbable as it seems today, Africa's earliest farming communities developed in the Sahara. In the immediate post-glacial period the Sahara was not desert but a wildlife-rich savanna dotted with vast lakes, while the Nile valley was a densely forested swamp that was unattractive to human settlement. Early human inhabitants of the Sahara settled around the lakes, living by fishing, hunting and gathering and, by 7000 BC, by cultivating cereals and herding cattle. Cave paintings preserve vivid scenes of this vanished way of life.

By 3500 BC climate change had turned the Sahara into desert, forcing most of the people out: it is possible that over-grazing contributed to the spread of the desert as it is still doing today in the Sahel. The same climate change that made the Sahara uninhabitable dried out the valley and delta of the river Nile, making it much more attractive to farming settlement. The earliest farming settlements in the Nile valley date to around 5000 BC and belong to the Badarian culture. This movement of farmers into the valley marks the beginning of Egypt's Predynastic Period, the period which ended with the unification of Egypt as a single kingdom.

The annual flood of the Nile spread silt on the flood plain, creating fertile soils that were ideally suited to intensive agriculture and the valley soon became densely populated. By *c.* 4500 BC a more complex culture, the Naqada I (or Amratian) culture, had arisen. This culture was characterized by polished black-rimmed pottery, ceremonial stone mace heads and other objects worked in hard stone, such as palettes for mixing cosmetics made in the shapes of animals. Naqada I was confined mainly to Upper Egypt but the Naqada II (or Gerzean), which appeared *c.* 4000 BC, is found throughout Egypt and shows increasing craft specialization and the influence of cultural contacts with the Levant.

The First Kingdoms

It was during Naqada II times that the first evidence for the emergence of towns and kingdoms in Egypt appears. The most important site of this culture is Hierakonpolis in Upper Egypt. By 3500 BC Hierakonpolis was already a large city with Egypt's oldest known temple complex. Excavations of burials at Hierakonpolis have shown that mummification, one of the trademarks of ancient Egyptian civilization, was already practiced. An industrial complex in the city had a brewery capable of producing 300 gallons of beer a day and at least 13 pottery kilns, suggesting that the centralized control of the food supply and craft production that was a characteristic of royal government in historic times had already developed by this time.

The Nile floods were not entirely reliable. About once every ten years the flood would fail and there would be famine. Those who could control the supply of food during these disasters could force others into dependence, so concentrating power in their own hands. In this way the first local chiefdoms and kingdoms emerged. Competition between these rulers gradually eliminated the weaker until only the kingdoms of Upper and Lower Egypt were left. Finally *c.* 3100 BC King Narmer of Upper Egypt led his armies north and conquered Lower Egypt. The history of the early dynasties that ruled Egypt after its unification by Narmer is very shadowy and it is only with the accession of the Third Dynasty *c.* 2649 BC that the country truly emerges from prehistory.

A ceremonial palette recording King Narmer's victory over Lower Egypt. This reverse side of the palette depicts Narmer wearing the red crown of Lower Egypt and inspecting prisoners. A pair of giant, long-necked cats held on leashes are also featured.

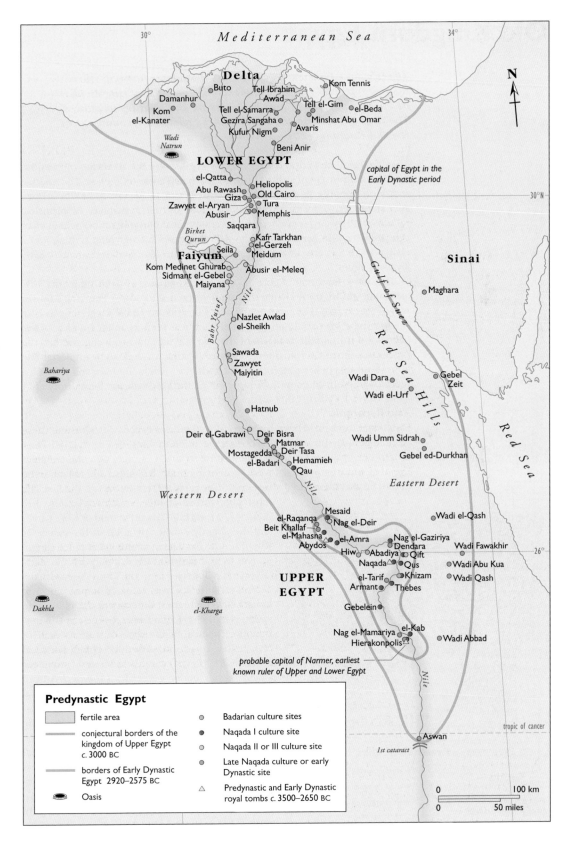

Mediterranean Sea

Delta

Buto
Damanhur
Kom
el-Kanater
Tell el-Samarra
Gezira Sangaha
Kufur Nigm

Tell Ibrahim
Awad
Kom Tennis
Tell el-Gim
el-Beda
Minshat Abu Omar
Avaris

Beni Anir

Wadi Natrun

LOWER EGYPT

el-Qatta
Abu Rawash
Giza
Zawyet el-Aryan
Abusir
Heliopolis
Old Cairo
Tura
Memphis

capital of Egypt in the
Early Dynastic period

Saqqara

Kafr Tarkhan
el-Gerzeh

Birket Qurun

Seila
Meidum

Faiyum

Kom Medinet Ghurab
Sidmant el-Gebel
Maiyana

Abusir el-Meleq

Sinai

Maghara

Nazlet Awlad
el-Sheikh

Sawada
Zawyet
Maiyitin

Bahariya

Wadi Dara
Gebel
Zeit

Wadi el-Urf

Hatnub

Deir el-Gabrawi
Deir Bisra
Matmar
Deir Tasa
Mostagedda
el-Badari
Hemamieh
Qau

Wadi Umm Sidrah

Gebel ed-Durkhan

Western Desert

Eastern Desert

Red Sea Hills

Red Sea

el-Raqanqa
Beit Khallaf
el-Mahasna
Abydos
Mesaid
Nag el-Deir

el-Amra
Hiw
Abadiya
Naqada
el-Tarif
Armant
Gebelein
Nag el-Gaziriya
Dendara
Qift
Qus
Khizam
Thebes

Wadi el-Qash

Wadi Fawakhir

Wadi Abu Kua
Wadi Qash

**UPPER
EGYPT**

Dakhla

el-Kharga

Nag el-Mamariya
Hierakonpolis
el-Kab
Wadi Abbad

probable capital of Narmer, earliest
known ruler of Upper and Lower Egypt

tropic of cancer

Aswan

1st cataract

Nile

Gulf of Suez

Bahr Yusuf

Predynastic Egypt

fertile area	

conjectural borders of the
kingdom of Upper Egypt
c. 3000 BC

borders of Early Dynastic
Egypt 2920–2575 BC

Oasis

○ Badarian culture sites

● Naqada I culture site

○ Naqada II or III culture site

○ Late Naqada culture or early
Dynastic site

△ Predynastic and Early Dynastic
royal tombs *c.* 3500–2650 BC

0 — 100 km

0 — 50 miles

Old Kingdom Egypt

The history of ancient Egypt has a compulsive pattern – three ages of imperial greatness and strong centralized rule divided by shorter periods of political division and military weakness. The first of these periods of greatness was the pyramid age of the Old Kingdom (2649–2134 BC).

"The pyramids are feared by time, although everything else in our present world fears time."

Umara al-Yamani
c. AD 1300

The Old Kingdom Period conventionally begins with the accession of Zanakht, the first king of Egypt's third historical dynasty, around 2649 BC. The sudden transition from the shadowy Early Dynastic Period to the Old Kingdom is, however, a modern construct, influenced more by the availability of historical records than by any decisive event. In reality most of the practices which characterized the Old Kingdom – theocratic kingship, hieroglyphic writing and a civil service – were already present during the less well-documented Early Dynastic times.

The most important figure of the Old Kingdom was the king (the title 'pharaoh' still lay more than a thousand years in the future). The king's power was in theory, and often in practice, absolute and the whole kingdom was considered to be his private property. The king was seen as an incarnation of the falcon god Horus, who was son of the Sun god Ra, and as a living god had the power to control the Nile flood. As a god, the king was held to be immortal. The king's soul was believed to rejoin the gods after death and his tomb became a place of worship. Mummification preserved the king's corpse for eternity.

The Pyramids

Early royal tombs had been built on brick platforms called *mastabas* but these were superseded by pyramids during the reign of King Djoser (r. 2630–2611 BC). Djoser's pyramid was a stepped stone structure, designed by the architect Imhotep, but true pyramids were soon being built. Pyramids were linked to the cult of Ra and their flared shape may have represented the rays of the Sun. The most noteworthy of the pyramids were the 146 metre (479 feet) high Great Pyramid of King Khufu and the slightly smaller pyramid of his successor Khephren at Giza. The pyramids are as much a monument to the organizational ability of the early Egyptian civil service as to the kings themselves.

The civil service was an extension of the royal household. The highest official was the vizier, who supervised the collection of taxes and the administration of justice. Below the vizier was a staff of chancellors, quartermasters and scribes. For local government, Egypt was divided into provinces called *nomes* under governors (*nomarchs*) from royal or noble families. Old Kingdom Egypt was a long and narrow state. Royal control did not extend far beyond the confines of the Nile valley: the southern border was at the First Cataract.

The Old Kingdom was destroyed by a natural disaster. Around 2150 the Nile entered a period of low floods. The resulting famine threw the authority of the kings into question and Egypt split into two rival kingdoms of Upper and Lower Egypt in what is known as the First Intermediate Period.

Pyramids at Giza

- Pyramid complex of Khufu
- Pyramid complex of Kephren
- Pyramid complex of Menkaure

0   300m
0   1000ft

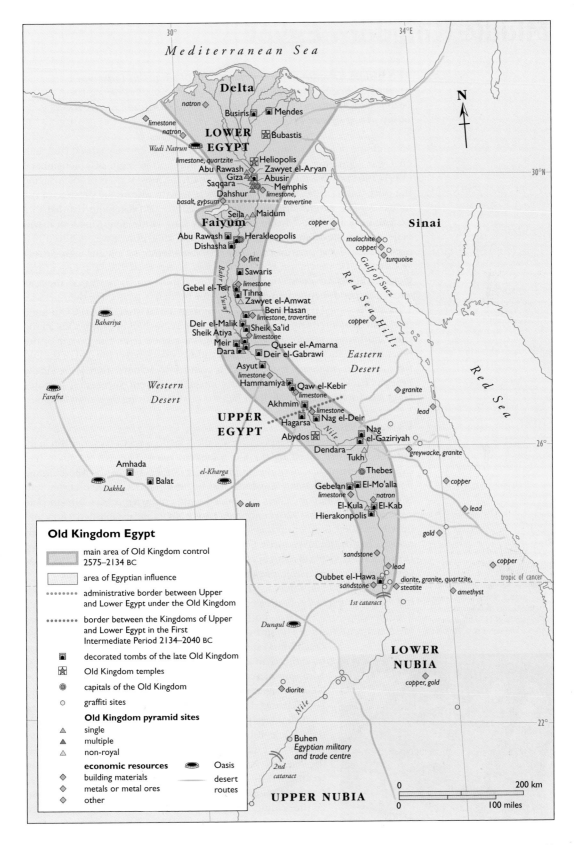

Old Kingdom Egypt

main area of Old Kingdom control 2575–2134 BC

area of Egyptian influence

administrative border between Upper and Lower Egypt under the Old Kingdom

border between the Kingdoms of Upper and Lower Egypt in the First Intermediate Period 2134–2040 BC

decorated tombs of the late Old Kingdom

Old Kingdom temples

capitals of the Old Kingdom

graffiti sites

Old Kingdom pyramid sites
single
multiple
non-royal

economic resources   Oasis
building materials   desert
metals or metal ores   routes
other

Middle Kingdom Egypt

The Middle Kingdom, the second of Egypt's ages of imperial greatness, began around 2040 BC with the reunification of the country by Mentuhotpe, the king of Thebes in Upper Egypt, after many years of hard fighting.

"A king shall come from the south called Amenembet, the son of a woman of Nubia and born in Upper Egypt.... The Asiatics shall fall before his slaughter and the Libyans shall fall before his flame. His foes will succumb to his wrath and the rebels to his might."

The prophecy of Neferti

Mentuhotpe enjoyed a long reign of 51 years but the country lapsed back into civil war soon after his death and it was only in the reign of Amenemhet I (1991–1962 BC) that full stability was restored. The most serious problem facing the early rulers of the Middle Kingdom was how to restore the prestige of the monarchy. The natural disasters which ended the Old Kingdom had led to a decline in belief in the divine nature of the king. In the Old Kingdom it was believed that the afterlife was in the gift of the king, now it was believed that even the humblest peasant could aspire to an afterlife simply through correct worship of the vegetation god Osiris. Kings compensated for the loss of religious authority by cultivating a new iconography which portrayed them as care-worn 'good shepherds' who took on the burden of protecting their people. They also resumed pyramid building, but not on the lavish scale of the Old Kingdom, and promoted the production of literature, including prophecies, moral tales and hymns, which showed the kings in a good light. The power of the nomarchs had increased greatly as royal authority declined at the end of the Old Kingdom and, although it took over a century to achieve, they were finally brought back under effective royal control. To prevent succession disputes kings also took to appointing their heirs as co-rulers during their own lifetimes.

Changing World

The world faced by the rulers of the Middle Kingdom was a far more threatening one than that faced by the Old Kingdom rulers. The Old Kingdom had existed in splendid isolation behind its desert borders but by the Middle Kingdom chiefdoms and small kingdoms had begun to develop in the Levant and Nubia. Middle Kingdom rulers responded with a more aggressive foreign policy. Senwosret I (1971–1926) conquered Lower Nubia and established a new, and heavily fortified, frontier on the Second Cataract of the Nile. Nubia's gold fields made it worth the investment. Senwosret III (1878–1841) campaigned in the Levant, forcing local rulers to become vassals of Egypt. Following this there was considerable peaceful immigration from Palestine into the Delta region.

In the later Middle Kingdom the civil service began to slip out of royal control and for much of the time effective power was exercised by the vizier rather than the king. Another period of irregular Nile floods seems to have damaged royal authority further. The growing weakness of Egypt was exploited by its neighbours and around 1640 the Middle Kingdom was brought to an end by the Hyksos, a people from the Levant who conquered Lower Egypt. Around the same time, the Nubian kingdom of Kush drove the Egyptians back to the First Cataract. Upper Egypt retained its independence under a native dynasty based at Thebes. Compared to the Near East, the Middle Kingdom had been technologically very backward. As a result of Hyksos influence the Egyptians adopted the use of wheeled vehicles, bronze technology, new weapons, fashions in dress and music, and new crops and domestic animals. However, as the Hyksos in their turn adopted the traditions of Egyptian government and religion, there was no sharp break in historical or cultural continuity.

This painted wooden funerary model of marching, armed soldiers was discovered in the tomb of Mesehti at Asyut and dates to c. 2000 BC.

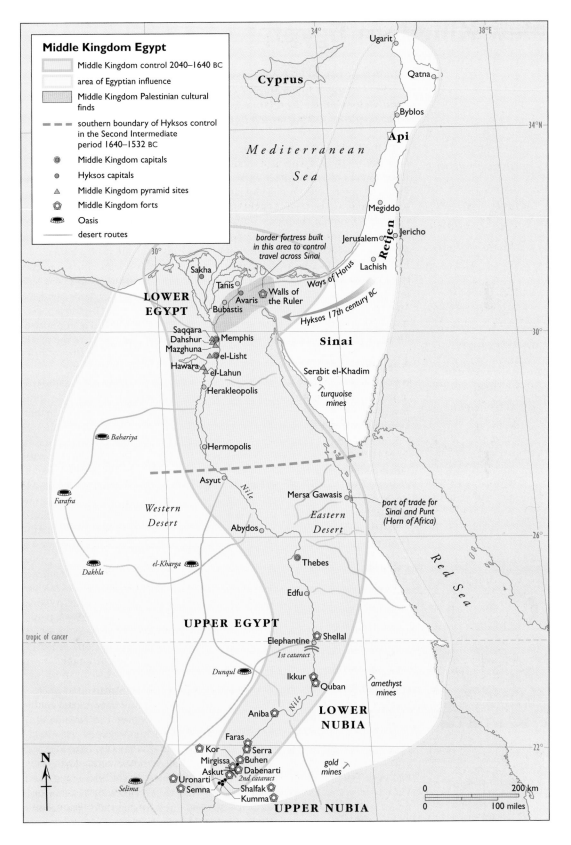

Middle Kingdom Egypt

Middle Kingdom control 2040–1640 BC

area of Egyptian influence

Middle Kingdom Palestinian cultural finds

southern boundary of Hyksos control in the Second Intermediate period 1640–1532 BC

Middle Kingdom capitals

Hyksos capitals

Middle Kingdom pyramid sites

Middle Kingdom forts

Oasis

desert routes

Ugarit

Cyprus

Qatna

Byblos

Api

Mediterranean Sea

Megiddo

Retjen

Jericho

Jerusalem

Lachish

border fortress built in this area to control travel across Sinai

Ways of Horus

Sakha

LOWER EGYPT

Tanis

Avaris

Walls of the Ruler

Bubastis

Hyksos 17th century BC

Saqqara

Dahshur

Mazghuna

Memphis

el-Lisht

Hawara

el-Lahun

Sinai

Serabit el-Khadim

Herakleopolis

turquoise mines

Bahariya

Hermopolis

Farafra

Asyut

Nile

Mersa Gawasis

port of trade for Sinai and Punt (Horn of Africa)

Western Desert

Eastern Desert

Abydos

el-Kharga

Dakhla

Thebes

Red Sea

Edfu

UPPER EGYPT

tropic of cancer

Elephantine

Shellal

1st cataract

Dunqul

Ikkur

Quban

amethyst mines

Aniba

LOWER NUBIA

Faras

Kor

Serra

Mirgissa

Buhen

Askut

Dabenarti

gold mines

Uronarti

2nd cataract

Selima

Semna

Shalfak

Kumma

UPPER NUBIA

N

0   200 km

0   100 miles

63

New Kingdom Egypt

Under the Theban king Seqenenre II (died c. 1601) the Egyptians began a struggle to reconquer Upper Egypt from the Hyksos. Their final victory under King Ahmose in 1532 marks the beginning of the New Kingdom during which Egypt reached the height of its power.

"You are a great warrior without equal.... All the lands, united as one, could not withstand you. You were victorious in the sight of the whole world.... You are the protector of Egypt, the conqueror of foreign lands."

Inscription of Ramesses II commemorating the battle of Qadesh, c. 1285 BC

Until the Hyksos conquered Lower Egypt, the Egyptian kingdom had survived for some 1500 years without a serious invasion. The Egyptians now realized that their borders were no longer secure and the rulers of the New Kingdom were, from the outset, overtly militaristic and expansionist. Under the great warrior King Tuthmosis I (r. 1504–1492 BC), Egyptian armies campaigned as far north as Carchemish on the Euphrates and as far south as the Fifth Cataract of the Nile. The Levant, Sinai, Lower and Upper Nubia and Kush all became part of the Egyptian empire. In the north, Tuthmosis' intention was to create a buffer zone between Egypt and the Mesopotamian empires; in the south the aim was to control Nubia's gold fields and suppress the Kushite kingdom. Nubia was subjected to full colonial government but in the Levant the Egyptians aped the Mesopotamian empires and ruled through local vassal kings. Diplomacy, conducted via gift exchange, marriage alliance and letters, kept good relations with Mesopotamia but the Hittites were always a threatening presence to the north.

The Pharaohs

It was during the New Kingdom that Egyptian kings first began to use the title 'pharaoh'. Meaning literally 'great palace', it was a sign of the central role of the royal household in government. The pharaohs were usually conservative in their attitudes to kingship and deliberately emphasized the continuity of tradition as a means of legitimizing their power. An important exception was Amenophis IV (r. 1353–1335), a radical religious reformer who tried to replace Egypt's traditional polytheism with a monotheistic cult of the Aten or sun disc. Amenophis changed his name to Akhenaten ('he who is pleasing to the Aten') and founded a new capital called Akhetaten ('horizon of the Aten'). Akhenaten's religious revolution failed and after his death Akhetaten (now el-Amarna) was abandoned.

In the period of instability after Akhenaten's death, Egypt lost control of the Levant and attempts by Sethos I (r. 1305–1290) and his son Ramesses II (r. 1290–1224) to restore the situation met with only partial success. Consummate self-publicist that he was, Ramesses claimed a great victory over the Hittites at Qadesh in 1285 but, as the Hittites still controlled the area after the battle, to Egypt the outcome was probably less favourable. Egypt also suffered, along with the rest of the eastern Mediterranean, from the migrating Sea Peoples (see page 40). Ramesses III decisively defeated them in the Delta in the 1180s but he could not prevent them settling in Palestine.

The end of the New Kingdom, c. 1070, is marked by another collapse of royal power. This time it was undermined by the priesthood, which had become hereditary and largely out of royal control. By the 11th century temples owned one third of Egypt's land and the most important, the temple of Amun at Karnak, was in effective control of all of Upper Egypt. By 1000 all of the New Kingdom empire had been lost and in 712 Egypt itself was conquered by the Nubians of Kush. Periods of Nubian, Assyrian and Persian rule were broken by brief revivals under native dynasties but after it was conquered by Alexander the Great in 332 BC, Egypt was permanently under foreign rule.

The youthful pharaoh Tutankhamun (c. 1370–1352 BC) is depicted attacking African enemies from his chariot in this detail from a painted wooden chest.

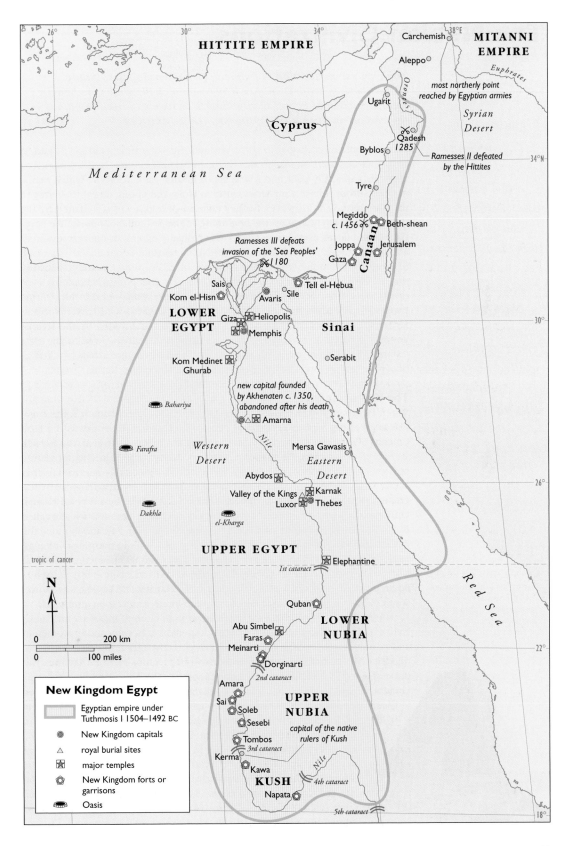

HITTITE EMPIRE

Carchemish

MITANNI EMPIRE

Aleppo

Euphrates

Ugarit

most northerly point reached by Egyptian armies

Cyprus

Syrian Desert

Qadesh
1285

Byblos

Ramesses II defeated by the Hittites

34°N

Mediterranean Sea

Tyre

Megiddo
c. 1456
Beth-shean

Ramesses III defeats invasion of the 'Sea Peoples'
1180

Joppa
Jerusalem

Gaza

Canaan

Sais
Tell el-Hebua
Sile

Kom el-Hisn
Avaris

30°

LOWER EGYPT
Giza
Heliopolis

Memphis

Sinai

Kom Medinet Ghurab

Serabit

Bahariya

new capital founded by Akhenaten c. 1350, abandoned after his death

Amarna

Farafra

Western Desert

Nile

Mersa Gawasis

Eastern Desert

Abydos

26°

Valley of the Kings
Karnak

Dakhla

Luxor
Thebes

el-Kharga

UPPER EGYPT

tropic of cancer

Elephantine

1st cataract

Red Sea

N

0   200 km

0   100 miles

Quban

LOWER NUBIA

22°

Abu Simbel
Faras

Meinarti

Dorginarti

2nd cataract

Amara

UPPER NUBIA

Sai
Soleb

Sesebi

capital of the native rulers of Kush

Tombos
3rd cataract

Kerma

Nile

Kawa

KUSH
4th cataract

Napata

5th cataract

18°

New Kingdom Egypt

	Egyptian empire under Tuthmosis I 1504–1492 BC
◉	New Kingdom capitals
△	royal burial sites
⊞	major temples
⬡	New Kingdom forts or garrisons
⬭	Oasis

65

The Nubian Civilizations

The earliest civilization of tropical Africa developed in Nubia, in the north of modern Sudan. The Nubian civilization was heavily influenced by the Egyptian civilization to its north and, like it, was dependent on the waters of the Nile for its existence.

"South of Elephantine the country is inhabited by Ethiopians. After forty days' journey by land, there follows another boat journey of twelve days to reach a great city called Meroë. The people there worship only Zeus and Dionysus amongst the gods, but show them the greatest reverence. "

Herodotus, *Histories*

A Kushite pyramid at Meroë in Sudan. The Kushites emulated the Egyptians by burying their dead royalty in pyramids. The pyramids at Meroë were built from local red sandstone blocks.

Farming settlement began in Nubia around the same time as in Egypt and its early cultures were similar to the Egyptian Naqada culture. Nubia was rich in minerals, especially gold, and it was also a natural trade route by which exotic products from sub-Saharan Africa, such as ivory and ebony, found their way to the Mediterranean. However, further cultural development was halted by the unification of Egypt around the beginning of the 3rd millennium BC. The Egyptians sent military expeditions into Lower Nubia to exploit its mineral resources and to capture cattle and slaves. Lower Nubia became depopulated as a result of these depredations. It was only in the period of Egyptian weakness following the fall of the Old Kingdom around 2150 that the first Nubian kingdom developed, centred on the city of Kerma near the Third Cataract of the Nile. During the Middle Kingdom the Egyptians conquered and garrisoned Lower Nubia as far south as the Second Cataract but after Egypt was invaded by the Hyksos around 1640 BC, Kerma extended its control north all the way to the First Cataract. Raids were made into Egypt itself and many fine artefacts taken as booty have been found in the huge royal burial mounds at Kerma.

The Kush Kingdom

When Egyptian power revived under the New Kingdom, Pharaoh Tuthmosis I (1504–1492 BC) sacked Kerma and conquered Nubia as far south as the Fifth Cataract. Monuments, such as the colossal statues of Ramesses II at Abu Simbel, were built as stark reminders to the Nubians of their subjection. The population of Lower Nubia became fully Egyptianized, but Nubian culture survived further south. Egypt lost control over Nubia at the end of the New Kingdom (1070 BC), creating a power vacuum which was filled around 900 BC by a revived Nubian kingdom centred on Napata. In Egyptian sources this kingdom is usually called Kush. The Kushite king Piye managed to conquer Egypt in 712 and founded the 25th dynasty of pharaohs. The Kushite dynasty adopted the trappings of Egyptian kingship, even being buried in cemeteries of small, steep-sided pyramids at Kurru and Nuri. The Kushites were finally expelled from Egypt in 663 BC. In 593 BC an Egyptian army invaded Kush and sacked Napata. The capital was moved south to Meroë, beyond the reach of Egyptian interference, soon afterwards.

The move south led to a lessening of Egyptian cultural influence in Nubia. Native Nubian gods, such as the Lion God Apedemak, became more prominent and a new Meroitic alphabet was developed. By exploiting rich local ore deposits, Meroë became the major ironworking centre in tropical Africa but trade and gold were the main sources of wealth. The Meroitic state was at its height around the beginning of the Christian era. In 24 BC the Kushites raided deep into Egypt; among the loot they carried off was a bronze head of the Roman emperor Augustus, which was buried at the entrance of a temple in Meroë to commemorate the event. Decline set in around AD 200 as a result of trading competition from the rising kingdom of Axum on the Red Sea coast. Desertification and soil erosion, probably the result of over-grazing, was adversely affecting agriculture and the population in many areas was declining. The kingdom experienced increasing difficulty fighting off raids by desert nomads and it finally collapsed around AD 350 following an attack by Axum.

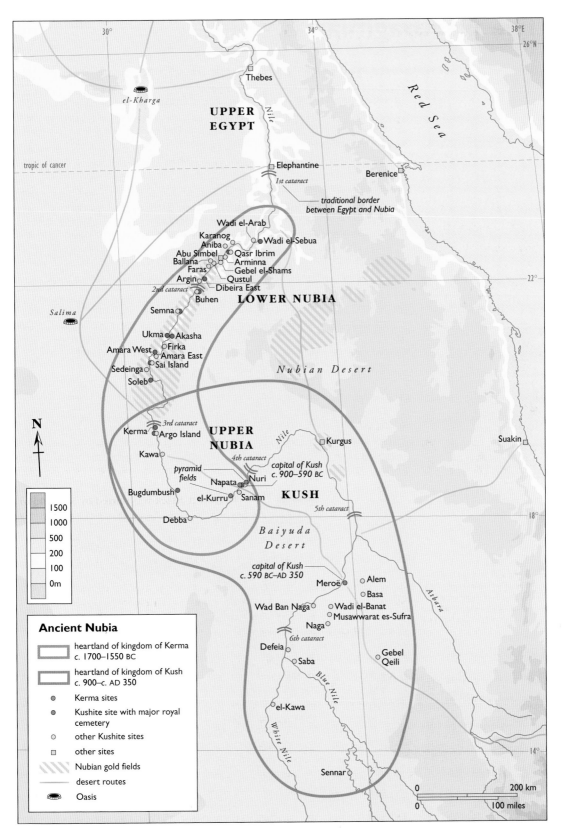

30°   34°   38°E

26°N

Thebes

el-Kharga

**UPPER
EGYPT**

*Red
Sea*

Nile

tropic of cancer

Elephantine

Berenice

1st cataract

traditional border
between Egypt and Nubia

Wadi el-Arab

Karanog

Aniba   • Wadi el-Sebua

Abu Simbel   Qasr Ibrim

Ballana   Arminna

Faras   Gebel el-Shams

Argin   Qustul

Dibeira East

2nd cataract   Buhen   **LOWER NUBIA**

Semna

Salima

Ukma   Akasha

Firka

Amara West   Amara East

Sai Island

Sedeinga

Soleb

Nubian Desert

22°

N

3rd cataract   **UPPER
NUBIA**

Kerma   Argo Island

Kawa   *4th cataract*   Kurgus

Nile

Suakin

pyramid
fields   Nuri   capital of Kush
c. 900–590 BC

Napata

Bugdumbush   el-Kurru   Sanam   **KUSH**

Debba   *5th cataract*

18°

*Baiyuda
Desert*

1500
1000
500
200
100
0m

capital of Kush
c. 590 BC–AD 350

Meroë   • Alem

• Basa

Wad Ban Naga   • Wadi el-Banat

• Musawwarat es-Sufra

Naga

Atbara

Defeia   *6th cataract*

Saba   Gebel
Qeili

Blue Nile

el-Kawa

14°

White Nile

Sennar

Ancient Nubia

heartland of kingdom of Kerma
c. 1700–1550 BC

heartland of kingdom of Kush
c. 900–*c.* AD 350

●   Kerma sites

●   Kushite site with major royal
cemetery

○   other Kushite sites

□   other sites

▨   Nubian gold fields

   desert routes

⬭   Oasis

0   200 km

0   100 miles

The Carthaginian Empire

In the 8th century the Phoenicians, a seafaring people from the Levant, founded merchant settlements around the western Mediterranean. The most important of these was Carthage.

According to tradition, Carthage was founded by settlers from Tyre around 814 BC but archaeological evidence suggests that the true date may have been up to a century later. Carthage was built on an easily defended site by a sheltered anchorage on a peninsula in northern Tunisia. The Carthaginians improved on nature by building two artificial harbours, one for merchant shipping, the other for its war galleys. Its position in the Mediterranean enabled Carthage to dominate the trade routes from the Near East to Atlantic Europe. Carthage quickly became the most prosperous Phoenician colony and, while subject to its parent city, in the 7th century began its own colonization of the Balearics. The city acted as protector to other Phoenician colonies in the western Mediterranean, intervening in Sicily in 580 to protect Motya from the Greeks and aiding Phoeni-

"The Carthaginians are a hard and gloomy people, obedient to their rulers and harsh to their subjects ... they keep stubbornly to their decisions, are austere and care little for amusement or the finer things of life. "

Plutarch, 2nd century AD

The ruins of the Roman baths at Carthage. Although it was destroyed by the Romans in 146 BC, the Phoenician city was refounded by Julius Caesar as a colony for veteran soldiers because of its strategic location.

cian colonies in Sardinia. After the overthrow of Tyre by the Babylonians in 573, Carthage became de facto independent and assumed leadership of Phoenicia's colonies in the western Mediterranean. This loose-knit maritime empire showed its growing power when it helped defeat a Greek attempt to colonize Corsica in 535 BC.

Carthage is remembered as Rome's rival for control of the Mediterranean but for several centuries the two cities were close. A treaty of friendship signed by the two cities in 509 BC, the first year of the Roman Republic, was renewed several times but Rome's conquest of peninsular Italy at the beginning of the 3rd century BC made conflict more likely. In 264 a Roman intervention in Sicily, which Carthage saw as part of its sphere of influence, led to the outbreak of the First Punic War. After Carthage was defeated in 241 it tried to compensate for its territorial losses by building an empire in Spain. When, in 218, the Carthaginian general Hannibal seized Saguntum, which was allied to Rome, the Second Punic War erupted. Despite surprising the Romans by invading Italy over the Alps and a string of great victories, Hannibal was unable to strike a decisive blow and Carthage conceded defeat in 201. Stripped of most of its empire, Carthage recovered too quickly for the Romans' comfort who laid siege to the city in 149 BC. When Carthage finally fell three years later, the Romans razed it to the ground and sold its surviving population into slavery.

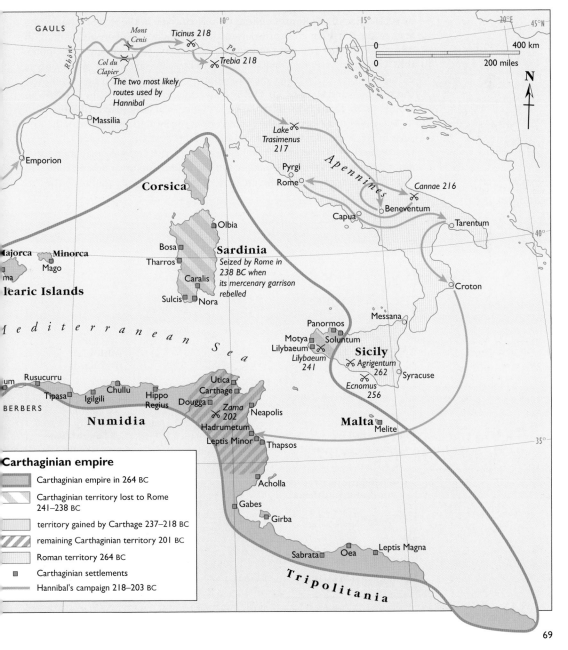

Carthaginian empire

- Carthaginian empire in 264 BC
- Carthaginian territory lost to Rome 241–238 BC
- territory gained by Carthage 237–218 BC
- remaining Carthaginian territory 201 BC
- Roman territory 264 BC
- Carthaginian settlements
- Hannibal's campaign 218–203 BC

Civilizations of Sub-Saharan Africa

Sub-Saharan Africa saw the development of a variety of indigenous civilizations between 500 BC and AD 1500. To a greater or lesser degree, the progress of all these civilizations was inhibited by European colonialism between the 16th and 19th centuries.

> *"Formerly the town of Axum was very famous among the Abyssinians ... they look upon it as most certain that the Queen of Sheba kept her court there, and that it was the residence of the emperors for many ages afterwards and they are crowned there to this day.*"
>
> Balthasar Tellez, 1660

The earliest centre of civilization in tropical Africa outside the Nile Valley was in northern Ethiopia and Eritrea. This was probably the land that the ancient Egyptians knew as Punt, the source of exotic aromatic resins, ivory and rhinoceros horn. Although maritime contacts with Egypt went back to Old Kingdom times, the strongest cultural influence came from the Sabeans of south-west Arabia, whose alphabet, architecture and religion were adopted around the 5th century BC. The rise of the Roman empire stimulated trade in the Red Sea and by the start of the Christian era a prosperous trading kingdom had arisen, centred on Axum (or Aksum). The most impressive monuments at Axum are huge monoliths carved to resemble multi-storey buildings; the tallest that still stands is 21 metres (69 feet) high. Axum reached its peak under King Ezana, who overthrew Yemen and Meroë *c.* AD 350. By converting to Christianity, the first African king to do so, Ezana helped lay the basis of medieval Ethiopian civilization.

Trade was also a factor in the emergence of the Swahili civilization of the East African coast and the 'Sudanic' civilization of the West African savanna. The peoples of the East African coast had begun trading with Greco-Roman merchants around the start of the Christian era but the main impetus to urbanization and state formation came after the creation of the Islamic Arab empire in the 7th

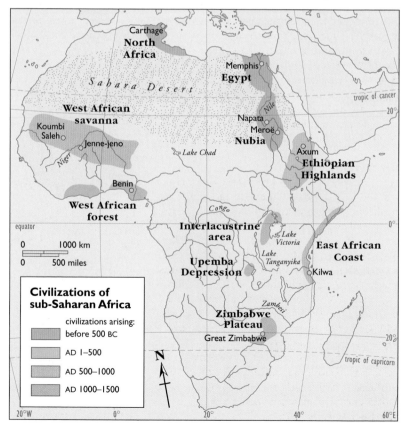

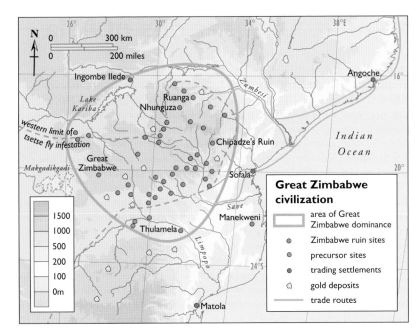

This soapstone carving is thought to have come from the ancient site of Great Zimbabwe. It is an excellent example of African tribal art.

century. Arab merchants introduced Islam, literacy and the beginnings of a cash economy, leading to the rise of an African-Islamic civilization by the Middle Ages. Muslim merchants from North Africa also had a major cultural influence on the civilizations which began to develop on the West African savanna from the 5th century AD. Early towns here, such as Jenne-jeno on the river Niger, developed as a result of local trade and intensive agriculture. The forging of caravan routes across the Sahara also enabled early kingdoms like Ghana (centred on Koumbi Saleh) to profit from being middlemen in the trade between North Africa and the tropical forests to the south, a source of gold, ebony, ivory and slaves. Cavalry armies, using horses imported from the north, were the basis of state power in the Sahel. Rich kingdoms with advanced bronze- and iron-working skills and highly centralized monarchies had developed in the forests too by the Middle Ages.

Great Zimbabwe

Much of central and southern Africa was either too arid or too wet for intensive agriculture but small kingdoms grew in the Middle Ages in fertile upland areas in the great lakes region. The most famous of sub-Saharan Africa's ancient civilizations developed on the Zimbabwe plateau and is named after its most important royal and ritual centre at Great Zimbabwe, which flourished around AD 1200. Great Zimbabwe's wealth came from intensive cattle rearing and a trade in gold with the cities on the East African coast, which supplied exotic products from as far afield as China in return. The scale of Great Zimbabwe's stone architecture was unequalled anywhere in sub-Saharan Africa and the first Europeans who visited the site refused to believe that it could have been built by Africans.

A view of the conical tower at the Iron Age site of Great Zimbabwe. The tower is solid, built of granite blocks, and was used for religious purposes.

Part III: The First Civilizations of Asia

Asia was home to two of the world's 'pristine' civilizations – the Indus valley civilization of Pakistan and northwest India, and the Shang civilization of China's Yellow River valley. After flourishing for 600 years the Indus civilization collapsed and it was a thousand years before another urban civilization grew in South Asia. The Shang civilization survived and is the ancestor of modern Chinese civilization. All subsequent civilizations of south and east Asia have developed under the influence of the Indian or Chinese civilizations.

Developing around 2600 BC, the Indus was the older of the two civilizations. As in the Near East, farming in south Asia began in upland areas with sufficient rainfall to support dry farming and only became widespread on the hot and dry Indus flood plain with irrigation. Excavations have revealed well-planned cities and extensive flood defences and irrigation systems that are evidence of a complex government with great organizational skills. However, less is known about the Indus civilization than any other of the Old World civilizations. This is because the Indus civilization's elegant writing system remains so far undeciphered. We do not even know what the relationship was between the cities of the valley; were they part of an Indus kingdom or independent city-states like those in Mesopotamia? There are no sculptures of rulers or depictions of military campaigns, as are common in Mesopotamia and Egypt, nor have any obvious elite burials been found.

Around 1800 BC the Indus civilization went into decline, the cities were gradually abandoned and writing fell out of use. It was formerly thought that the decline was caused by the invasions of the Aryans, a nomadic pastoralist people from central Asia who overran most of northern India in the 2nd millennium. However, it is now certain that the Aryans did not arrive in south Asia earlier than *c.* 1500 BC, so they could have had nothing to do with the decline of the Indus civilization. It is now thought more likely that environmental changes caused a collapse of agriculture, so the cities could not be sustained and life reverted to a pre-urban level.

A figurine, possibly of a priest-king, from the city of Mohenjo-Daro. The city was part of the Harappan civilization, one of the most ancient civilizations in the Indus valley in what is now the south of Pakistan and western India. Relatively little is known about the people who created this highly complex culture

The Aryan Influence

The Aryan invasion is arguably the most important event in the history of the Indian sub-continent. The Aryans' Indo-European language was the ancestor of the most widely spoken languages of modern India, Pakistan and Bangladesh, including Hindi (the fourth most widely spoken language in the world), Urdu, Bengali, Punjabi, Sindhi and Gujarati. The Aryans' religious beliefs were ancestral to modern Hinduism, which is central to modern Indian culture and identity.

There are no true historical records of the Aryan invasion but a mythic record of it is preserved in the *Vedas*, the oldest books of the Hindu religion. In Vedic times the Aryans were divided into four *varnas* or social classes - *kshatriyas* (warriors), *Brahmins* (priests), *vaishyas* (merchants), and the *shudras* (labourers) - which provided the foundation of the Hindu caste system. What became of the indigenous population after the Aryan invasion is not known for certain. The *Vedas* record a succession of different wars, however, it is more likely that the conquered natives were assimilated to Aryan culture and language, than exterminated.

Some historians see the subordinate *shudra* class as being derived from the conquered natives. There is certainly evidence of some continuity of pre-Aryan cultural traditions and there are disputed claims that the major Hindu god Shiva originated with the Indus civilization.

The revival of urban civilization in India began on the Ganges river flood plain in the 9th century when small towns and tribal kingdoms called *jana-padas* began to develop. The initial impetus for this probably came from the adoption of wet rice farming, and the resulting increase in population size and density. Rice is the highest yielding cereal and in the Ganges plain two or three crops a year were possible but it also required considerable, and well-organized, input of labour to build the irrigation and water control systems needed.

By around 700 BC the many *janapadas* had coalesced into 16 *mahajana-padas* ('great realms') and this was reduced to around six by 400 BC. Factors in this continuing centralization of power may have been an increase in regional trade and the spread of iron technology, which may have contributed either by aiding the further intensification of agriculture or by intensifying warfare between kingdoms – unlike the Indus cities, the cities of the Ganges plain were all well fortified. The age of the *mahajanapadas* saw important religious developments; the recording in written form of the early Hindu scriptures in the Sanskrit script (an adaptation of the Near Eastern Aramaic alphabet), and the foundation of Jainism and Buddhism.

Land of Local Kingdoms

Although the Gangetic civilization would eventually spread to most of the sub-continent, cultural unity would not, as it did in China, prove to be an aid to political unity. The Mauryan dynasty, which came to power in the Gangetic kingdom of Magadha in 321 came close to uniting the sub-continent under their rule but their achievement was too short-lived to begin to overcome India's many regional identities. From time to time powers emerged on the Indo-Gangetic plain that were strong enough to dominate northern India but they were never able to extend their control throughout the south, where powerful and wealthy kingdoms emerged early in the Christian era. These gained much of their wealth from trading gems and spices with the Roman empire. The north was always exposed to invasions from the Near East and central Asia, and hegemonic states rarely survived more than a few generations. India therefore remained a land of local kingdoms and short-lived regional empires until modern times.

The roots of Chinese civilization lie in the Longshan Neolithic culture (3200–1800 BC), which saw the development of warlike hierarchical societies in the Yellow River valley.

The Ashoka pillar with its capital of four standing lions at Sarnath, India. After his conversion to Buddhism, Ashoka, the ruler of the Mauryan empire, had many pillars erected in memory of his pilgrimages. Ashoka reigned over most of the Indian sub-continent from present-day Afghanistan to Bengal and as far south as Mysore.

According to later Chinese historical traditions, it was in the later half of this period that the Xia dynasty forged the first state in China. These traditions assert that the Xia kingdom arose out of conflicts between chiefdoms and the need to organize massive flood defences to try to contain the violent and unpredictable Yellow River. While this is a credible enough explanation in itself, there is no convincing evidence for the existence of states in China before the foundation of the Shang dynasty in the 18th century BC. Under the Shang the first Chinese writing system, based on pictographs, appeared and bronze casting and wheeled vehicles came into use.

A bronze ding, or ritual food vessel, from the Shang dynasty. The development of bronze metallurgy signified a settled and organized society. Bronze making led to better tools and weapons, but in ancient China it had another important use for casting food and wine vessels essential to their ancestor worship.

For patriotic reasons Chinese historians have always stressed the pristine nature of Chinese civilization, and there is no doubt that the reasons for its development are intimately connected to the intensification of farming in the Yellow River valley and the attendant rise in population. However, it is now clear that much of the technology that appeared in the Shang period was not invented independently by the Chinese but was introduced to China from the West through the intermediary of the Indo-Iranian nomads who dominated the Eurasian steppes in the Bronze and early Iron Ages. These introductions included the art of bronze casting itself as it was known on the eastern steppes two centuries before it was known in China. The fact that the Chinese words for the wheel, spokes, axles and the chariot come from Indo-Iranian suggests that knowledge of wheeled vehicles came by the same route. Many Chinese words associated with divination (including the word for magic), architecture and medicine also have Indo-Iranian origins.

In 1027 the last Shang king, Di-xin, was overthrown by one of his vassals, King Wu of Zhou in the west of China. Under the Shang, the Chinese had believed that the king was divine and that he was a descendant of the creator god Shang Di. To justify their usurpation the Zhou formulated one of the most influential ideas in Chinese history, the 'Mandate of Heaven'. The king was the 'Son of Heaven' and he was granted 'All under Heaven' to rule as his domain on condition that he was just and moral. If a ruler became unjust or immoral Heaven would send him a warning (a natural disaster or social disturbances for instance) and if he failed to heed it and reform, the Mandate would be given to another. Di-xin, it was claimed, had been a sadist who had invented new tortures, so Heaven gave the right to rule to the Zhou. The transfer of the Mandate was confirmed by Wu's victory over Di-xin. This flexible doctrine could be used equally to condemn unsuccessful rebellion against a legitimate dynasty as disobedience to the will of Heaven and to justify successful usurpation, as the failure of the ruling dynasty to defeat a rebellion proved that it had lost the Mandate. The idea could also provoke rebellions. If a ruler experienced problems, like a series of bad harvests, his subjects might take this as a sign that the Mandate was being withdrawn, encouraging them to rebel.

End of the Zhou Dynasty

Feudalism is a common response by rulers who lack the power, resources or administrative expertise to impose strong centralized government. The ruler grants out parcels of land, known as fiefs, to his supporters to administer, in return for their allegiance and services, which may consist of military service, forwarding tax revenues raised in the ruler's name and so on. In theory fiefs are revocable but there is always a tendency for them to become hereditary and pass out of the ruler's control. In extreme instances, the ruler may have direct control over little more of the kingdom than his own personal estates and so lack the resources to impose his will on his vassals should they prove disobedient. This was the fate of many European kings during the Middle Ages and it was also the fate of the Zhou dynasty kings, who had lost direct control of most of the kingdom to their dukes by 800 BC. The residual prestige of the dynasty sufficed to hold the kingdom in obedience but a barbarian invasion in 770 forced the Zhou to move their capital from Xian to a safer and more central location at Luoyang. This was a disaster for the dynasty's authority. The dukes were able to rule their fiefs in complete independence. Yet the Zhou dynasty was not overthrown. In theory, the authority of the dukes derived from the king, so it was convenient to retain him as a purely nominal overlord as it gave legitimacy to their own positions. The Zhou survived in this position until 256 BC when they were finally overthrown by the Qin dynasty, which went on to unify China under its rule in 221 BC.

The First Chinese Empire

In the 4th century, the Qin dukes had been among the first to reject the fiction of allegiance to the Zhou and had begun calling themselves kings. In the reign of King Xiao (361–338 BC), the prime minister Shang Yang had systematically destroyed all vestiges of feudalism and given the Qin state a strong centralized government with a professional non-hereditary bureaucracy. Shang introduced the political doctrine of Legalism, which held that humans were inherently evil and could only be restrained by fear of punishment. When King Zheng, better known by his imperial title Shi Huangdi ('First Emperor') united China between 228 and 221 BC, he ruthlessly imposed the same centralized system of government on the whole country and the old feudal aristocracy was destroyed. Frontier defences were built against the steppe nomads and for the first time large areas were brought under Chinese rule that were inhabited by non-Chinese peoples. An enormous burden of taxation was imposed on the peasantry to pay for the emperor's reforms and savage punishments were imposed for any disobedience. As a Legalist, the idea of using the carrot as well as the stick never occurred to Shi Huangdi, who saw this as weakness. The power Shi Huangdi wielded in life is amply demonstrated by his tomb. The famous 7000-strong terracotta army that was buried to protect him in the afterlife represents only a fraction of the grave goods in his tomb, most of which remains unexcavated.

Unsurprisingly, the Qin dynasty did not survive for long after Shi Huangdi's death in 210. In 206 rebels slaughtered the entire Qin royal family and after a civil war Gaodi, a former peasant, came to power founding the Han dynasty 210 BC–AD 220). Gaodi abolished Shi Huangdi's more draconian laws but he maintained the structure of the centralized bureaucratic state founded by the first emperor: it was regarded as the ideal form of government to be emulated by every successive Chinese dynasty and also by the founder of Communist China, the 'great helmsman' Mao Zedong. Shi Huangdi is usually described as the founder of the Chinese empire but, in reality, it was only the first of many Chinese empires. As Shi Huangdi had destroyed every vestige of the old feudal states, Gaodi was able to take over the Qin empire intact and his successors preserved its unity for 400 years. However, forces of localism eventually reasserted themselves, the Han were overthrown in AD 220 and China broke up into independent kingdoms for over 350 years.

The forces of centralization and localism have struggled in China ever since, with periods of strong centralized imperial rule being followed by periods of disunity or foreign rule. However, neither disunity nor foreign rule has significantly broken the continuity of Chinese civilization. Chinese historians have traditionally looked at the periods of disunion and retrospectively appointed whichever dynasty eventually reunited China as the official imperial dynasty, so maintaining the fiction of continuous imperial rule. Officially the last Chinese imperial dynasty, the Manchu or Qing, collapsed into warlordism and civil war in 1911 but it can be argued that the modern People's Republic of China, with its dozens of suppressed ethnic minorities, is as much an imperial state in disguise as was the late USSR (Union of Soviet Socialist Republics).

An oracle bone from the Shang dynasty, c. 1500 BC. Oracle bone inscriptions are the earliest examples of Chinese writing. The ancient Chinese used these bones in divinations. They applied heat to the bones, usually the shoulder bones of domestic cattle and water buffalo and tortoise shells, and interpreted the cracks that subsequently appeared. Many of the divinations refer to hunting, warfare, weather and auspicious days for ceremonies.

The Indus Valley Civilization

The least known of the important early civilizations of the Old World, the Indus valley civilization emerged around 2600 BC in what is now Pakistan and northwest India. In its origins the Indus valley civilization resembled the Sumerian civilization in that it developed on the fertile flood plain of a river where the need for irrigation and flood defences led to the rise of a well-organized hierarchical society.

"The Meluhhaites, the men of the black land, bring to Naram-Sin of Agade all kinds of exotic wares. "

The Curse of Agade
c. 2000 BC

Farming settlement on the Indus flood plain began *c.* 4000 BC. The first signs of urbanization were appearing by 3000 BC and by 2600 BC there were dozens of towns and cities on the plain. Most of the towns and cities in the Indus valley were small but there were at least two, probably three, pre-eminent cities, Mohenjo-Daro, Harappa and Ganweriwala, with populations of 30,000–40,000 people, making them comparable to the largest cities in Mesopotamia. The political organization of this civilization is unknown but these cities may have been the capitals of territorial kingdoms.

The Indus cities were well planned with orderly street plans. Mohenjo-Daro and Harappa had impressive mud brick city walls, a citadel with granaries and public buildings and an efficient system of underground drains and sewers. Houses were built to standardized plans and different occupations and social classes were segregated in different quarters of the cities. Long-distance trade was important to the Indus cities. Mountain peoples brought metals, precious stones and timber to the cities to exchange for grain. The cities then exported copper and other goods to Sumeria (see page 26).

Mysterious Civilization

The Indus civilization was literate, with a writing system that developed from symbols and pictographs used originally to decorate pottery: examples have been found on carved stamp seals, amulets, weights and copper tablets, which may have been an early form of coinage. Unfortunately, all attempts to decipher the Indus script have failed, so much less is known about the Indus civilization than about its contemporaries in Mesopotamia and Egypt. Even the ethnic identity of the Indus people is unknown, although most historians believe that they were related to the Dravidian peoples who now live mainly in southern India. The Sumerians knew the Indus valley as Meluhha and its people as Meluhhaites.

Around 1800 BC the Indus civilization went into decline: writing and standardized weights and measures used for trade and taxation fell out of use, trade links with Mesopotamia were broken and civic order disintegrated in

This engraved stamp seal from Mohenjo-Daro in the Indus valley features a mythological animal and pictographic symbols from the Indus language. The Indus script remains undeciphered.

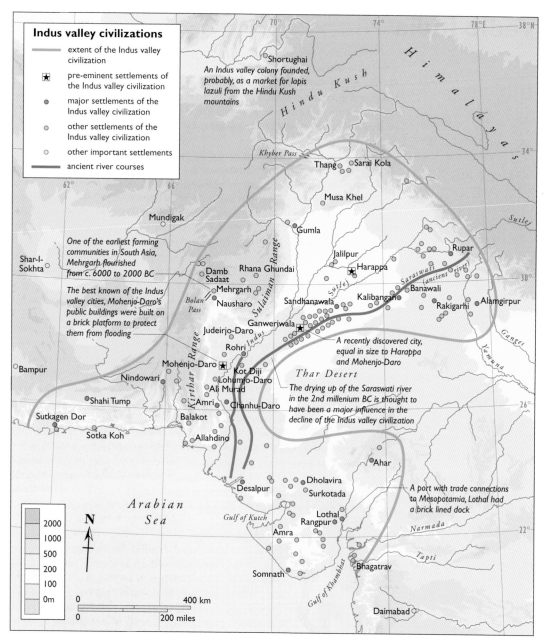

Indus valley civilizations

— extent of the Indus valley civilization

★ pre-eminent settlements of the Indus valley civilization

● major settlements of the Indus valley civilization

◉ other settlements of the Indus valley civilization

○ other important settlements

— ancient river courses

Shortughai
An Indus valley colony founded, probably, as a market for lapis lazuli from the Hindu Kush mountains

One of the earliest farming communities in South Asia, Mehrgarh flourished from c. 6000 to 2000 BC

The best known of the Indus valley cities, Mohenjo-Daro's public buildings were built on a brick platform to protect them from flooding

A recently discovered city, equal in size to Harappa and Mohenjo-Daro

The drying up of the Saraswati river in the 2nd millenium BC is thought to have been a major influence in the decline of the Indus valley civilization

A port with trade connections to Mesopotamia, Lothal had a brick lined dock

Hindu Kush
Himalayas
Khyber Pass
Suleiman Range
Kirthar Range
Bolan Pass
Indus
Sutlej
Saraswati (ancient river)
Ganges
Yamuna
Narmada
Tapti
Thar Desert
Arabian Sea
Gulf of Kutch
Gulf of Khambhat

Thang, Sarai Kola, Musa Khel, Gumla, Jalilpur, Rupar, Harappa, Banawali, Kalibangan, Rakigarhi, Alamgirpur, Sandhanawala, Ganweriwala, Judeirjo-Daro, Rohri, Mohenjo-Daro, Kot Diji, Lohumjo-Daro, Ali Murad, Amri, Chanhu-Daro, Nindowari, Shahi Tump, Balakot, Allahdino, Ahar, Desalpur, Dholavira, Surkotada, Lothal, Rangpur, Amra, Somnath, Bhagatrav, Daimabad, Mundigak, Damb Sadaat, Rhana Ghundai, Mehrgarh, Nausharo, Shar-I-Sokhta, Bampur, Sutkagen Dor, Sotka Koh

2000
1000
500
200
100
0m

N

0   400 km
0   200 miles

the cities, where public works, such as the sewers, fell into disrepair. The cities were not abandoned as suddenly or completely as was once thought – there was still some habitation at Harappa as late as 1300 BC – but life clearly reverted to a simpler social and economic level.

The reasons behind the collapse of the Indus civilization remain a mystery but, as many aspects of Indus culture survived in the countryside, it seems unlikely that an outside invasion was to blame. The most likely explanation is that the end of the civilization was somehow connected with the drying up of the river Saraswati, which began around 1900 BC. This would have had a devastating effect on agriculture and robbed the cities of their economic base. Displaced peasants may have sought refuge in the cities, hastening the break down of civic order.

Vedic India

Around 1500 BC the Aryans, nomads from central Asia, crossed the Hindu Kush mountains into the Indian sub-continent. The Aryan language gained ascendancy over the indigenous languages and was the ancestor of Sanskrit, the language of classical Indian literature, and of the modern Indic languages, including Hindi and Urdu.

"When they divided the man, into how many parts did they apportion him?... His mouth became the Brahmin *(priest); his arms were made into the* Kshatriya *(warrior), his thighs the* Vaishya *(common people), and from his feet the* Shudras *(servants) were born. "*

Rig Veda
(c. 1500–1000 BC)

For several centuries after their arrival in the sub-continent, the Aryans continued a semi-nomadic lifestyle based on cattle rearing, adopting settled agriculture only around 1000 BC. There are no historical records of this period but a mythic record of the Aryan migrations and wars with the native peoples is preserved in the *Vedas*, the holiest books of the Hindu religion. The four *varnas*, or social classes, of the *Vedas* provided the foundation of the Hindu caste system. The *Vedas* were transmitted orally for centuries until they were committed to writing in the 6th century BC. Despite the tradition of mutual hostility shown in the *Vedas*, it is thought that the religious traditions they record were an amalgamation of Aryan and indigenous influences as many features of Hinduism, such as ritual bathing, appear to have had precedents in the Indus civilization. Survival of indigenous traditions is also evident in the Black-and-Red Ware pottery which spread across most of southern India in the early 1st millennium: this was derived from the indigenous styles of late Indus times.

The distribution of Painted Grey Ware pottery, which appeared around 1000 BC, is often associated with the spread of the Aryans across the Gangetic plain but this is far from certain. By the 9th century dozens of small tribal kingdoms and aristocratic tribal republics, known as *janapadas*, had developed on the plain. Competition for power was intense and by 700 BC the *janapadas* had coalesced to form 16 *mahajanapadas* or 'great realms'; by 400 BC there were only around half a dozen. The most important of the survivors was Magadha, which achieved a dominant position in the 6th century under its expansionist king Bimbisara. The capitals of the *mahajanapadas* were small cities protected by walls of mud brick or stone. Writing, using an adaptation of one of the Semitic scripts of the Near East, came back into use in India in this period.

Factors in Urbanization

Urbanization is associated with a dramatic increase in iron production. First made in India as early as 1000 BC, it was only around 550 BC that iron tools and weapons came into widespread use. Some historians have argued that the availability of iron tools made possible an increase in agricultural productivity, leading to population increase. Others argue that it was iron weapons leading to an intensification of warfare that promoted the growth of states and cities for reasons of defence. A third view is that it was an increase in regional trade, rather than iron tools or weapons, that was really the key factor in urbanization. The period of the *mahajanapadas* was one of great importance in the history of religion. Not only did it see the recording of the early traditions of Hinduism but also the birth of Jainism and Buddhism. By 500 BC the Gangetic civilization had spread to most of India north of the river Godavari. To the south of the river were tribal farming peoples who buried their dead in megalithic tombs. It would be another 500 years before state formation began in this area.

This 14th-century bronze statue is of Vishnu, one of the major Hindu gods. Although Vishnu is a minor deity in the *Rig Veda*, by 500 BC he had assumed the role of the Great God, protector and preserver of the world.

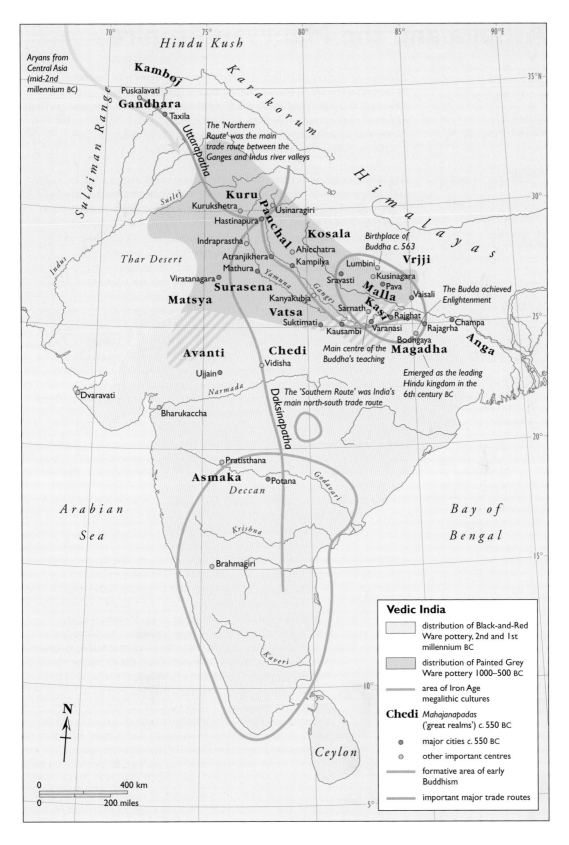

Aryans from Central Asia (mid-2nd millennium BC)

Hindu Kush

Karakorum

Kamboj

Puskalavati

Gandhara

Taxila

Sulaiman Range

Uttarapatha

The 'Northern Route' was the main trade route between the Ganges and Indus river valleys

Himalayas

Sutlej

Kuru

Kurukshetra

Usinaragiri

Hastinapura

Panchal

Indraprastha

Kosala

Ahicchatra

Birthplace of Buddha c. 563

Thar Desert

Atranjikhera

Kampilya

Lumbini

Vrjji

Mathura

Viratanagara

Yamuna

Sravasti

Kusinagara

Indus

Surasena

Ganges

Malla

Pava

Vaisali

The Budda achieved Enlightenment

Matsya

Kanyakubja

Sarnath

Kasi

Vatsa

Suktimati

Kausambi

Varanasi

Rajghat

Rajagrha

Champa

Sarnath

Bodhgaya

Anga

Avanti

Chedi

Main centre of the Buddha's teaching

Magadha

Vidisha

Ujjain

Emerged as the leading Hindu kingdom in the 6th century BC

Narmada

Daksinapatha

The 'Southern Route' was India's main north-south trade route

Dvaravati

Bharukaccha

Pratisthana

Asmaka

Potana

Godavari

Deccan

Arabian

Sea

Krishna

Bay of

Bengal

Brahmagiri

Kaveri

Ceylon

N

0   400 km
0   200 miles

Vedic India

distribution of Black-and-Red Ware pottery, 2nd and 1st millennium BC

distribution of Painted Grey Ware pottery 1000–500 BC

area of Iron Age megalithic cultures

Chedi *Mahajanapadas* ('great realms') *c.* 550 BC

major cities *c.* 550 BC

other important centres

formative area of early Buddhism

important major trade routes

Ashoka and the Mauryan Empire

The age of the mahajanapadas *was brought to an end by the Mauryan dynasty, which came to power in Magadha in 321 BC. Through military and diplomatic skill, the Mauryans created the greatest empire of ancient India and came closer to uniting the entire sub-continent into a single state than any future rulers would do before the Mughals in the 16th century AD.*

> *"All men are my children. As on behalf of my own children, I desire that they be provided by me with complete welfare and happiness in this world, and in the other world also."*
>
> Edict of Ashoka, 3rd century BC
> Translated by H. Kulke and D. Rothermund, *History of India* (Routledge, 1986)

Magadha was already established as the most powerful of the surviving *mahajanapadas* when it came under the control of the Nanda dynasty in 364 BC. The Nandas were expansionist rulers and within 25 years they had conquered all of the Ganges plain. However, the Nandas were also avaricious rulers and resentment over high taxation led to their overthrow in 321 BC in a coup by one of their generals, Chandragupta Maurya. Chandragupta more than doubled the size of the kingdom by conquering the Indus valley and the uplands to its west. Chandragupta imposed a harsh penal code on his subjects and created an efficient centralized government which controlled the economy and carried out public works programmes, such as road building and irrigation schemes. Chandragupta retired from office around 293 BC to become a Jain monk and was succeeded by his son Bindusara (r. 293–268 BC). Bindusara continued his father's policies with successful campaigns in southern India. The Mauryan empire was brought to its greatest extent by Bindusara's son Ashoka (r. 268–233 BC), one of the most remarkable rulers in Indian history. Following his bloody conquest of the kingdom of Kalinga in 261 Ashoka suffered a personal crisis of remorse for the suffering he had caused and converted to Buddhism.

Ashoka and Buddhism

The Buddhist religion had originated in Magadha with the teachings of Siddhartha Gautama, the Buddha (c. 563–483 BC), but it was still only a minor cult at the time of Ashoka's conversion. Ashoka attempted to apply the Buddhist principles of right conduct and non-violence to all aspects of his rule. He sought to rule by moral authority alone, moderating Chandragupta's penal code, ending militaristic expansion and assuring neighbouring states that he had no hostile intentions. To spread Buddhist values, Ashoka had edicts on morality and compassion carved onto rock faces and stone pillars throughout the empire. Over 30 of these have survived providing the most important source of information about Ashoka's reign. From them we learn that he encouraged his subjects to become vegetarians. Some of the earliest stupas (Buddhist monasteries) were built in his reign. Ashoka actively promoted Buddhism abroad, sending missions to Ceylon, south-east Asia and central Asia. These missions helped transform Buddhism from a minor Indian sect into one of the world's major religions. The majority of Ashoka's subjects never adopted Buddhism and Hinduism later made such a strong recovery that Buddhism became virtually extinct in India. But by this time, the religion was secure in the lands whose conversion was begun by Ashokan missionaries.

Sadly, moral authority was not enough to sustain the Mauryan empire in the long term and it declined after Ashoka's death. By the time the last Mauryan ruler was overthrown in 185 BC the empire had been reduced to its heartland of Magadha. No native dynasty would ever again rule so much of India.

The Great Stupa at Sanchi in India. Ashoka was the first to encourage the building of these dome-shaped monuments to house sacred Buddhist relics. Stupas can be found in every country in which Buddhism has been practised.

Herat

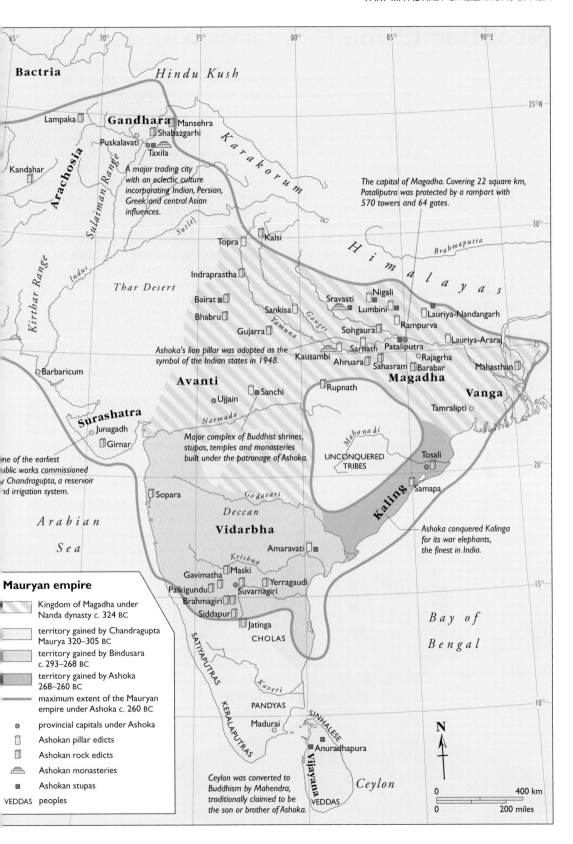

Bactria

Hindu Kush

Lampaka

Gandhara Mansehra

Shabazgarhi

Puskalavati

Taxila

A major trading city with an eclectic culture incorporating Indian, Persian, Greek and central Asian influences.

Kandahar

Arachosia

Sulaiman Range

Karakorum

The capital of Magadha. Covering 22 square km, Pataliputra was protected by a rampart with 570 towers and 64 gates.

Surlej

Topra Kalsi

Himalayas

Brahmaputra

35°N

30°

Kirthar Range

Indus

Thar Desert

Indraprastha

Bairat

Bhabru

Sankisa

Gujarra

Sravasti

Nigali

Lumbini

Rampurva

Lauriya-Nandangarh

Ganges

Yamuna

Sohgaura

Lauriya-Araraj

Ashoka's lion pillar was adopted as the symbol of the Indian states in 1948.

Kausambi

Sarnath Pataliputra

Ahruara

Sahasram Barabar

Rajagrha

Mahasthan

25°

Barbaricum

Avanti

Magadha

Vanga

Rupnath

Surashatra

Junagadh

Girnar

Ujjain Sanchi

Narmada

Tamralipti

Major complex of Buddhist shrines, stupas, temples and monasteries built under the patronage of Ashoka.

Mahanadi

UNCONQUERED TRIBES

Tosali

20°

ne of the earliest ublic works commissioned y Chandragupta, a reservoir nd irrigation system.

Sopara

Godavari

Deccan

Vidarbha

Amaravati

Krishna

Kaling

Samapa

Ashoka conquered Kalinga for its war elephants, the finest in India.

Arabian Sea

Gavimatha Maski

Palkigundu

Brahmagiri

Siddapur

Yerragaudi

Suvarnagiri

Jatinga

CHOLAS

Bay of Bengal

15°

Satiyaputras

Keralaputras

Kaveri

PANDYAS

Madurai

SINHALESE

10°

Anuradhapura

Ceylon

Vijayana

VEDDAS

Ceylon was converted to Buddhism by Mahendra, traditionally claimed to be the son or brother of Ashoka.

Mauryan empire

- Kingdom of Magadha under Nanda dynasty c. 324 BC
- territory gained by Chandragupta Maurya 320–305 BC
- territory gained by Bindusara c. 293–268 BC
- territory gained by Ashoka 268–260 BC
- maximum extent of the Mauryan empire under Ashoka c. 260 BC
- provincial capitals under Ashoka
- Ashokan pillar edicts
- Ashokan rock edicts
- Ashokan monasteries
- Ashokan stupas

VEDDAS peoples

N

0   400 km

0   200 miles

Neolithic China

The roots of Chinese civilization can be traced to the Longshan culture which developed in the Yellow River valley during the later Neolithic period.

"People spread manure on the fields and planted cereals. They dug the ground and drank water from wells. ... They built walls to protect themselves. They captured wild animals and made them into domesticated livestock."

Huainanzi, late 2nd century BC

Farming in China began around 6500 BC with the domestication of wild rice in the wetlands of the Yangtze basin. In northern China farming developed independently about 700 years later on the band of loess soils which extends across the Yellow River basin. This was an attractive area for early agriculturalists. Formed from wind-blown sediments at the end of the Ice Age, loess is fertile and light enough to be worked with simple stone tools like hoes.

The staple crop of these early Neolithic farmers was millet, a grain that is nutritionally much inferior to wheat and barley being deficient in important proteins and amino acids. As a result early Chinese farmers were frail-boned and much shorter than their hunter-gatherer forbears. Domesticated chickens and pigs were also bred and hunting remained an important source of food. There was considerable local diversity among the early millet farming cultures, the most important of which were the Peiligang and Cishan cultures.

Yangshao and Longshan

The later Neolithic period of the Yellow River basin is characterized by two main cultures. The earliest of these was the Yangshao culture, which developed around 5000 BC and was confined mostly to the loess belt. The Yangshao culture was characterized by coarse painted pottery with great regional diversity of styles and a small-scale, kinship based social organization. The Yangshao culture was succeeded around 3200 BC by the Longshan culture, which saw steady development to more hierarchical forms of society and laid the foundations for the emergence of the first Chinese kingdoms in the 2nd millennium BC.

The development of the Longshan culture was a result of the population increase following the introduction of rice farming to the Yellow River valley. Rice has a much higher yield than millet and is more nutritious but northern China has a relatively dry climate so rice farming was possible only with irrigation. The need to organize the communal effort required to construct irrigation systems may have been one of the factors that encouraged more hierarchical leadership to emerge.

The Longshan culture developed many of the features that were characteristic of the Bronze Age Shang civilization. Finely carved tools and ritual vessels of jade, a hard translucent stone that was highly prized in China in historical times, appeared. The first copper tools and ornaments were produced. Regional trade networks blossomed, promoting a greater degree of cultural homogeneity over wide areas. A militaristic warrior class emerged and there is also evidence of organized warfare, such as massacres or sacrifices of

This lid from a Yangshao pot dates to c. 2500 BC. The crude painting is typical of Yangshao earthenware. The face on the lid may be that of a shaman.

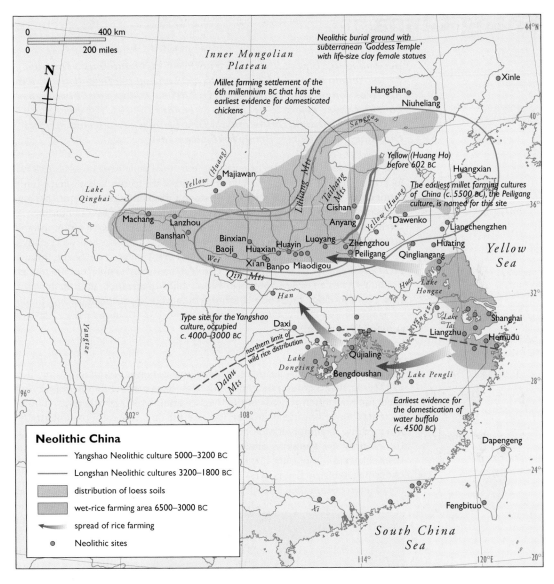

Neolithic burial ground with subterranean 'Goddess Temple' with life-size clay female statues

Millet farming settlement of the 6th millennium BC that has the earliest evidence for domesticated chickens

Yellow (Huang Ho) before 602 BC

The earliest millet farming cultures of China (c. 5500 BC), the Peiligang culture, is named for this site

Type site for the Yangshao culture, occupied c. 4000–3000 BC

northern limit of wild rice distribution

Earliest evidence for the domestication of water buffalo (c. 4500 BC)

Neolithic China

—— Yangshao Neolithic culture 5000–3200 BC

—— Longshan Neolithic cultures 3200–1800 BC

◼ distribution of loess soils

◼ wet-rice farming area 6500–3000 BC

◀ spread of rice farming

● Neolithic sites

prisoners and the proliferation of fortifications constructed using the *hangtu* or pounded earth technique.

Chiefs displayed their power even in death, with burials accompanied by grave goods and animal and human sacrifices. Cinnabar, a mercury oxide, known to be associated in later Chinese culture with immortality, was placed in burials. Elegant wheel-thrown pottery was made. A system of divination using oracle bones came into use.

The degree to which wealth and power had become centred in an elite minority by the late 3rd millennium is highlighted by a very large cemetery discovered at Taosi (north of Luoyang) containing thousands of graves. High status individuals had large graves with wooden coffins and up to 200 objects of jade, furniture, musical instruments and fine pottery. Individuals of medium status had smaller graves with similar but fewer grave goods to the large graves. Low-status individuals were buried in small graves with few or no grave goods. Medium-sized graves made up 11.4 percent of the total, while large graves made up just 1.3 percent.

Shang China

According to Chinese historical traditions, civilization was founded by the Yellow Emperor Huang Di in 2698 BC and the first dynasty, the Xia, was founded by Yu the Great in 2205 BC. Today, most historians consider these rulers to be purely legendary figures. The emergence of China's first civilization and its first historically attested dynasty, the Shang, both belong firmly to the Bronze Age.

"The Yellow Emperor gained the power of Earth, and a yellow dragon and an earthworm appeared. The Xia gained the power of wood, and a green dragon appeared, and the grass and trees grew luxuriantly. The Shang gained the power of metal, and silver flowed forth from the mountains. "

Sima Qian, Historical Records (c.100 BC)

The earliest known Chinese bronzes are four ritual wine vessels cast *c.* 1800 BC at Erlitou, one of a number of cities that grew up in the Yellow River basin around this time. The vessels were cast using a piece-mould technique that was constantly refined in the centuries that followed until the Chinese became the most accomplished bronze casters of the ancient world, able to cast shapes of amazing complexity. Erlitou contained two palace complexes and was clearly a royal centre of some importance, possibly the first capital of the Shang dynasty of kings. Shang palaces were large but architecturally simple timber framed buildings with thatched roofs. However, their appearance was made more impressive by siting them on platforms which were approached by long flights of stone steps. This concept remained typical of Chinese palace designs throughout imperial times.

Chinese Writing

According to traditional histories, the Shang dynasty was founded by King Tang in 1766 BC, that is around the time of the emergence of the Erlitou culture, but there are no written records of the dynasty until *c.* 1500 BC when a system of pictographic writing came into use. This was the direct ancestor of modern Chinese writing. Examples of pictographic writing are found on bronze vessels but the majority are found on oracle bones used for divination. The Shang kings would make no important decision about war, hunting or agriculture without consulting their ancestors who they believed resided in Heaven where they could intercede on their behalf with the creator god Shang Di. A question was inscribed on the bone (usually the shell of a turtle or the shoulder blade of an ox), which was then struck with a hot implement. The pattern of cracks created was then interpreted and the answer was recorded on the bone.

The majority of oracle bones have been found at Anyang, the last and greatest of the Shang dynasty capitals. Anyang covered 62 square kilometres and consisted of specialized craft quarters, residential quarters, temple complexes and cemeteries, including 11 royal burials in elaborate

This bronze ritual cooking vessel decorated with human faces is from the Shang dynasty. It would have been used for religious ceremonies and for entertaining honoured guests. Bronze had great ritual significance in ancient China, relating to power and divinity.

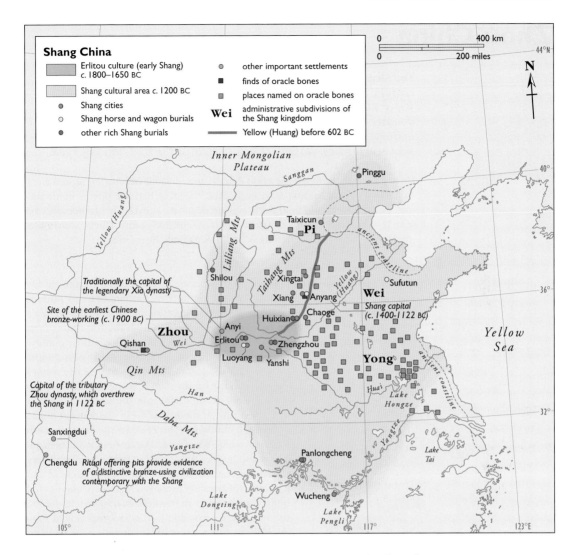

Shang China

- Erlitou culture (early Shang) c. 1800–1650 BC
- Shang cultural area c. 1200 BC
- ● Shang cities
- ○ Shang horse and wagon burials
- ● other rich Shang burials
- ● other important settlements
- ■ finds of oracle bones
- ■ places named on oracle bones
- **Wei** administrative subdivisions of the Shang kingdom
- ── Yellow (Huang) before 602 BC

0 400 km
0 200 miles

Inner Mongolian Plateau

Sanggan

Pinggu

Yellow (Huang)

Lüliang Mts

Taihang Mts

Taixicun
Pi

ancient coastline

Shilou
Xingtai
○Sufutun

Traditionally the capital of the legendary Xia dynasty

Xiang ●Anyang
Yellow (Huang)
Wei

Site of the earliest Chinese bronze-working (c. 1900 BC)

Huixian ○○
Chaoge
Shang capital (c. 1400–1122 BC)

Zhou
Anyi
Erlitou ○○
○○Zhengzhou
Yellow Sea

Qishan ■ *Wei*
Luoyang ■ Yanshi
Yong

Qin Mts

Han

Capital of the tributary Zhou dynasty, which overthrew the Shang in 1122 BC

Hua'
Lake Hongze

Daba Mts

Sanxingdui
Yangtze

Chengdu *Ritual offering pits provide evidence of a distinctive bronze-using civilization contemporary with the Shang*

Panlongcheng
Lake Tai

ancient coastline

Lake Dongting

Wucheng
Lake Pengli

105° 111° 117° 123°E

44°N
40°
36°
32°

N

shaft tombs. These burials were all robbed in ancient times except for that of Lady Fu Hao, which was furnished with over 400 ritual bronze vessels, nearly 600 jade carvings, thousands of other objects, and sacrificed retainers and guards. Inscriptions found in her tomb record that Fu Hao was the wife of King Wu Ding and had taken part in military campaigns. Many of the royal tombs contained chariots, which first came into use in China in this period, together with their teams of horses and their drivers.

Shang Influence

Although it was the dominant culture of a wide area of northern China by 1500 BC, it is far from certain that the area of Shang cultural influence was the same as the area actually ruled by the Shang dynasty. Identifiable places mentioned on oracle bones probably give a truer idea of the extent of the Shang's direct influence. Certainly the Shang state was not unique in early Bronze Age China. In the 1990s evidence of an independent civilization contemporary with the Shang was discovered at Sanxingdui in central China. Sanxingdui was a major city with vast ceremonial buildings including one 200 metres square. Sacrificial pits here were filled with jade and ivory objects and cast bronze statues of gods, all executed in artistic styles very different from those of the Shang.

Zhou China

The Shang dynasty came to an end in 1027 (some sources suggest a century earlier) when its last king Di-xin was overthrown by King Wu of Zhou, a vassal state in the west of the Shang kingdom. The dynasty established by Wu became the most long-lived in Chinese history, surviving for over 700 years. By the time the last Zhou king was overthrown, classical Chinese civilization had fully emerged.

"When the sounds of war are heard, personal wealth is diminished to make soldiers rich."

Su Qin, 4th century BC

Historians usually divide the Zhou dynasty into periods before 770 BC and after. In the first period, known as Western Zhou, the kings had real power; in the second period, Eastern Zhou, royal power declined and the kings became the merely nominal overlords of a decentralized feudal kingdom. The Western Zhou made their capital at Xian in their traditional family heartlands.

Golden Age of the Zhou

In later periods, the early years of Zhou rule came to be regarded as a golden age of peace and prosperity. The Zhou were masters of propaganda and skilfully legitimized their usurpation through the new doctrine of the 'Mandate of Heaven'. Consequently the Zhou faced only one rebellion from the remnants of the old Shang regime. The change of regime did not result in any dramatic cultural discontinuity either. Shang-style ritual vessels continued to be used for sacrifices and oracle bones remained in use for divination. It was only later, when the decline of the dynasty's authority had really destroyed faith in them, that these elements of Shang culture fell out of use. The Zhou divided the kingdom into fiefs which were granted to members of the royal family and important retainers. There was a small central bureaucracy attached to the royal household and a number of standing armies, which were augmented by troops levied from the fiefs in wartime. In theory, the fiefs were revocable but, as in other feudal societies, there was an inevitable tendency for them to become hereditary and therefore fall out of the king's control. Gradually, royal power was eroded.

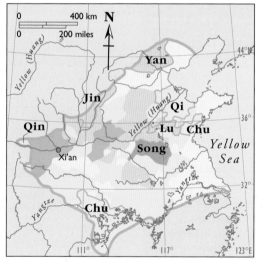

Springs and Autumns Period

In 770 BC the Zhou dynasty decided to move their capital to Luoyang because Xian had become too vulnerable to barbarian raids. This move marks the beginning of the period of disorder and fragmentation known as the Springs and Autumns period (named after the title of the state annals of Lu). Luoyang was more centrally situated than Xian but the decision to remove the dynasty from its traditional heartland sent its prestige and authority into freefall.

The territory directly controlled by the king was now smaller than those controlled by most of his dukes, who to all intents and purposes became the rulers of independent states, which made constant war on one another. Although the dukes continued to recognize the king as sovereign, they also recognized the duke of the strongest state of the time as hegemon, who exercized primacy over the other states in the king's name. Each state had its own government, laws and hierarchy of ranks and classes; their rulers had civic, military and religious duties and were concerned (or at least said they were concerned) for the welfare of their people.

Western Zhou Kingdom

—— approximate border of Zhou kingdom

▨ Zhou royal domain

▨ fiefs held by members of the Zhou royal family

▨ fief held by the Shang royal family

▨ fiefs held by other noble families

● Western Zhou capital

In spite of, or because of, the conflicts of the time, the Springs and Autumns was a period of great creativity in literature and in political, religious and philosophical thought. Towards the end of the period, the sage Confucius (551–479) formulated his ethical system, which with its emphasis on respect for legitimate authority, remains central in Chinese thought today. The major religious figure of the age was Lao Zi, whose teachings inspired Daoism (perhaps better known by its alternative transliteration as 'Taoism').

There is no sharp division between the Springs and Autumns period and the Warring States Period (480–221 BC) that followed it: 481 is simply the last year covered by the Springs and Autumns annals. The Warring States saw the development of centralized government, a decline in feudalism and the first widespread use of iron tools and weapons. Competition between states intensified as the stronger eliminated the weaker, a process which eventually culminated in the unification of China.

This globe-shaped food container, or *dui*, is from the Eastern Zhou kingdom (4th–3rd century BC). It is bronze and is richly decorated with inlaid gold and silver.

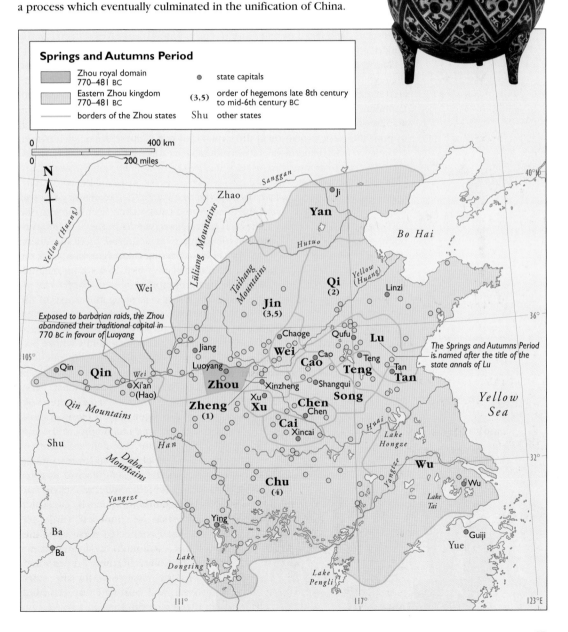

Springs and Autumns Period

- Zhou royal domain 770–481 BC
- Eastern Zhou kingdom 770–481 BC
- borders of the Zhou states
- state capitals
- (3,5) order of hegemons late 8th century to mid-6th century BC
- Shu other states

Exposed to barbarian raids, the Zhou abandoned their traditional capital in 770 BC in favour of Luoyang

The Springs and Autumns Period is named after the title of the state annals of Lu

The Unification of China

When the Warring States Period began in 480, China was divided into some 17 competing states. Although nominally still subject to the Zhou dynasty, the rulers of these states increasingly regarded themselves as kings in their own right. The Warring States Period was one of frequent conflict as the stronger states began to conquer the weaker ones. By 256 BC there were just seven states left. The strongest of the survivors was the state of Qin in western China.

> *"A state that uses good people to rule the wicked will always suffer from disorder.... A state that uses the wicked to rule the good will always enjoy order."*
>
> The Book of Lord Shang, early 3rd century BC

Qin began to rise to prominence in the reign of King Xiao (361–338). Xiao's prime minister, the capable but somewhat cynical Shang Yang, better known as Lord Shang, turned Qin into an absolutist centralized state. Shang Yang broke the power of the feudal aristocracy by making military service the basis of nobility. Aristocrats who failed to win glory in battle found themselves reduced to the rank of commoner or even slave.

Meritocratic reforms made it possible for commoners of ability to rise through the hierarchy and achieve nobility. Paramilitary organizations were created to secure social order and the extended family was declared abolished. Economic reforms encouraged trade and agriculture and increased the resources of the state. Qin was aided by its peripheral position which gave it opportunities for expansion at the expense of non-Chinese states, such as Shu, conquered in 316, and made it less vulnerable to attack by other Chinese states.

The First Emperor

Qin made steady territorial advances in the first half of the 3rd century. War was waged with great ruthlessness and the defeated could expect little mercy. In one battle against Zhao in 260 BC the victorious Qin reputedly buried 400,000 prisoners alive. The final unification of China was achieved by King Zheng (r. 246–210 BC) in just nine years by a series of daring campaigns which left the other states no time to make common cause against him. To mark his triumph Zheng took the name Shi Huangdi or 'First Emperor'.

To consolidate his rule, Shi Huangdi set about destroying all vestiges of the old states; their aristocracies were deported and he ordered all historical records of them destroyed (although some were preserved by brave scholars at risk to their own lives). China was divided into 48 commanderies whose borders were not based on the old states. Qin laws and institutions were extended to the whole of China. Feudalism, with its decentralizing tendency, was then abolished and professional, non-hereditary bureaucracies were created and kept under close control. Cultural and economic unity was imposed by the standardization of coins, weights and measures, writing scripts and the axle sizes of wagons. Many of the Warring States had defended their borders by constructing walls of pounded earth. Shi Huangdi connected these up to create a continuous defensive barrier along China's northern border which was the inspiration for the stone Great Wall built later by the Ming dynasty (1368–1644).

Terracotta soldiers from the 7000-strong army buried with Shi Huangdi. Chinese peasants came across some pottery while digging for a well in 1974 and helped make one of the most significant archaeological discoveries of the 20th century.

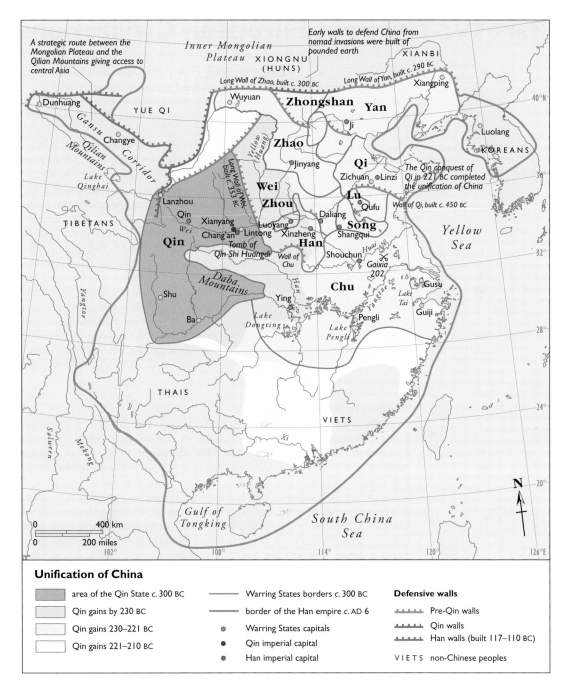

A strategic route between the Mongolian Plateau and the Qilian Mountains giving access to central Asia

Early walls to defend China from nomad invasions were built of pounded earth

Inner Mongolian Plateau XIONGNU (HUNS)

XIANBI

Long Wall of Zhao, built c. 300 BC

Long Wall of Yan, built c. 290 BC

Xiangping

Dunhuang

YUE QI

Wuyuan

Zhongshan **Yan**

Ji

Luolang

KOREANS

Gansu

Changye

Qilian Mountains

Corridor

Lake Qinghai

Zhao

Jinyang

Long Wall of Wei, built c. 353 BC

Yellow (Huang)

Qi

Zichuan ○Linzi

The Qin conquest of Qi in 221 BC completed the unification of China

Lanzhou

Qin

Wei

Zhou

Lu

Wall of Qi, built c. 450 BC

Yellow Sea

TIBETANS

Xianyang

Wei

Chang'an ○Lintong Xinzheng

Luoyang

Daliang

Qufu

Qin

Tomb of Qin Shi Huangdi

Han

Song

Shangqui

Wall of Chu

Shouchun

Huai

Gaixia 202

Daba Mountains

Shu

Ying ○

Chu

Yangtze

Gusu

Lake Tai

Guiji

Bao ○

Lake Dongting

Pengli

Lake Pengli

Yangtze

Yangtze

THAIS

Xi

VIETS

Salween

Mekong

N

Gulf of Tongking

South China Sea

| 0 | 400 km |
| 0 | 200 miles |

102° 108° 114° 120° 126°E

Unification of China

- area of the Qin State *c.* 300 BC
- Qin gains by 230 BC
- Qin gains 230–221 BC
- Qin gains 221–210 BC

—— Warring States borders *c.* 300 BC
—— border of the Han empire *c.* AD 6
○ Warring States capitals
● Qin imperial capital
● Han imperial capital

Defensive walls

⊥⊥⊥ Pre-Qin walls
⊥⊥⊥ Qin walls
⊥⊥⊥ Han walls (built 117–110 BC)

VIETS non-Chinese peoples

Emperor Shi Huangdi's despotical rule was highly unpopular and after his death rebels massacred the entire Qin royal family in 206 BC. However, there was no attempt to resurrect the old China of independent states and the empire passed virtually intact under the rule of the capable Han dynasty (206 BC–AD 220). Adopting Confucian principles, the Han somewhat relaxed Shi Huangdi's savage penal code, and reduced taxes, however, they did not significantly change the pattern of centralized totalitarian government he had created: despite long periods of renewed political disunity and foreign rule, it has endured in China to the present day.

Part IV: The First European Civilizations

Until the late 19th century, European civilization was believed to have begun with the Classical Greeks and Romans but, with the advent of modern archaeology, it was discovered that the history of civilization in Europe is far more ancient than had been imagined.

The earliest European civilization, the Minoan, developed on the eastern Mediterranean island of Crete in the early Bronze Age *c*. 2000 BC. In terms of its geographical spread, the Minoan civilization was the smallest of the Old World's primary civilizations and was the only primary civilization to develop in Europe. Partly under the influence of the Minoans a second European civilization, the Mycenaean, developed on the Greek mainland about 400 years later. Despite their impressive achievements, these Bronze Age civilizations died out without direct heirs. The Minoan civilization vanished after it was conquered by the Mycenaeans around 1450 BC, while the Mycenaean civilization collapsed in mysterious circumstances shortly after 1200 BC.

Folk memories alone survived of the Minoans and Mycenaeans to be transformed into a glorious semi-legendary past by Homer and other Greek poets of later ages. After this false start, civilizations did not arise again in Europe for four centuries. When they did, in Greece, Italy and Iberia, the stimulus came not so much from internal developments but from the Near East, where demand in the mighty Assyrian empire for imported luxuries led to the growth of trade throughout the Mediterranean.

Farming in Mesolithic Europe

As was the case everywhere in the world, the emergence of civilizations in Europe depended upon the development of intensive agriculture. Although Europe had a number of plants and animals suitable for domestication, farming probably did not develop there independently. The period of European prehistory between the immediate post-Glacial period and the adoption of farming is known as the Mesolithic or Middle Stone Age. Mesolithic Europe was a land of diverse environments and rich natural resources. In some areas hunter-gatherers were able to adopt semi-sedentary lifestyles and, burials reveal, there were even emerging distinctions of social status. The pressures on Mesolithic Europeans to adopt farming were few but their lifestyle meant that many of them were 'pre-adapted' to adopt agriculture should the opportunity or need arise.

This fresco of a leaping bull and three acrobats comes from the Minoan palace of Knossos in Crete. The Minoans, who created the first civilization in Europe, are famous for their lavish palaces with their vibrant wall paintings. The use of colour, pattern and dynamic movement in Minoan art makes it distinct from that of other Mediterranean cultures.

The transition from hunting and gathering to farming in Europe began in Greece and the Balkans *c.* 6500 BC. There are similarities between the material cultures of Anatolian and early Greek and Balkan farming peoples, suggesting that agriculture may initially have been intro-duced to Europe by immigrants. Emmer wheat and barley were certainly introduced from Anatolia but other crops and animals used by early farmers in this area, including einkorn wheat, sheep, goats and cattle, could have been domesticated locally. Farming spread quickly around the Mediterranean but its spread to central and northern Europe was slower, progress depending on the development of strains of crops and livestock which were resistant to colder and wetter climates. As farming became established native plants and animals were domesticated including oats, grapes, olives and horses. Farming had spread through most of Europe by 4000 BC but hunting and gathering persisted in the far north into the modern age.

A Neolithic chamber tomb at Hanöbukten in southern Sweden. This is a typical megalithic chamber tomb because of its small size. It would have been used for communal burials by a single family group.

The spread of farming was probably accomplished by a mixture of small-scale migrations and by indigenous Mesolithic hunter-gatherers adopting the way of life. When the population of a farming village became too large, a daugh-ter settlement would be founded on virgin land a few kilometres away. A single hunter-gatherer needs about 25 square kilometres to make a living, whereas even the most primitive forms of agriculture can support up to 20 people on one square kilometre. The steady encroachment of farming peoples would have put pressure on the wild resources needed by the hunter-gatherers (early farm-ers still hunted, gathered and fished when they could), forcing them to adopt farming too: their semi-sedentary way of life would have made the transition from one way of life to the other a fairly smooth one.

Neolithic Europe

The adoption of farming marks the beginning of the Neolithic or New Stone Age. The best known monuments of Neolithic Europe are the megalithic tombs, circles and alignments of the Atlantic west, which are still a prominent and enig-matic presence in the landscape. Due to its rich natural resources, Atlantic Europe was already densely populated in the Mesolithic Age. The population would have increased even more after the adoption of farming and it is thought that the megalithic tradition may have arisen from a concern by communities to mark their ownership of territory. A prominently sited tomb, for example, made the visible statement: 'This is where our dead are, this is our land.' Although often described as a megalithic civilization, most megalithic monuments were built by small-scale societies based on extended families or clans, working part-time over several seasons. The greatest megalithic structures, such as the Newgrange chamber tomb in Ireland, the vast stone alignments at Carnac in Brittany and the stone circle at Stonehenge, could only have been built by territorial chiefdoms with strong centralized leadership that were able to command labour and resources over a wide area, yet even these relatively complex societies had no towns or cities and were not literate.

The reason why Crete became the location of the first European civilization has much to do with its location, which made the island a natural focus of long-distance trade routes. Crete had a prosperous agriculture based on the 'Mediterranean Triad' of wheat, olives and vines, and mountain sheep herding: grain, oil, wine and wool are all valuable and are easily stored and transported. The most distinctive feature of the Minoan civilization is its palaces, the capitals

This stone carving comes from the King's Grave, known as Kungagraven, at Kivik southern Sweden. The figure on a chariot pulled by horses is thought to be influenced by Mycenaean culture. Unusual carvings such as this one decorated the King's Grave which is the largest circular burial site in Sweden and a unique example of Northern European Bronze Age culture.

of the half dozen small kingdoms that arose on the island *c.* 2000 BC. The palaces incorporated large storehouses where grain, wine and olive oil were kept in huge pottery jars. This shows that it was control and redistribution of surplus food, and no doubt other products such as cloth and metals, that was the main factor in state formation in Crete. The need to manage these surpluses efficiently led to the development of writing. The earliest Minoan writing system was hieroglyphic and may have been inspired by the Egyptian hieroglyphs (the Minoans traded with Egypt), however, the symbols themselves are uniquely Minoan. A syllabic script, known as Linear A, was developed later. Neither script has been deciphered and the ethnic identity of the Minoans remains unknown.

The Mycenaeans

Europe's second civilization, the Mycenaean, was founded by early Greeks. Although influenced by the Minoans, whose syllabic script they adopted, the Mycenaeans were more warlike. Mycenaean kings ruled from strongly fortified towns; they had their palaces but they were much smaller than those on Crete. Like the Minoans, the Mycenaeans were engaged in long-distance trade and their kings gained much of their power from their control over the distribution of surplus food and craft products. The Mycenaeans were expansionist, they conquered the Minoans and established the first Greek settlements on the coast of Anatolia and in Cyprus.

Mycenaean civilization collapsed abruptly and violently around 1200 BC. It is not known who the attackers were: the late Bronze Age was a turbulent time throughout the eastern Mediterranean, marked by folk movements, wars and the disruption of long-distance trade (see page 40). In the 400 year 'dark age' that followed writing fell out of use and iron tools came into widespread use in southern Europe: by 500 BC their use had spread to all except the far north of Europe. By 800 BC urban life was beginning to revive in Greece, the population was rising and long-distance trade was on the increase.

The Bronze Age civilizations were remembered as a legendary time but this revival of civilization in Greece was really a new beginning, the true origin of European civilization. As the old Mycenaean script had been long forgotten, the Greeks adapted the Phoenician alphabet to their own needs. Architectural and artistic ideas were adopted from the Egyptians and mathematics and astronomy from the Mesopotamians. If it initially absorbed many foreign influences, Greek civilization soon proved itself to be brilliantly inventive in almost every aspect of the arts and sciences and in the field of political thought. Although the basic political unit throughout Greece was the city-state, by the 6th century there was a wide range of governing institutions including monarchies, oligarchies, tyrannies (popular dictatorships) and, in Athens, the first democracy. The full flowering of Greek civilization, which took place in the Classical Period (*c.* 480–356 BC) is outside the scope of this book.

The Phoenicians had been important cultural intermediaries in the revival of civilization in Greece and they played a similar role further west in the Mediterranean. By 800 BC the Phoenicians had pioneered trade routes right across the Mediterranean and through the Pillars of Hercules into the Atlantic Ocean (see page 44). Along these routes the Phoenicians founded colonies. The most famous of these was Carthage in North Africa, but there were smaller colonies in Malta, Sicily, Sardinia, the Balearic Islands and the southern coast of Iberia. Each of these became a centre from which the influence of the eastern Mediterranean civilizations spread to the hinterland. By the 8th century Phoenician influences had pushed the native Iberian peoples on the road towards state formation. The Phoenicians were interested in Atlantic Europe because it was rich in metal ores and especially tin ore, the rarer of the two ingredients of bronze. Tartessos had rich mineral deposits of its own but it was also ideally situated to play the role of middleman in the trade in metal ores from northern Spain, Gaul and Britain, re-exporting them to the Phoenicians. Striking evidence for this trade comes from a shipwreck found at Huelva, dated to *c*. 800 BC, which contained over 200 bronze artefacts manufactured in the Loire region.

The Etruscan and Italian City-states

The Greeks soon became competitors of the Phoenicians and began an even more vigorous policy of colonization to defuse social tensions caused by overpopulation. Although the indigenous peoples were often hostile to the Greek colonies, they could not escape their powerful influence. The Greeks were most influential in Italy where Etruscan and Latin peoples had begun to form city-states in the 8th and 9th centuries. Long-distance trade was important to the Etruscans but it was probably not the major factor in the growth of their civilization. Etruria, roughly modern Tuscany, was an exceptionally fertile agricultural area with the added advantage of rich reserves of copper and iron ores. Etruscan civilization undoubtedly arose because of the production and exploitation of agricultural surpluses. It was, however, trade that brought the Etruscans into contact with the Greeks, from whom they borrowed their alphabet, art and architectural styles. The Latin city-states grew up under the cultural influence of both the Greeks and Etruscans. By 500 BC Rome had become the largest of the Latin city-states and one of the largest cities in Italy. Rome's days of imperial greatness still lay a long time in the future, but it had already distinguished itself with its republican system of government, introduced in 509 BC.

The Greeks also had a considerable influence on the Celtic peoples of Gaul and central Europe through their colony of Massalia (Marseille), founded *c*. 600 BC. Massalia was well situated to take advantage of the trade routes which ran north from the Mediterranean into Gaul and southern Germany up the valley of the river Rhône. The Celtic elite was eager to acquire Mediterranean luxuries, especially wine, because the control of their use and distribution was a major source of their authority. The Greeks introduced the cultivation of vines and olives and southern Gaul soon developed a typically Mediterranean economy. By the later centuries BC state formation was well advanced among the Celts of southern Gaul and central Europe. They had adopted versions of the Greek and Latin alphabets, coinage and institutions of government modelled on those of the Mediterranean world. However, Celtic civilization never got the chance to flower before it was overtaken by the growing might of Rome.

Part of the fortress wall of the ring fort at Dún Eochla on the Aran island of Inishmore. Built in the late Iron Age, Dún Eochla belongs to the last age of the ancient Celts, after the Romans had destroyed Celtic civilization in most of Europe.

Neolithic Europe

Europe's temperate climate was an obstacle to the adoption of a way of life that had developed in a region with mild winters and dry, sunny summers. Early farmers were adaptable and by 3000 BC agriculture had spread as far north as Scandinavia.

The Ring of Brodgar stone circle in Orkney. Neolithic stone circles are among the megalithic monuments that have endured as part of the landscape of western Europe. The Ring of Brodgar is one of the most impressive stone circles in Britain, with 27 of the original 60 stones remaining.

Europe's earliest farming communities developed in Greece and the Balkans around 6500 BC. As the staple crops, emmer wheat and barley, were of Near Eastern origin, it is likely that the farming way of life was introduced by settlers from Anatolia. Thereafter farming spread through Europe by a mixture of small-scale migrations by farming peoples and the adoption of farming techniques by hunter-gatherers. Not surprisingly, farming spread most rapidly through Mediterranean Europe. Its spread through central and northern Europe hinged on the discovery of crop strains suited to the wetter, colder climates of these regions. The spread of farming to temperate Europe is marked by the appearance of the Linear Pottery Culture in central Europe *c.* 5600 BC, which spread north from the Balkans following a belt of fertile and easily worked loess soil. After a hiatus of several centuries farming made a new advance into the wet and cool maritime areas of north-west Europe.

In most of Europe, few traces of Neolithic settlement have survived above ground but in western Europe Neolithic megalithic monuments, such as chambered tombs and stone circles, are prominent features of the landscape. The earliest megalithic tombs were built *c.* 4300 and stayed in use as communal bur-

"It was in those days that men first sought covered dwelling places.... Then corn, the gift of Ceres, first began to be sown in long furrows, and straining bullocks groaned beneath the yoke. "

Ovid, *Metamorphoses* (*c.* AD 8) Translated by M. M. Innes (Penguin Classics, 1955)

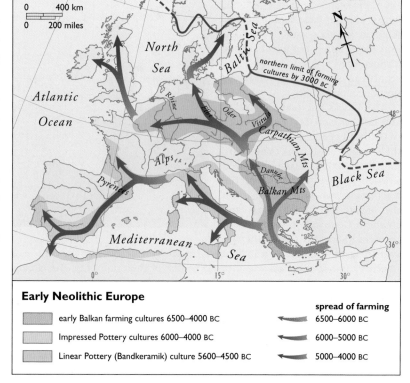

Early Neolithic Europe

- early Balkan farming cultures 6500–4000 BC
- Impressed Pottery cultures 6000–4000 BC
- Linear Pottery (Bandkeramik) culture 5600–4500 BC

spread of farming
- 6500–6000 BC
- 6000–5000 BC
- 5000–4000 BC

ial places for generations. Most megalithic tombs are modest enough to have been built by small-scale, kinship based communities but some, such as the Newgrange tomb, built *c.* 3000 BC in Ireland, are evidence of the evolution of more hierarchical societies, such as chiefdoms, that could command the labour and resources of wide areas. Evidence for the emergence of hierarchical societies becomes more common in the later Neolithic period. In the Bell Beaker cultures which developed in western Europe *c.* 2500 BC burial customs reflected social status with a minority of graves containing prestige goods, such as gold and copper ornaments, while most contained simpler items, such as stone tools.

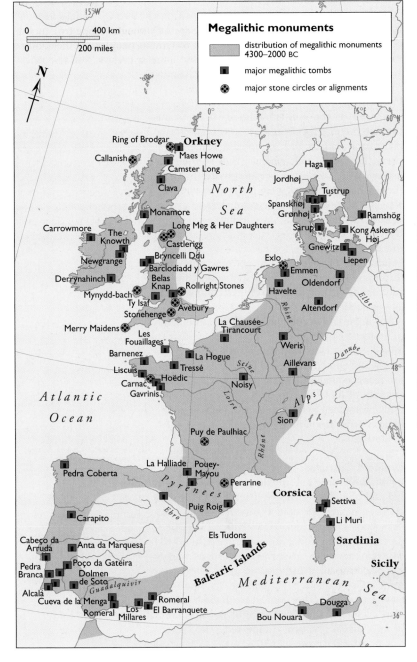

Megalithic monuments

distribution of megalithic monuments 4300–2000 BC

major megalithic tombs

major stone circles or alignments

One of the famous standing stones of Stenness on the island of Orkney in Scotland. This stone once formed part of a circle of 12 stones; now only four of the stones remain. The tallest megalith stands six metres (19 feet) high. The site is thought to date from about 3000 BC, making it one of the earliest stone circles in Britain.

The Bronze Age and the Rise of Elites

The earliest bronze-using culture in Europe, the Únětice culture of modern Poland, developed around 2500 BC. With no demonstrable links with bronze-using civilizations in the Near East, it was probably an entirely indigenous development. Bronze came into use in Greece, the Balkans and Italy around 2300 BC, in Spain and Britain by 1800 BC, and finally in Scandinavia by 1500 BC.

"After that came the third age, the age of bronze, when men were of a fiercer character, more ready to turn to cruel warfare."

Ovid, *Metamorphoses* (*c.* AD 8)
Translated by M. M. Innes, (Penguin Classics, 1955)

The introduction of bronze accelerated the development of hierarchical societies. Social elites were able to increase their power through control over the trade, production and use of metal weapons. As a result the Bronze Age saw chiefdoms established across Europe. The chiefdoms were highly competitive societies and evidence of organized warfare, such as hillforts, and specialized weapons, such as the sword, became more common.

Prestige Objects
The need of the elite to reinforce their status through the display of prestige objects stimulated craftsmanship and the production of fine jewellery, tableware, cult objects and weapons in bronze, gold and silver. Very large quantities of these valuable artefacts were interred in elite burials, such as those of the early Bronze Age Wessex culture, or sunk into bogs as offerings to the gods. It was common practice across much of Europe in the early Bronze Age for the elite to be buried beneath barrows. These were not only prominent features in the landscape but also practical demonstrations of the power of the elite to command the labour needed to build them.

An important consequence of the introduction of bronze technology was a substantial increase in long-distance trade. Copper and tin ores are less widely distributed than good tool-making stone so for many communities, the only way to obtain supplies of metal was to trade. The expansion of trade promoted the transmission of ideas, resulting in considerable uniformity of culture across much of Europe.

Urnfield Cultures
By the late Bronze Age, the diverse cultures of central Europe had been replaced by Urnfield cultures, named for their distinctive burial practices. Bodies were cremated and placed in pottery funerary urns for burial in cemeteries of hundreds or even thousands of graves. High-status burials were accompanied by valuable grave goods and sometimes marked by a barrow. In south-east Europe trade and other contacts with the Near East were factors in the emergence of the first European states, which appeared in Crete *c.* 2000 BC and Greece *c.* 1650 BC.

A ship setting on the Swedish island of Gotland. Ship settings, stones set in the layout of a ship, date from the late Bronze Age. Nobody knows for certain what the stones symbolized, but they are generally regarded as burial monuments. Many of the settings, widespread in Scandinavia, contain graves.

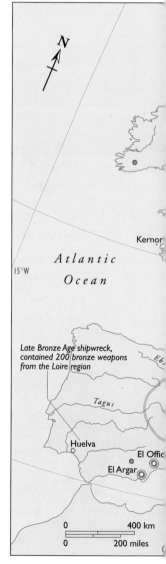

N

Atlantic Ocean

15°W

Kernor

Late Bronze Age shipwreck, contained 200 bronze weapons from the Loire region

Eb

Tagus

Huelva

El Offic

El Argar

0   400 km
0   200 miles

The European population increased substantially during the Bronze Age. Population pressure in this period is confirmed by evidence of the spread of enclosed field systems, which could be managed more intensively, by clear property boundaries and by the spread of settlement into marginal uplands. Settlement retreated again at the end of the Bronze Age, either because of climatic deterioration or because poor upland soils had been worked to exhaustion. Other developments of the Bronze Age included the domestication of European wild oats and the introduction of wheeled vehicles.

The period we characterize as the Bronze Age started to come to an end around 1200 BC, following the introduction of iron-working to Greece from Anatolia, where it is thought to have been invented about 300 years earlier. Not only does iron keep an edge better than bronze, but it is also less expensive to manufacture because iron ore is very common: it occurs not only as rock ores but also as easily workable rusty deposits in bogs (known as bog iron ore). From Greece, iron-working spread to Spain and central Europe by 750 BC and to northern Europe by 500 BC.

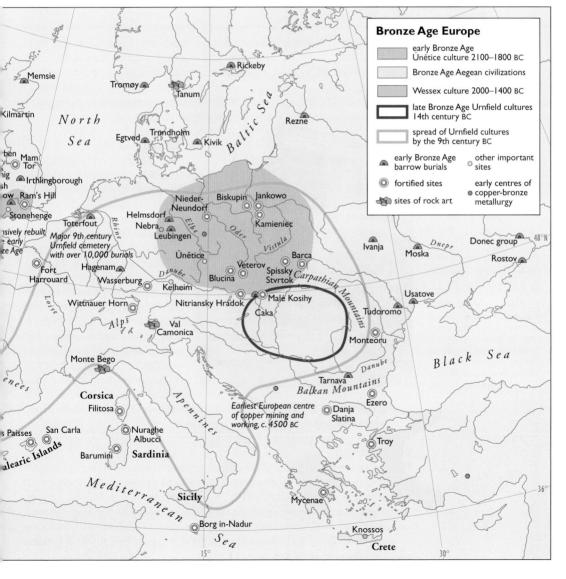

Bronze Age Europe

- early Bronze Age Únětice culture 2100–1800 BC
- Bronze Age Aegean civilizations
- Wessex culture 2000–1400 BC
- late Bronze Age Urnfield cultures 14th century BC
- spread of Urnfield cultures by the 9th century BC
- early Bronze Age barrow burials
- other important sites
- fortified sites
- early centres of copper-bronze metallurgy
- sites of rock art

The Minoans

The earliest European civilization, the Minoan, developed on the mountainous Aegean island of Crete c. 2000 BC. Named for Minos, a legendary king of Crete, the Minoan civilization flourished for over 500 years until it was brought to a sudden end by invaders from Greece.

"Out in the dark blue sea there is a land called Crete, a rich and beautiful land … densely populated and boasting ninety cities… The greatest of the ninety cities is called Knossos, and there, for nine years, king Minos ruled and enjoyed the friendship of mighty Zeus. "

Homer, *The Odyssey* (7th or 8th century BC)

The north entrance of Knossos, the most important palace of the Minoan civilization. After the first palace was completely destroyed by fire in 1700 BC, it was rebuilt according to a more complex plan.

The origins of the Minoan civilization were quite different from those of its contemporaries in Mesopotamia, Egypt and the Indus valley: Crete has no flood plains of fertile alluvium or great rivers which can be tapped for irrigation. The basis of Minoan subsistence was the 'Mediterranean Triad' of wheat, olives and vines. Olives and vines grew well on the island's rugged mountainsides and produced valuable, easily stored, commodities – oil and wine – that were traded widely around the eastern Mediterranean.

The limited areas of fertile valley land on Crete could be devoted to growing wheat. Flocks of sheep, kept on the high mountain pastures, produced wool that supplied a textile industry that exported cloth as far away as Egypt. In ways such as these the Minoan people maximized the productivity of what at first sight was not a very promising environment for intensive agriculture. Other craft products produced by the Cretans, such as metalwork, dyes and pottery, were

also exported as a sideline to the primary trade in oil, wine and cloth.

Grand Palaces

By 2000 BC Crete's prosperity and dense population had led to the development of towns and small kingdoms centred on magnificent palace complexes at Knossos, Phaistos, Mallia and Khania. A number of smaller palaces are thought to have been subordinate power centres. As well as being residences for the rulers, the palaces also acted as religious, economic and administrative centres. The palaces also housed workshops, shrines, audience chambers and storerooms where food surpluses and trade goods were stored for redistribution. The great central courtyards were probably the scene of religious rituals and communal feasting.

The Minotaur

The size and complex plans of the palaces probably gave rise to the later Greek legend of the Labyrinth in which King Minos kept the Minotaur, a half-human, half-bull monster. Bulls certainly had a special significance in Minoan religion. There are painted frescoes on the walls of the palace at Knossos showing youths leaping over the backs of bulls in a ritual game and stone bulls' horns are a common religious symbol. Another popular religious figure was a goddess often shown holding snakes.

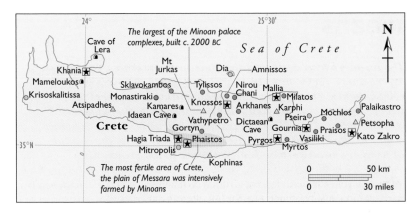

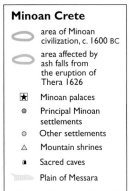

The map legend reads:

Minoan Crete

- area of Minoan civilization, c. 1600 BC
- area affected by ash falls from the eruption of Thera 1626
- ★ Minoan palaces
- ● Principal Minoan settlements
- ○ Other settlements
- △ Mountain shrines
- ◪ Sacred caves
- Plain of Messara

The needs of palace administration led to the development of writing, first using hieroglyphs and later a syllabic script known as Linear A. Neither script has been deciphered, so the ethnic identity of the Minoans is unknown. As it is clear that the Minoans did not speak an Indo-European language, they were certainly not Greeks. As in the Near East, documents were written on clay tablets and stored in archives.

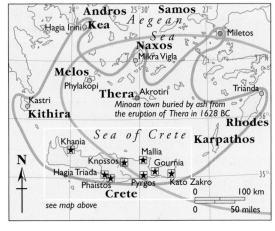

Destruction by Fire

Around 1700 BC the Minoan palaces were destroyed by fires, probably as a result of wars between the palace kingdoms. All the palaces were rebuilt but as only Knossos regained its former splendour it would seem that it had conquered the whole island and reduced the other palaces to tributary status. The power of Knossos may have extended well beyond Crete. Later traditions describe King Minos' fleets dominating the Aegean and taking tribute from the Greeks. The Minoans certainly had many colonies in the Aegean and there was a Minoan quarter in the Egyptian city of Avaris. One of the Minoan colonies, Akrotiri, on the volcanic island of Thera, was buried by ash in a huge eruption in 1628 BC. Described as a Minoan Pompeii, preservation was so good that even wall paintings survived. Earthquakes associated with the eruption of Thera caused extensive damage on Crete. Ashfalls from the eruption destroyed crops and buried fields, causing famine and social instability.

A final disaster befell the Minoans around 1450 BC when almost all of Crete's palaces, towns and farmsteads were destroyed or damaged by fire and many were abandoned, never to be occupied again. Knossos alone escaped the destruction but only because it was wanted by the island's new rulers, who introduced new burial practices, new gods, new art forms and a new script, bringing an end to the Minoan civilization.

The palace at Knossos was built on a sloping site, and in places was up to five storeys high. The reconstructed ruins seen here give a good impression of its complex architecture and high standard of masonry.

The Mycenaeans

The invaders who destroyed the Minoan civilization were the Mycenaean Greeks or, as they probably called themselves, the Achaeans. The Mycenaeans were relative newcomers to Greece, having only migrated into the area from the Balkans around 2000 BC. The Mycenaeans take their name from Mycenae, a hilltop citadel which features in Homer's epics as the capital of King Agamemnon, who led the Greeks in the Trojan War.

Mycenaean Greece was a land of fortified settlements, each one an independent power centre ruled by a petty king who controlled the surrounding countryside with the support of a warrior aristocracy. According to a list preserved in Homer's *Iliad* called the 'Catalogue of Ships', the king of Mycenae was recognized as having an ill-defined primacy over the other kings. The kings' palaces were smaller than those on Crete but they served the same functions.

"In the ruins of Mycenae is a water source called Perseia, and the underground chambers of king Atreus and his sons Agamemnon and Menelaus which were the treasure houses of their wealth."

Pausanias, *Guide to Greece* (c. AD 150)

Linear B Script

Administrative records were written on clay tablets in a syllabic script called Linear B. Although based on the Minoan Linear A, Linear B has been deciphered and found to record an early form of Greek. From inscriptions on these tablets, it is known that the Mycenaeans worshipped some of the Greek gods of the Classical Period, including Zeus, Apollo, Athena and Poseidon. The earliest evidence for the emergence of the Mycenaean civilization is a series of richly furnished shaft graves discovered at Mycenae. The objects in these graves, including gold, silver and electrum tableware, jewellery, fine bronze weapons and sheet gold death masks. Later Mycenaean kings were buried in vaulted tholos ('beehive shaped') tombs where it is thought kingship rituals were performed. Being rather more obvious than the older shaft graves, any grave offerings were looted long ago but they remain impressive structures.

War and the Mycenaeans

War was central to Mycenaean society. Mycenaean warriors used chariots as battlefield transport, dismounting to fight on foot with spear, sword and dagger. For protection they used large, ox hide shields, distinctive helmets covered with boars teeth and, rarely, crude bronze armour. Mycenaean towns had strong walls built of massive stone blocks, bastioned gateways and tunnels to underground springs that provided secure water supplies when under siege.

In the 15th century the Mycenaeans started to expand their territory across the Aegean, conquering Crete c. 1450 BC, raiding Egypt and the Hittite empire (see page 36), and establishing colonies on Rhodes and the coast of Anatolia. It is possible that the Trojan War happened during this period of Mycenaean expansion (the traditional date given by Classical Greek historians is 1184 but this is too late to be really likely).

The Mycenaeans were also active as traders around the eastern Mediterranean and as far west as Malta, Sicily and Italy. A Mycenaean shipwreck, discovered off the southern coast of Turkey, had a cargo of pottery and copper ingots from Cyprus, tin from Anatolia, resin, glass and ivory from Phoenicia, ebony jewellery and weapons from Egypt and ostrich eggs from Libya.

Remains of the walls of the city of Tiryns. The huge size of the stones used to build the walls of Mycenaean cities led to later legends that they were built not by humans but by the giant Cyclops.

There are clear signs that the Mycenaeans were feeling increasingly insecure in the later 13th century. Many cities, including Tiryns, Mycenae and Athens strengthened their defences and a wall was built across the Isthmus of Corinth to close off the only land route to the Peloponnese. An archive of writing tablets from Pylos indicates that the city was preparing for an attack from the sea. The tablets survived because they were baked hard in a fire which destroyed the city soon after they were written. By around 1200 BC every major Mycenaean centre had suffered the same fate and the civilization collapsed. Writing fell out of use in Greece for 400 years.

The identity of the attackers is unknown; the best guess is that they were associated with the so-called Sea Peoples who ravaged the eastern Mediterranean around this time (see page 40). An alternative possibility is that the attackers were Dorians, another Greek-speaking people from the Balkans who established themselves in the Peloponnese, Crete and Rhodes sometime in the 'dark age' which followed the fall of the Mycenaean civilization.

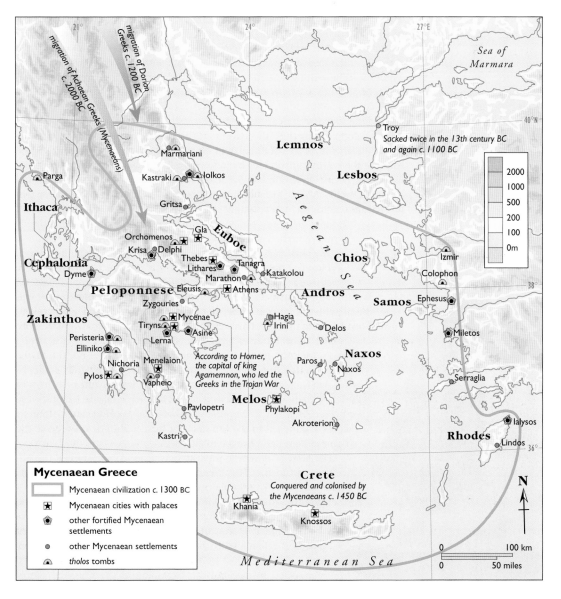

Mycenaean Greece

- Mycenaean civilization c. 1300 BC
- ★ Mycenaean cities with palaces
- ◉ other fortified Mycenaean settlements
- • other Mycenaean settlements
- ▲ *tholos* tombs

Troy
Sacked twice in the 13th century BC and again c. 1100 BC

According to Homer, the capital of king Agamemnon, who led the Greeks in the Trojan War

Crete
Conquered and colonised by the Mycenaeans c. 1450 BC

The Greek City-states

The Classical civilization of ancient Greece is acknowledged as one of the most inventive and influential in human history. The foundations of this civilization were laid by the city-states which emerged from the post-Mycenaean 'dark age'.

"Again there is the Greek nation – the common blood, the common language ... the whole way of life we understand and share together."

Herodotus, *Histories*

This statue of Nike, the goddess of victory, was found perched in the outstretched hand of a colossal statue of the Greek god Zeus at Olympia.

Little is known about the four centuries following the disaster that destroyed the Mycenaean civilization. The population declined and town life and trade decayed so that there was no need for writing, which fell out of use. When recovery began in the 8th century much had changed. Bronze had given way to iron as the most important metal for tools and weapons. The institution of monarchy was in decay as power passed into the hands of the warrior aristocracy: by *c.* 600 BC Sparta and Argos were the only major Greek states with monarchies. The *polis*, or city-state, had emerged as the main form of political organization. The revival of urban life was made possible by an increase in trade and general prosperity. The needs of trade led to the revival of writing. As the Mycenaeans' Linear B was long forgotten, the Greeks adopted the Phoenician consonantal alphabet and improved on it by adding separate letters for vowels. This created a more flexible writing system that was easily learned, with the result that literacy became more widespread than in any earlier civilization.

Early Democracy

The development in the 7th century of the phalanx, a new way of fighting involving large numbers of infantry in disciplined formations, undermined the status of the warrior aristocracy by involving a larger section of the community in warfare. The newly wealthy in particular resented their exclusion from power on the grounds of birth. In many Greek cities this led to the overthrow of aristocratic government in revolutions led by popular leaders called 'tyrants'.

Tyrants were not initially oppressive rulers; the term meant simply a ruler who had gained power by his own efforts, but their reaction to any challenge to their power was to become more authoritarian. Tyrannies rarely lasted more than a few decades before they were overthrown and replaced by oligarchic governments based on wealth rather than birth. The most radical experiment in government was in Athens where a form of direct democracy was introduced, giving every freeborn Athenian man aged over 20 the right to vote in the citizen assembly.

Despite their bitter rivalries, the Greeks had developed a strong common identity by the 6th century. All Greeks used the name 'Hellenes' to describe themselves, worshipped the same gods and celebrated pan-Hellenic festivals, such as the Olympic games. Shrines of pan-Hellenic importance, such as the Oracle of Apollo at Delphi, were protected by leagues (amphictonies) of neighbouring states. Homer's epics, composed in the 8th century, were admired and seen as the common cultural heritage of all Greeks.

The Greeks' common identity was tested at the start of the 5th century BC. In the 540s Greek cities on the Anatolian coast came under Persian rule. Athenian assistance to a rebellion there led to a Persian punitive attack. After this was defeated at Marathon in 490 the Persians launched an invasion of Greece in 480 BC. The Greeks united under Sparta and Athens and defeated the Persians again, at Salamis (480) and Plataea (479). Their victory is generally recognized as marking the beginning of the Classical age of

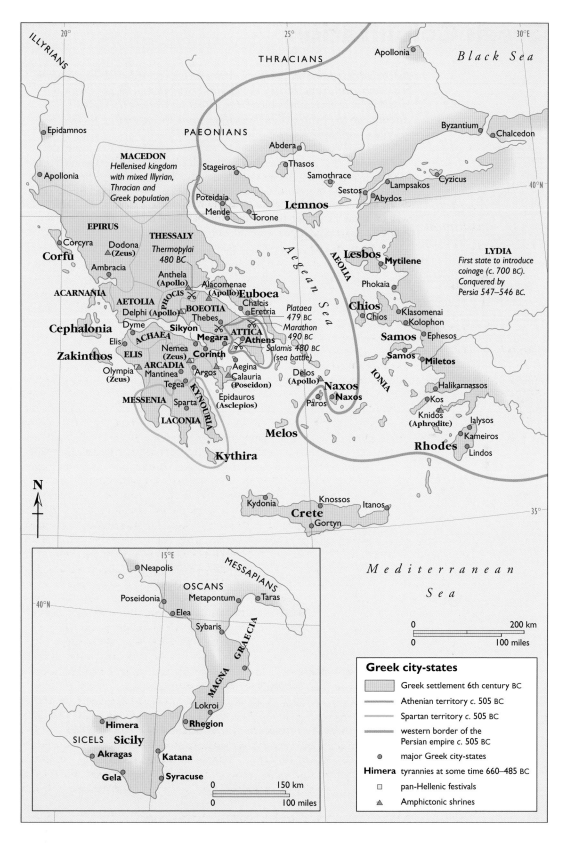

ILLYRIANS
20°
25°
30°E
THRACIANS
Apollonia
Black Sea

Epidamnos
PAEONIANS
Apollonia
Byzantium
Chalcedon

MACEDON
Hellenised kingdom with mixed Illyrian, Thracian and Greek population
Stageiros
Abdera
Thasos
Samothrace
Lampsakos
Cyzicus
40°N
Sestos
Abydos

Poteidaia
Mende
Torone
Lemnos

EPIRUS
Corcyra
Dodona △ (Zeus)
THESSALY
Thermopylai 480 BC
Corfu
Ambracia
Anthela (Apollo)
Lesbos •Mytilene
Phokaia

LYDIA
First state to introduce coinage (c. 700 BC). Conquered by Persia 547–546 BC.

ACARNANIA
AETOLIA
Alacomenae (Apollo) △
Euboea
Chalcis
Eretria
Platea 479 BC
Chios Chios
Klasomenai
Kolophon

Delphi (Apollo)
BOEOTIA
Thebes
Marathon 490 BC
Ephesos

Cephalonia
Dyme
Sikyon
ATTICA
Athens
Salamis 480 BC (sea battle)
Samos Ephesos

ACHAEA
Megara
Samos
Miletos

Elis
Nemea (Zeus)
Corinth

Zakinthos
ELIS
ARCADIA
Mantinea
Aegina
Calauria (Poseidon)
Delos (Apollo)
Naxos
Halikarnassos

Olympia (Zeus) △
Tegea
Argos
Naxos
Kos

MESSENIA
Sparta
Epidauros (Asclepios)
Paros
Knidos (Aphrodite)
Ialysos

KYNOURIA
LACONIA
Melos
Rhodes
Kameiros
Lindos

Kythira

N

Kydonia
Knossos
Itanos
Crete
Gortyn

15°E
MESSAPIANS
Neapolis
OSCANS
40°N
Poseidonia
Metapontum
Taras
Elea
Sybaris
MAGNA GRAECIA

Mediterranean Sea

0   200 km
0   100 miles

Lokroi
Rhegion

Himera
SICELS **Sicily**
Akragas
Katana
Gela
Syracuse

0   150 km
0   100 miles

Greek city-states

	Greek settlement 6th century BC
	Athenian territory c. 505 BC
	Spartan territory c. 505 BC
	western border of the Persian empire c. 505 BC
●	major Greek city-states
Himera	tyrannies at some time 660–485 BC
□	pan-Hellenic festivals
△	Amphictonic shrines

103

Greek Colonization

By the close of the 6th century BC the influence of Greek civilization was very apparent across the Mediterranean world. This was the result of a remarkable colonizing effort by Greek city-states attempting to resolve their social tensions by exporting their surplus populations.

"The Theraeans have reached a firm decision to send Battus to Cyrenaica as leader and king, and that Theraeans shall sail with him as his companions. They shall sail on equal and fair terms. One son shall be enlisted from each household.... Any man who refuses to sail when ordered by the city shall suffer the death penalty. "

Sworn agreement of the settlers of Cyrene, 7th century BC

The growth of the Assyrian empire in the 9th century BC led to a general revival of trade in the Mediterranean. The Phoenicians were among the first to benefit from this but the Greeks soon followed suit, re-establishing links to the Levant and Italy which had been forsaken since the fall of the Mycenaean civilization.

Colonization Begins

As prosperity returned to Greece, the population began to rise leading many city governments to see colonization as a means of relieving population pressure and social tensions. Colonists were chosen by lot and any who refused to go faced severe penalties. Unlike the Phoenician colonies, which remained subject to their founding cities, Greek colonies were independent city-states from the outset. Relations with parent cities generally remained close. The most active colonizers were the Ionians, generally believed to be descendants of the Mycenaeans, and the Dorians, who arrived in Greece early in the 'dark age'.

Greek colonization reached its peak during the 8th and 7th centuries. One of the first attempts at colonization was at Al Mina in Syria, but it never became a

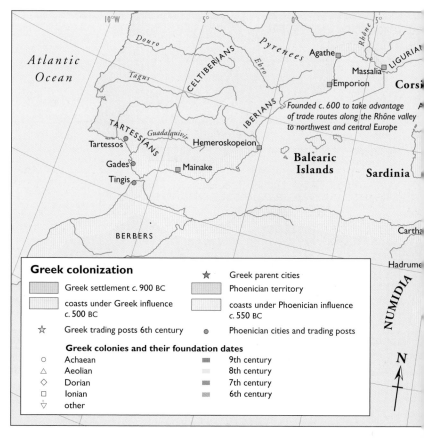

wholly Greek settlement and was often dominated by its strong neighbours. In the 8th century the Greeks generally looked west to Sicily and southern Italy, where there was fertile land, good harbours and no strong empires to curtail their independence.

Influence of Greek Culture

Despite frequent hostilities between the colonists and the indigenous peoples, Greek culture had great influence in Italy, especially among the Etruscans and early Romans. The Greeks also attempted to establish colonies further west in the Mediterranean region but they found their activities severely limited by the Phoenicians. However, the colony of Massalia (modern Marseille) was enormously successful and first exposed the Celts to Mediterranean civilization.

During the 7th and 6th centuries, the colonizing effort shifted direction to the Black Sea. The Greek colonies traded wine and other luxuries with the Scythians in exchange for grain to feed people of their parent cities. Colonies were also established in Cyrenaica and Egypt. The pharaohs welcomed the Greeks for their military skills, while the Greeks were influenced by the art and architecture of Egypt.

The remains of a Doric temple at Agrigento in Sicily. The Greeks founded their colony of Akragas there in *c.* 580 BC and it became one of the most prosperous in the Greek world.

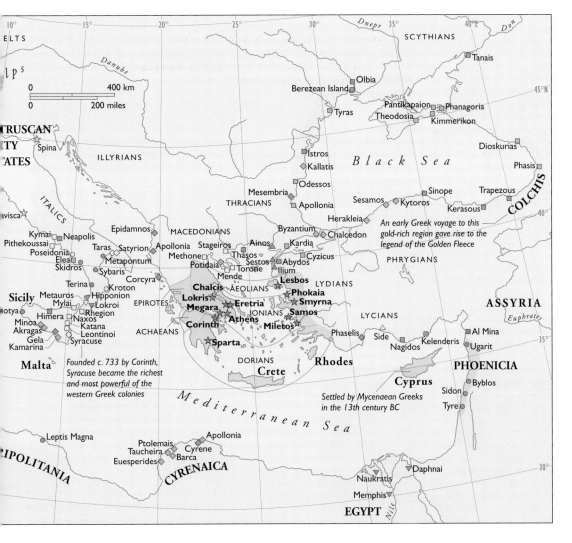

Italy before the Romans

Pre-Roman Italy was inhabited by a great diversity of peoples of different ethnic, cultural and linguistic backgrounds. The Sicilians, Ligurians and Etruscans were probably descendants of the original post-Ice Age population of Italy. All are believed to have spoken non-Indo-European languages. The Italics, Messapians, Gauls and Greeks all spoke different Indo-European languages and had arrived in the peninsula at various times between 1000 and 700 BC.

"The Etruscans originated that dignity which surrounds rulers, providing their rulers with lictors and an ivory stool and a toga with a purple band ... and these things were in general adopted by the Romans. "

Diodorus Siculus
1st century BC
Translated by
C. H. Oldfather
(Loeb Classical
Library, 1933)

As the founders of the first civilization of western Europe, the Etruscans were the most important of the peoples of pre-Roman Italy. The forerunner of the Etruscan civilization was the early Iron Age Villanova culture which developed in Etruria (roughly modern Tuscany) *c.* 900 BC from the local Bronze Age Urnfield cultures. Etruria had the benefits of good farmland, plentiful reserves of iron and copper ores and good natural harbours, which encouraged the Etruscans to become maritime traders.

Each Etruscan city was an independent state with its own king, but they were loosely federated in the Etruscan League. The Etruscans saw the Greek colonies of southern Italy as a threat to their commercial interests but this hostility did not prevent them taking a great interest in Greek culture and by the 6th century their civilization had become very Hellenized. Most of what we know about the Etruscans comes from their cemeteries which were planned formally like cities. Tombs were cut directly from the bedrock and richly furnished and decorated with wall paintings.

The Ligurians were a tribal people who lived around the Gulf of Genoa and had colonies in Corsica and Sardinia. Sardinia was also home to other peoples who built circular stone towers, or *nuraghe,* for defence: their identity is unknown but they may have included the Shardana who joined the Sea Peoples in the late Bronze Age (see page 40). The Sicilians (Sicels) were divided into two main peoples, the Siculi and Sicani. Although they maintained their independence against Greek and Phoenician colonists, they both eventually became Hellenized in culture and language. The most impressive of the monuments left by the Sicels is the vast necropolis of Pantálica, where thousands of tombs were cut into the faces of sheer limestone cliffs.

The Italics

The necropolis of Pantálica in Sicily is the largest rock necropolis in Europe. The large number of tombs cut into the rock is staggering considering that iron tools did not exist at the time the Sicels excavated them.

The Italics were divided into eight main groups: the Veneti, Umbrians, Sabines, Apulii, Latins, Samnites, Lucanians and Bruttii. In the 6th century BC the Italics were still predominantly tribal, but the Latins were organized in city-states; one of these was Rome. The culture of the Latins was strongly influenced by contact with both the Etruscans and the Greeks. The Italics were descended from peoples who had migrated into Italy *c.* 1000 BC. At about the same time the Messapians had settled in the 'heel' of Italy. They were an Illyrian people from across the Adriatic. By around 500 the Messapians formed a loose confederation of city-states and had developed a literate culture using an adaptation of the Greek alphabet.

The main Gaulish immigration to Italy did not take place until around 400 BC but one Celtic-speaking people, the Insubres, had occupied the western part of the Po valley possibly from as early as 1000 BC. In the 6th century the Insubres became the earliest of the Celtic peoples to adopt writing, using a version of the Etruscan alphabet.

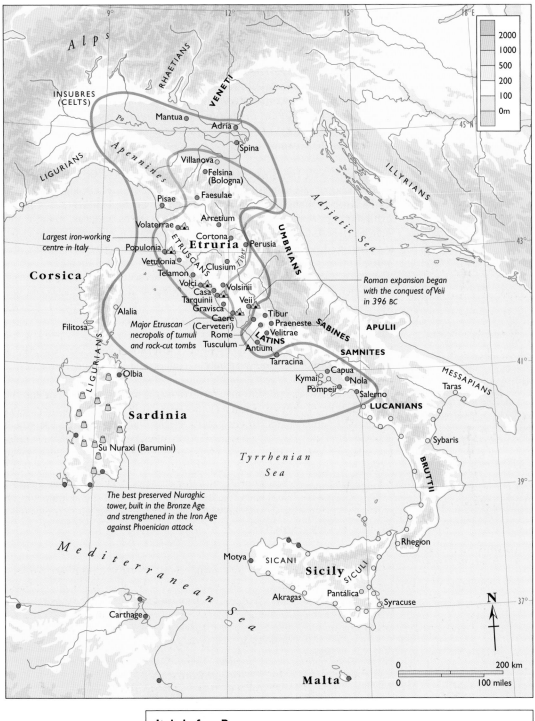

Largest iron-working
centre in Italy

Roman expansion began
with the conquest of Veii
in 396 BC

Major Etruscan
necropolis of tumuli
and rock-cut tombs

The best preserved Nuraghic
tower, built in the Bronze Age
and strengthened in the Iron Age
against Phoenician attack

Italy before Rome

▬▬ Early Iron Age Villanova culture c. 900 BC	● Etruscan cities	△ Etruscan rock-cut tombs	
▬▬ maximum area of Etruscan domination late 6th century BC	● Latin cities		
	○ Greek colonies	⬤ Nuraghe (Nuraghic towers)	
	● Phoenician colonies	**APULII** Italic peoples	

Early Rome

According to tradition, Rome was founded in 753 BC by the twins Romulus and Remus. The twins quarrelled over who should be king of the city and Romulus killed Remus and named the city Rome after himself. The Romans dated all events in years 'from the foundation of the city' but they had probably underestimated its true age as there is archaeological evidence of habitation on the site going back to the 10th century BC.

The Romans were Latins, one of the Italic group of peoples. Although they lived in independent city-states, the Latins had a close sense of kinship, manifested through their common language (Latin), shared religious beliefs and a common myth that they were all descendants of Latinus – the father-in-law of the Trojan Aeneas. The annual festival of Jupiter Latiaris on Mons Albanus (Monte Cavo) was attended by all the Latins, including the Romans. The Latin states also extended common rights of residence and trade to one another. Latin culture was much influenced by the Greeks and the Etruscans. The Latin (or Roman) alphabet, used from the 7th century, and now the world's most widely used, was derived from the Etruscan alphabet.

First Rulers

Romulus is most likely a legendary figure, however, his successor Numa Pompilius (r. 673–642 BC) was probably a real person. Although Numa was a peaceful king, those who followed, Tullus Hostilius and Ancus Marcius, were more warlike and extended Roman territory to the sea at Ostia and out into the hills of Latium. Rome first began to look like a city of some importance under Tarquin I (r. 616–579 BC). Tarquin supervized the draining of the Forum, which

> *"It seems to me that Romulus must at the very beginning have had a divine intimation that Rome would one day be the seat and hearthstone of a mighty empire; for scarcely could a city placed upon any other site in Italy have more easily maintained our present widespread domination. "*
>
> Cicero (106–43 BC), *De Republica* Translated by C. W. Keyes (Loeb Classical Library, 1928)

Rome and Latium

- ▭ Roman territory c. 700 BC
- ▭ Roman territory c. 500 BC
- ☆ sanctuary of Jupiter Latiaris

The Capitoline She-wolf shows the brothers Romulus and Remus, the legendary founders of Rome, suckling from the wolf. The bronze Etruscan sculpture of the she-wolf dating to the 5th century BC has long been the traditional icon of ancient Rome. The figures of the twins were added in the 15th century.

was then a marsh, and laid it out as a public square with shops and monumental buildings. Rome benefited from its central position in Italy and as it was the lowest crossing place on the river Tiber, it was a natural crossroads. The sea was near enough for Rome to benefit from maritime trade but not so near that it was vulnerable to pirate raids. By the 6th century Rome had become a prosperous commercial city with a growing population. The temple of Jupiter Capitolinus, completed in 509 was, at 64 metres (210 feet) long by 55 metres (180 feet) wide and 40 metres (130 feet) high, one of the largest temples of its time. Rome's growth was aided not only by its position but by its willingness to extend citizenship to immigrants who accepted its values. It was even possible for an immigrant to become king – Ancus Marcius was a Sabine and Tarquin I was an Etruscan. This ability to assimilate new populations would be critical to its later success as an imperial power.

The last king of Rome was Tarquin the Proud (r. 535–509). Tarquin alienated the aristocracy by refusing to rule with the advice of the Senate, the assembly of leading citizens. When his son raped a noblewoman, Tarquin was overthrown and Rome became a Republic, ruled by the Senate. With a population nearing 40,000, Rome was by this time one of the largest cities in Italy and it had come to dominate Latium. After the fall of the monarchy in 509 the Latins rebelled and founded an alliance, the Latin League, based at Aricia. Peace was patched up in 493 but it did not last and in 338 Rome conquered Latium as the prelude to its conquest of Italy and, ultimately, the Mediterranean world.

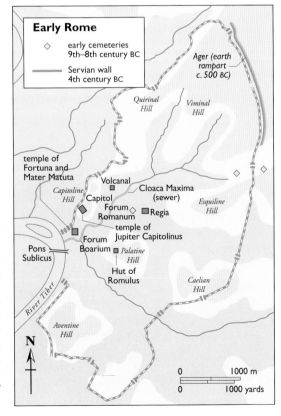

Early Rome

◇ early cemeteries 9th–8th century BC

— Servian wall 4th century BC

Ager (earth rampart c. 500 BC)

Quirinal Hill
Viminal Hill

temple of Fortuna and Mater Matuta
Capitoline Hill
Volcanal
Capitol
Cloaca Maxima (sewer)
Forum Romanum
Regia
Esquiline Hill
temple of Jupiter Capitolinus
Pons Sublicus
Forum Boarium
Palatine Hill
Hut of Romulus
Caelian Hill
River Tiber
Aventine Hill

N

0   1000 m
0   1000 yards

The Ancient Celts

The term 'Celt' was first used by Greek writers of the 6th century BC to describe the peoples of central and western Europe. The Romans called these same peoples Gauls. Today, the word is used generally to describe all the peoples of Europe who speak Celtic languages.

"Their possessions consisted of cattle and gold, because these were the only things they could carry about ... and shift when they chose. They treated comradeship as of the greatest importance."

Polybius

Mousa Broch in the Shetland Islands, Scotland is the best-preserved example of an Iron Age fortified tower. It was built over 2000 years ago as a refuge against raiding local tribes.

At the time their recorded history began, Celtic-speaking peoples were already spread over a wide area of western Europe. How they came to be there is much disputed. Some historians believe the Celts originated in the same part of central Europe where the Hallstatt culture developed in the late Bronze Age. The Celts subsequently migrated across western Europe and into Iberia and Britain, taking the Hallstatt culture with them. Other historians take the view that Celtic languages actually emerged over a wide area of western Europe and that the Hallstatt culture was spread not by migration but by trade and social contact between peoples who already had much in common.

The Hallstatt and La Tène Cultures

The Hallstatt Celts were ruled by chiefs or 'princes' who lived in hillforts, such as the Heuneburg in southern Germany, and gained their power by controlling the production of bronze weapons and jewellery and the distribution of imported foreign luxuries, like wine. The Hallstatt culture was replaced c. 450 BC by the La Tène culture. The La Tène culture was more warlike than the Hallstatt culture, with a wealthy and influential warrior aristocracy who used success in war and the display of fine weapons and jewellery as a means to underpin their elite status. Around 400 BC the Celts began a series of migrations which expanded their territories into northern Italy, eastern Europe and Anatolia. The causes of these migrations is unclear: overpopulation is the most commonly cited cause.

Although the type of aristocratic warrior society typical of early La Tène times survived in Ireland and northern Britain into the Middle Ages, those areas of the Celtic world that were in closer contact with the Mediterranean civilizations all began to show signs of the centralization of power and state formation in the later centuries BC. The first signs of urbanization can be seen in the abandonment of hillforts in favour of semi-urban settlements on lower ground called *oppida*. Although usually fortified, *oppida* were trade and administrative centres as well as chiefly residences and tribal refuges. In many areas the Celts adopted writing systems; the Insubres of northern Italy from the Etruscans, the Celtiberians from the Phoenicians, the Gauls from the Romans and Greeks. Writing was mainly used for memorials but by the first century BC some Celtic peoples had developed a high level of administrative abilities. When Caesar defeated the Helvetii in 58 BC he captured census

records, written in Greek letters, recording the names of all the tribe's warriors, the numbers of dependents and the numbers of the tribe's allies amounting in all to 368,000 people. Except in northern Britain and Ireland coins were in widespread use in the Celtic world by the 1st century BC. Celtic coins were often of a high quality and bore portraits of rulers and inscriptions in Latin or Greek letters. Coins were mainly used by rulers to reward their followers rather than as a means of everyday exchange and nowhere had a true cash economy yet developed. Many Gaulish tribes had political institutions, such as elected magistracies and advisory 'senates', that were comparable to those of the Mediterranean world. Unfortunately for the Celts, their progress through to a fully developed urban civilization was cut short by the Roman conquest in the 1st century BC.

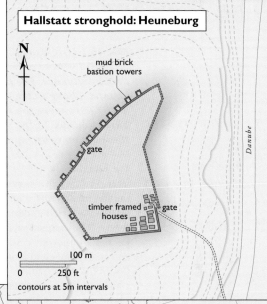

records written in Greek letters

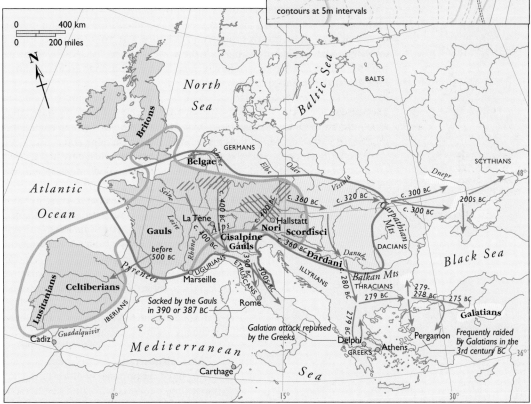

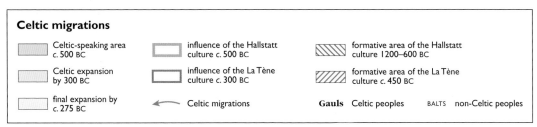

Celtic migrations

Celtic-speaking area c. 500 BC	influence of the Hallstatt culture c. 500 BC	formative area of the Hallstatt culture 1200–600 BC
Celtic expansion by 300 BC	influence of the La Tène culture c. 300 BC	formative area of the La Tène culture c. 450 BC
final expansion by c. 275 BC	← Celtic migrations	**Gauls** Celtic peoples BALTS non-Celtic peoples

The Iberians

"The country of the Iberians contains richer and more numerous silver mines than any other."

Diodorus Siculus

Like Italy, pre-Roman Iberia was a land of considerable ethnic diversity, where early civilizations developed under Phoenician and Greek influence. The peoples of Iberia were divided into two broad groups. Living in the south and east in a band from the Atlantic to the Ebro were the Iberians and the related Tartessians and Turdetanians. In the northwest and on the high Meseta of central Iberia lived Celtic-speaking peoples.

The Iberians spoke so-far untranslated, non-Indo-European languages of unknown origin: it is possible that they were descendants of the first modern human inhabitants who settled in the Iberian peninsula around 30,000 years ago. Iberia is rich in minerals, especially copper and tin, the main ingredients of bronze. This mineral wealth attracted Phoenician merchants from around 1000 BC and by the 8th century they had founded permanent settlements in the Balearic Islands and along the south coast, the most important of which was Gades (modern Cadiz).

The Greeks arrived in the 6th century and established a few colonies on the east coast. The Phoenician and Greek colonies linked Iberia into the cultural worlds of the eastern Mediterranean and the Near East. These contacts had led to the introduction of iron technology, the potter's wheel, the growth of towns, state formation and the adoption of writing by 500 BC. Iberian art and architecture was also influenced by such contact.

Tartessos

The most important of the early Iberian states was Tartessos, which emerged as early as 750 BC. Its capital was probably at Huelva and its territory extended over much of the valley of the Guadalquivir. Tartessos exploited its mineral wealth and was also an important intermediary on the long-distance trade route linking Britain and Atlantic Europe with the Mediterranean. The Iberians were conquered by the Carthaginians in the 3rd century BC and then passed under Roman rule after Carthage's defeat in the Second Punic War (218–202 BC). Under Roman rule the Iberians lost their distinctive identity. Their language died out, replaced by a local dialect of Latin. It is possible that Euskara, the language of the Basques, which is unrelated to any modern language, may be a descendant of the languages spoken by the Iberians.

The Celtiberians

The most important of Iberia's Celtic-speaking peoples were the Celtiberians, who lived on the Meseta, and the Lusitanians of the west coast. According to ancient Greek writers, the Celtiberians were formed by the assimilation of Celtic immigrants with native Iberian peoples. Their material culture was influenced by both the Celts and Iberians and they eventually adopted a version of the Iberian script, although they never developed a fully literate culture. By the 3rd century the Celtiberians were living in

gate

city wall

N

gate

gate

houses

early towers
(6th century BC)

houses

Acropolis

market place

main gate

gate

houses

0   50 m

0   50 yards

Iberian city: Ullastret

excavated area

Iberia in the mid-1st millennium BC

Celtiberians	● native settlements
Tartessians and Turdetanians	◑ Phoenician settlements
Iberians	○ Greek settlements
Phoenicians	⬈ mineral resources
approximate borders of the kingdom of Tartessos *c.* 600 BC	VACCEI main tribes

fortified semi-urban *castros*, the equivalent of the *oppida* of other parts of Celtic Europe. The Lusitanians were probably an indigenous people, Celticized through contacts with their neighbours.

Left: the sculpture of the Lady of Elche shows a woman wearing an elaborate style of headdress. Many historians believe that the bust is Iberian in origin although some date it to the Hellenistic or Roman periods.

Carthaginian Control

The Carthaginians attempted to conquer the Celtiberians and Lusitanians in the 3rd century. Through alliances with friendly chiefs and occasional punitive expeditions, the Carthaginians did succeed in exercizing a measure of control over the Celtiberians but the Lusitanians resisted successfully.

Both peoples also put up fierce resistance to the Romans but were conquered eventually, the Lusitanians between 197 and 139 BC, the Celtiberians by 133. However, the Romans faced frequent rebellions and their control over Celtic Iberia was not finally secure until as late as 14 BC. Under Roman rule the Celtiberians and Lusitanians shared the same fate as the Iberians, becoming Romanized in culture and adopting a dialect of Latin.

Part V: The Ancient Americas

The pre-Columbian Americas were home to spectacular civilizations which developed entirely independently from those of the Old World. However, their development was brought to a catastrophic halt by the arrival of Europeans in the 16th century.

Until the end of the 15th century, the Old World and New World civilizations might as well have been on different planets as each was quite unaware of the existence of the other. It is true that the Norse sometimes visited Newfoundland and Labrador, Polynesians certainly visited South America and took the sweet potato home with them, and medieval north Europeans occasionally found a bewildered Eskimo in a kayak washed up on their shores, but these fleeting contacts had no cultural consequences.

While the primary civilizations of the Old World were in, albeit tenuous, contact with one another, the primary civilizations of the New World developed entirely without outside influences. Some people have found this hard to accept, pointing in particular to the superficial similarity between the pyramids of ancient Egypt and the temple pyramids of Mesoamerica. A variety of improbable theories have been advanced to explain this similarity, however, as the first pyramids of Mesoamerica were not built until 1400 years after the last pyramids had been built in Egypt, a connection can be ruled out on chronological grounds alone. The different symbolic meaning and uses of the structures in each civilization also points to separate development. The similarity of these structures, and the ziggurats of Mesopotamia and the ceremonial platforms of Peru, are easily explained. All of these civilizations lacked advanced architectural skills and in such circumstances gathering together what is in effect a large pile of stone, earth or brick is the only way to build a tall and imposing structure. Faced with similar problems it is really no surprise that people in different parts of the world and at different times came up with similar solutions.

The Olmec

The earliest civilization of the Americas began to develop *c.* 1200 BC among the Olmec people of the tropical rainforests of Mexico's southeastern Gulf coast.

The striking Maya ruins of Palenque in southern Mexico are situated on a fertile alluvial plain. Palenque's high rainfall meant that a large population could be sustained at this site.

Rainforest soils are thin and easily leached of nutrients by the high rainfall. This is an obstacle to intensive agriculture because fields cleared from the forest lose their fertility in four or five years at most and have to be abandoned. This was not a problem faced by the Olmec, who lived on low lying flood plains and farmed the river levees where soil fertility was naturally maintained by fresh river silt. With year-round warmth and rainfall, the Olmec were able to grow four crops of maize (corn) a year, producing the food surpluses needed to support a complex hierarchical society. Although it never became truly urbanized, and only in its later stages did it use writing, the Olmec was the 'mother culture' of Mesoamerica and its ideas and art styles had a widespread influence on other emerging civilizations of the region, such as the Maya and the Zapotec.

Like the Olmec, the Maya civilization developed in a rainforest environment, south and west of the Olmec lands, in the Guatemalan highlands and the Petén lowlands. City-states with monumental ceremonial centres and semi-divine rulers had begun to arise in these areas by *c.* 400 BC. In flood-plain areas the Maya farmed levees intensively, as the Olmec did. They also created fertile raised fields by draining and canalizing extensive areas of swamp. Tree crops, such as cacao and avocado, were exploited and, in drier areas, irrigation canals were built. This diverse subsistence base allowed the Maya to build what was, at its height in the Classic Period (AD 300–800), without doubt the most sophisticated civilization of the

A detail of one of the precious Bonampak wall paintings from Chiapas, Mexico. These colourful murals, despite being difficult to study because of their age and fragmentation, reveal vital information about the life of the Maya. This scene is thought to depict music-makers. The sophisticated Maya civilization occupied what is now Mexico, Guatemala and the Yucatán peninsula before the Spanish conquered them during the 16th century.

pre-Columbian Americas. However, the rulers of the Maya city-states were war-like and extremely competitive and their demands strained even this productive system of agriculture to breaking point and after 800 most of the cities in the Petén were abandoned. The Maya civilization survived until the Spanish conquest in the Guatemalan highlands and the drier Yucatán peninsula but it never regained the cultural heights of the Classic Period.

Other early centres of civilization in Mesoamerica were located in the drier uplands of Oaxaca and the Valley of Mexico. In Oaxaca irrigation and terracing to retain soil and water were the basis of intensification of agriculture. The Zapotec civilization which began to develop here *c.* 800 BC was the first pre-Columbian society to use writing, a system of hieroglyphs which was the ancestor of all later Mesoamerican scripts. In the Valley of Mexico so-called floating gardens or *chinampas* were built around the edges of Lake Texcoco. *Chinampas* were built on long rectangular mats of floating water plants. The surface of the *chinampa* was raised above the water level by piling on lake mud and household waste. *Chinampas* were laid out in a grid pattern and secured to the lake bed with wooden stakes. Canals were left between the *chinampas* to provide access by boat and irrigation water. *Chinampas* were extremely productive: about one hectare (roughly 2.5 acres) of *chinampa* was sufficient to support ten people.

South American Civilizations

In South America the first complex societies developed among fishing peoples on the arid Pacific coast of Peru. Marine resources here were so rich that permanent villages developed as early as 3500 BC and ceremonial centres were being built by 2600 BC. The earliest crops to be cultivated by these peoples were cotton, for its fibres, and gourds, which were grown not for food but to use, hollowed out, as floats for fishing nets. Around the same time as these developments on the coast alpacas, llamas, potatoes, quinoa (a cereal) and other crops were being domesticated in the Andean highlands, where farming gradually replaced hunting and gathering as the main source of food. As the population rose highland farmers terraced hillsides to increase the area of arable land. With the development of irrigation techniques *c.* 1800 BC farming also became increasingly important in the coastal lowlands.

The first true civilization of South America was the Moche state which emerged *c.* 100 BC in the coastal lowlands of Peru. States emerged at Tiwanaku and Wari in the highlands a century or so later. A key factor in the subsequent history of the Andean civilizations is the interaction between the highlands and lowlands. Their great vertical range means that the Andes encompass a wide variety of environments. The Pacific coast provided dried fish and salt, the coastal lowlands grain and cotton, the highlands root crops and wool, while the forested eastern foothills on the edge of the Amazon basin provided exotic products such as feathers. Not surprisingly, trade networks between the different environmental zones developed early and facilitated the spread of cultural ideas and art styles across the Andean region. The desire of rulers to control the resources of as many different zones as possible provided the motive for the creation of a succession of Andean empires, culminating in the Inca empire which brought the entire region under its control in the 15th century.

The Andean civilizations never developed writing but used a complex system of record keeping based on coloured and knotted strings called *quipus*. Information was conveyed by the colour and ply of the cord and the type of knots. No civilizations developed in the South American rainforests to compare with those of Mesoamerica but complex, hierarchical societies did develop in the Amazon basin. Intensive agriculture was made possible by the painstaking creation of deep fertile soils using vast quantities of charcoal and organic matter. Little is known about these societies, which collapsed in the 16th century because of depopulation resulting from epidemics of European diseases.

North America

It is debatable whether there were any fully developed civilizations in North America before the Europeans arrived. However, in the eastern woodlands and the southwestern deserts, complex societies developed which had many of the characteristics of early states such as monumental ceremonial structures, towns and cities, and long-distance trade. In both regions there are some parallels with the Mesoamerican civilizations, ceremonial ball courts in the southwestern deserts and temple pyramids in the eastern woodlands for example, but the importance of Mesoamerican influences in North America is uncertain.

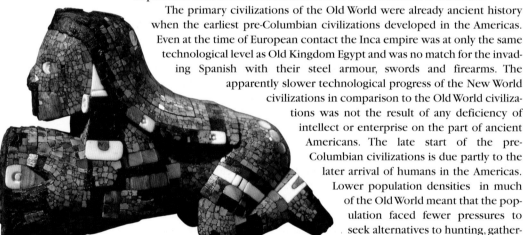

The primary civilizations of the Old World were already ancient history when the earliest pre-Columbian civilizations developed in the Americas. Even at the time of European contact the Inca empire was at only the same technological level as Old Kingdom Egypt and was no match for the invading Spanish with their steel armour, swords and firearms. The apparently slower technological progress of the New World civilizations in comparison to the Old World civilizations was not the result of any deficiency of intellect or enterprise on the part of ancient Americans. The late start of the pre-Columbian civilizations is due partly to the later arrival of humans in the Americas. Lower population densities in much of the Old World meant that the population faced fewer pressures to seek alternatives to hunting, gathering and fishing. The Americas also had fewer plants and, particularly, animals that were suitable for domestication than the Old World. Even those that were suitable, proved difficult to domesticate. This was especially true of teosinte, the wild ancestor of maize, the most important staple crop of the Americas. Teosinte is a wild grass which bears its small seeds on spikes and it took centuries of selective breeding before anything remotely resembling the familiar corn cob appeared. Only when this had been achieved, around 2300 BC in southern Mexico, could communities which depended on farming for the majority of their food begin to develop. Once this is taken into account, the development of the pre-Columbian civilizations no longer seems backward.

The handle of an Aztec ritual knife. The Aztecs produced such knives to cut out the hearts of their victims, sacrificed to appease their gods. The handle is wooden and carved in the shape of a crouching figure with an inlaid mosaic of turquoise, malachite and shell fragments.

In various respects it could even be said to be more rapid. In Mesoamerican states, writing, advanced astronomical and calendrical knowledge, monumental architecture and official art had all appeared within 2000 years of the advent of full-time farming. In the Near East the interval was more like 4000 years. Looked at like this their failure to use the wheel no longer seems surprising: neither did the pyramid builders of Old Kingdom Egypt (pre-Columbian Americans certainly understood the principle of the wheel but they applied it only to children's toys). Wheels are not quite as essential as they seem to us, in the ancient Old World heavy loads were usually moved on sleds even by peoples such as the Assyrians who did also use wheeled vehicles.

The ancient city of Machu Picchu is situated high in the Andes Mountains between two peaks. There the Incas planted crops, such as potatoes and maize, by using advanced terracing and irrigation methods. They also integrated their architecture into the landscape in a unique way.

The only continent in which indigenous civilizations had not developed by the age of European colonialism was Oceania. In Australia the obstacle was a complete absence of animals and plants suitable for domestication rather than the harsh, arid climate which prevails over most of the island continent. New Guinea has been densely populated by farming peoples since ancient times but small-scale societies prevailed until modern times; chiefdoms and states did not develop. Part of the reason for this may be the limitations on agricultural productivity imposed by the rainforest environment which dominates the island. Soils are quickly exhausted and farmers practice a shifting slash and burn type of agriculture. Another factor is New Guinea's exceptionally rugged mountainous geography which makes overland travel extremely arduous, limiting contacts between communities and preventing the formation of larger social and political units. As a result New Guinea is a land of great cultural diversity with literally hundreds of distinct ethnic groups, with their own customs and languages, many confined to a single valley.

Pacific Cultures

Although coral atolls are too infertile to support intensive agriculture and large populations, the larger volcanic islands in the Pacific have very fertile soils and were more favourable to the development of complex societies. By the 13th century AD chiefdoms had developed in many archipelagos, including Tahiti, Fiji, Tonga, Hawaii, Easter Island, and in New Zealand. At the time of the first European contacts in the 18th century state formation was in progress in many of these places and the Hawaiian islands had been united into a single kingdom under the Kamehameha dynasty by 1810. However, the native cultures could not withstand the shock of contact with the Europeans. European diseases caused depopulation, Christian missionaries undermined native beliefs and by 1900 the entire Pacific was under the control of European empires, Japan or the USA. The most fascinating of the Pacific cultures is that which developed on Easter Island or Rapa Nui. Best described as a 'pre-civilization', this Polynesian society developed impressive monumental art and even a rudimentary writing system before its reckless over-exploitation of the environment brought catastrophe in its wake.

The Preclassic Civilizations

The first civilizations and the main cultural traditions of Mesoamerica developed during the Preclassic Period (2000 BC–AD 300). The earliest of these civilizations emerged among the Olmec, a maize farming people who lived on fertile flood plains in the tropical forests of Mexico's southern Gulf coast.

"In a certain era, which no one knows and no one remembers, there was a kingdom for a long time."

Nahuatl poem recorded in the 16th century

By the 13th century BC the Olmec people were living in chiefdoms or small kingdoms. The Olmec built massive ceremonial platforms, which were the prototypes for the more elaborate pyramids constructed by later Mesoamerican cultures. These ceremonial centres were decorated with monumental sculptures of altars and colossal heads of rulers wearing helmets for taking part in a sacred ball game. These games, which were a ritual method of communication with the supernatural world, were another Olmec innovation that became popular in Mesoamerica.

Small towns grew up around the ceremonial centres. The ceremonial centres were periodically demolished and the sculptures destroyed or buried. This may have been a result of warfare but it is thought more likely to have served a ritual purpose, perhaps to mark the end of a calendrical cycle. Later in their history, the Olmec developed a hieroglyphic script, used mainly for astronomical inscriptions, and they began to use (and probably had invented) the Mesoamerican 260-day sacred year and the 52 year 'long-count' calendar.

A jade pectoral carving dating to 1000–600 BC. The Olmec were the first jade-sculptors in Mesoamerica. Jade is extremely hard and difficult to carve. The small-scale and fine detail of this face demonstrates the skill of Olmec craftmanship.

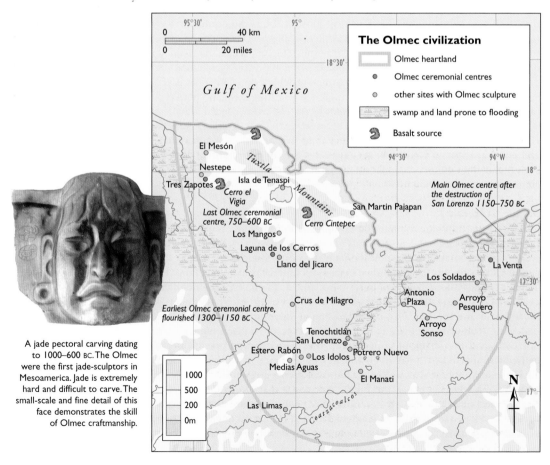

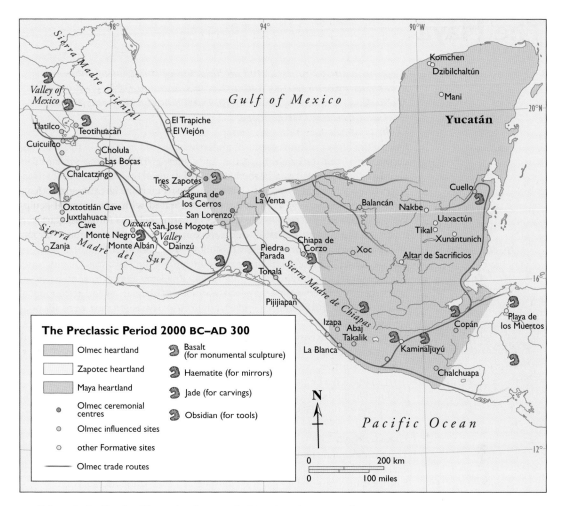

The Preclassic Period 2000 BC–AD 300

Although fertile, the Olmec lands were lacking in other natural resources. This led the Olmec to create a long-distance trade network which also helped disseminate their culture throughout Mesoamerica, influencing other early civilizations. Basalt for monumental sculpture and grindstones was brought from the Tuxtla Mountains. Haematite (an iron ore) for polished mirrors came from Oaxaca while jade for carvings and ritual artefacts came from as far away as Costa Rica. In return the Olmec traded jungle products such as jaguar pelts and feathers which were status symbols.

By *c.* 300 BC the Olmec were in relative decline as other Mesoamerican civilizations overtook them. In environmental terms the Maya, who originated in the densely forested Guatemalan highlands *c.*1200 BC, were the most similar to the Olmec. The Maya created a system of intensive agriculture by draining and canalizing swamplands. By 600 BC, towns such as Kaminaljuyú and Nakbe, with monumental stone temple pyramids, had developed.

Other centres of civilization developed in the drier, more open uplands to the west. In the Oaxaca valley intensive agriculture using irrigation and terracing led to the rise of city-states among the Zapotec people by 400 BC. The most important Zapotec site was Monte Albán: a ceremonial centre with the earliest hieroglyphic inscriptions in Mesoamerica. There are also relief carvings of *danzantes*, so called because they resembled dancers. The carvings are thought to be of tortured captives and shamans trying to achieve trance-like states through painful bloodletting ceremonies.

The Maya

By far the most sophisticated civilization of the pre-Columbian Americas was the Maya civilization of Guatemala, Petén and Yucatán. At its peak between AD 300 and 800, the Maya civilization survived into the 17th century.

"America, say historians, was peopled by savages; but savages never reared these structures … standing as they do in the depths of a tropical forest … strange in design, excellent in sculpture, rich in ornament."

J. L. Stephens,
Incidents of Travel in Central America
(1841)

One of the biggest achievements of archaeologists and linguists in the late 20th century was the deciphering of the Maya hieroglyphic writing system. This enabled the reconstruction of the histories of many Maya states and revolutionized our understanding of their civilization. Once, idealistically, thought to have been a peaceful society of astronomer-priests, it is now known to have been as violent as most other early civilisations. The Maya was the last native American civilization to fall to the Spanish: one kingdom held out until 1697. However, the civilization was at its peak in the Classic Period (AD 300–800).

The normal form of political organization among the Maya was the city-state. The first city-states developed during the late Preclassic Period (300 BC–AD 300). In the same period the Maya acquired advanced mathematical and astronomical knowledge, the 'long-count' calendar and the 260-day sacred year were adopted (possibly from the Olmecs) and a system of hieroglyphic writing came into use on commemorative stelae (upright stone slabs). Although the Maya did not invent the idea of writing, their hieroglyphic script was the only one used in Mesoamerica that could fully transcribe the spoken language. Most of these early cultural developments originated in the southern highlands but this area declined in importance after a devastating volcanic eruption *c.* AD 200–250 and the centre of the Classic Maya world was in the Petén lowland rainforests.

Classic Maya Life

The development that marks the beginning of the Classic Maya Period is the erection of the first commemorative stelae at Tikal and Uaxactún: the custom later became common across the central Maya area. These stelae record dynastic histories, frequent wars between cities and the capture, torture and sacrifice of rival rulers. Human sacrifice was a key part of Maya ritual, essential for the dedication of temples, at the completion of calendrical cycles and to accompany important people to the afterlife when they died. The Maya never created any territorial empires to compare with those of central Mexico; cities fought primarily to impose tributary relationships on their neighbours and to capture prisoners for sacrifice. The cities of Calakmul, Copán, Palenque and Yaxchilán arose as major regional powers but for most of the Classic Period the dominant Maya state was Tikal, which had close links with Teotihuacán. Maya cities were built around ceremonial centres with impressive temple pyramids, ball courts and palaces. The Maya built their magnificent cities with Neolithic technology and without the use of the wheel.

The Classic Period ended *c.* 800 with the collapse of the city-states in the Petén. The population dropped, commemorative stelae were no longer erected, the long-count calendar fell out of use and the cities were all abandoned by *c.* 909. The causes of the collapse have never been satisfactorily established but overexploitation of the fragile soils of the rainforest environment is thought to have been a major factor. The collapse in the Petén did not lead to the end of the Maya civilization, which continued to flourish in Yucatán and the southern highlands until the arrival of the Spanish in the 16th century.

This well-preserved stone relief from Yaxchilán in Mexico shows the great Maya king, Yaxun Balam IV, taking part in a religious bloodletting ritual.

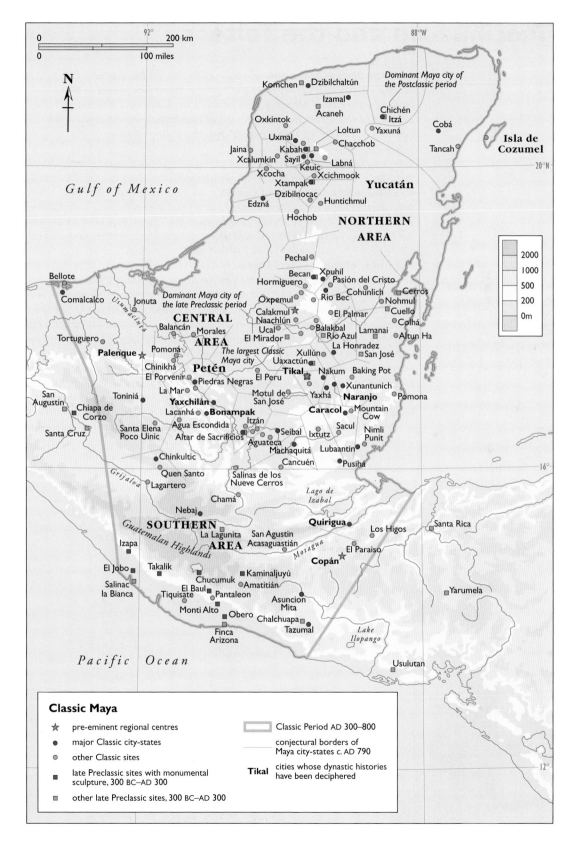

0   200 km

92°

0   100 miles

88°W

N

Gulf of Mexico

Komchen ■ Dzibilchaltún

Dominant Maya city of
the Postclassic period

Izamal
Acaneh
Chichén
Itzá

Oxkintok
Loltun
Yaxuná
Cobá

Uxmal
Chacchob

Jaina Kabah
Sayil
Tancah

Xcalumkin
Labná
Keuic

Xcocha
Xcichmook

Xtampak
Dzibilnocac

Edzná Huntichmul

Hochob

Yucatán

**Isla de
Cozumel**

20°N

**NORTHERN
AREA**

Pechal

Becan Xpuhil
Hormiguero Pasión del Cristo

Bellote

Comalcalco Jonuta
*Dominant Maya city of
the late Preclassic period*

Oxpemul
Río Bec
Cohunlich Cerros

Calakmul ☆
Naachlún

El Palmar
Nohmul
Cuello

CENTRAL
Balancán
Ucal
Balakbal
Colhá

Tortuguero
Morales
AREA
El Mirador ■
Río Azul
Lamanai
Altun Ha

Palenque ☆
Pomoná
*The largest Classic
Maya city*
Xullún
La Honradez
■ San José

Chinikhá
Petén
Uaxactún

El Porvenir
Tikal ☆
Nakum Baking Pot

San
Augustin
Piedras Negras
El Peru
El Peru

Toniniá
Motul de
San José
Yaxhá
Naranjo
Pomona

Chiapa de
Corzo
Yaxchilán
Lacanhá
Bonampak
Caracol
Mountain
Cow

Santa Cruz
Santa Elena
Poco Uinic
Agua Escondida
Itzán
Seibal
Ixtutz
Sacul
Nimli
Punit

Chinkultic
Altar de Sacrificios
Aguateca
Machaquitá
Lubaantin

Cancuén
Pusihá

16°

Quen Santo
Lagartero
Salinas de los
Nueve Cerros
*Lago de
Izabal*

Chamá

Nebaj

SOUTHERN
La Lagunita
San Agustin
Acasaguastián
Quirigua
Los Higos
Santa Rica

AREA

Izapa
Guatemalan Highlands

Copán ☆
El Paraiso

El Jobo
Takalik
Kaminaljuyú

Salinac
la Bianca
El Baul
Pantaleon
Amatitián

Tiquisate
Chucumuk
Yarumela

Monti Alto
Obero
Asuncion
Mita
Chalchuapa

Finca
Arizona
Tazumal

*Lake
Ilopango*

Usulutan

Pacific Ocean

12°

2000
1000
500
200
0m

Classic Maya

☆ pre-eminent regional centres

● major Classic city-states

○ other Classic sites

■ late Preclassic sites with monumental
sculpture, 300 BC–AD 300

▪ other late Preclassic sites, 300 BC–AD 300

▭ Classic Period AD 300–800

conjectural borders of
Maya city-states c. AD 790

Tikal cities whose dynastic histories
have been deciphered

Teotihuacán and the Toltecs

With the decline of the Olmec civilization the main centres of Mesoamerican civilization shifted to the Maya lands and to the central uplands of Mexico. Two powers in particular dominated the history of the latter before the rise of the Aztec empire in the 15th century – the city of Teotihuacán and the Toltec empire.

> *"The remains of their pottery, of their cups and figurines, their dolls and their bracelets can be seen everywhere, their ruins are everywhere, truly the Toltecs lived here once. "*
>
> Nahuatl poem recorded in the 16th century

Teotihuacán ('place of the gods') was one of several small market towns which grew up *c.* 200 BC in the fertile Valley of Mexico. The city's rise began *c.* 50 BC when the neighbouring city of Cuicuilco, then the dominant city in the valley, was overwhelmed by a volcanic eruption. By AD 100 Teotihuacán's population was about 40,000; when it was at its height in the Classic Period (AD 300–700) the population reached 150,000, making it one of the largest cities in the world.

Pyramids of the Sun and Moon

Teotihuacán was planned on a grid pattern of streets around a vast ceremonial centre; although less densely populated, its area, at 20 square kilometres, was greater than ancient Rome's. The ceremonial centre was dominated by the huge Pyramids of the Sun and Moon. With a base 210 metres square and a height of nearly 65 metres (213 feet), the Pyramid of the Sun is the largest structure of pre-Columbian America. Beneath the pyramid was a sacred cave, which, it is believed, attracted pilgrims from a wide area. Teotihuacán was also a major commercial centre and it controlled much of Mexico's trade in obsidian, a volcanic glass that makes high quality stone tools. The influence of Teotihuacán can be seen in the art and architecture of cities across Mesoamerica. What is not clear is whether this was the result of conquest or because local elites emulated the styles of what was the largest and most powerful city of its day. For unknown reasons Teotihuacán was violently destroyed and abandoned *c.* 700.

A Toltec stone warrior figure on top of a pyramidal platform at Tula in Mexico. These huge stone warriors were once used as columns to support a temple dedicated to Quetzalcóatl.

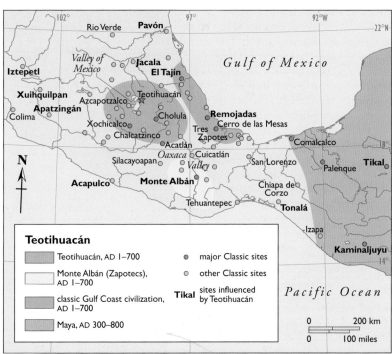

Teotihuacán

- Teotihuacán, AD 1–700
- Monte Albán (Zapotecs), AD 1–700
- classic Gulf Coast civilization, AD 1–700
- Maya, AD 300–800

- ● major Classic sites
- ◎ other Classic sites
- **Tikal** sites influenced by Teotihuacán

0   200 km
0   100 miles

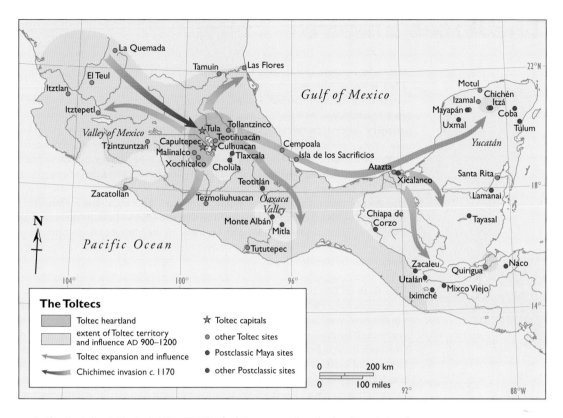

The Toltecs

▨ Toltec heartland	☆ Toltec capitals
▨ extent of Toltec territory and influence AD 900–1200	● other Toltec sites
⬅ Toltec expansion and influence	● Postclassic Maya sites
⬅ Chichimec invasion c. 1170	● other Postclassic sites

0 _____ 200 km
0 _____ 100 miles

In the Postclassic Period (700–1100) Cholula emerged as the leading state of central Mexico. As the centre of the Quetzalcóatl (Feathered Serpent) cult which swept Mesoamerica, Cholula inherited Teotihuacán's prestige. Cholula did not entirely fill the vacuum left by the fall of Teotihuacán, allowing the Chichimec and Nonoalca peoples to migrate into the Valley of Mexico c. 900 where they merged to form the Toltec nation. Toltec influence became much more widespread than that of Teotihuacán. One of the most striking examples of this is the similarities between the Toltec capital Tula and Chichén Itzá in the Puuc Maya area of Yucatán. Both cities share an almost identical plan and other features, such as relief carvings of feathered serpents. However, there are few similarities between the everyday items used in the two cities, indicating that the general populations were culturally distinct. It could be either that Chichén Itzá's Maya elite had chosen to emulate Toltec style or that a Toltec dynasty was ruling over a largely Maya population. There is a legend of a Toltec ruler called Topiltzin-Quetzalcóatl, a historical figure born in 935 or 947, who came to be identified with the god Quetzalcóatl. Topiltzin-Quetzalcóatl was overthrown because of his opposition to human sacrifice and fled east, over the sea, vowing to return to reclaim his kingdom. Maya sources record that in 987 a man called Kukulcán ('Feathered Serpent' in Mayan) conquered Yucatán. The Toltec empire fell after Tula was sacked in 1168 but its cultural heritage was claimed by the Aztecs.

The Pyramid of the Sun, built in the 2nd century AD, dominates the landscape of the ancient city of Teotihuacán in Mexico. It is the third biggest pyramid in the world. At its height, Teotihuacán had a population of around 150,000 people.

The Aztec Empire

Like the Toltecs, the Aztecs were immigrants to the Valley of Mexico. They were a farming people who originated in a mythical land in northwest Mexico called Aztlán. During their migration, their tribal god Huitzilopochtli gave them a new name, the Mexica. For over a century after their arrival in the valley c. 1200 the Aztecs moved from one site to another until in 1325 they founded a permanent settlement at Tenochtitlán on an island in Lake Texcoco. There they constructed chinampas, highly productive raised fields, along the lake shore.

"Tenochtitlán is spread out in circles of jade.... Beside it the Aztec lords are borne in boats and over them floats a flowery mist. "

Nahuatl poem recorded in the 16th century

The Aztecs had a reputation as good warriors and they were frequently employed as mercenaries by rulers of the numerous city-states in the valley. In 1367 they signed on to serve King Tezozomoc of Azcapotzalco. With Aztec help Tezozomoc conquered many of the neighbouring cities, giving the Aztecs a generous share of the loot.

The Rise of Tenochtitlán

Tezozomoc also elevated Tenochtitlán to a city-state in its own right by appointing the first Aztec king or *tlatoani* ('speaker'). Tezozomoc's son Maxtlatzin was concerned by the rising power of Tenochtitlán and tried to get rid of the Aztecs. However, he was defeated and overthrown in 1428 by Itzcóatl, the fourth Aztec king (r. 1427–40). In 1434 Tenochtitlán formed the Triple Alliance with Texcoco and Tlacopán and together they conquered the whole Valley of Mexico. Expansion continued under Itzcóatl's successors, reaching its peak during the reign of Moctezuma II (1502–20), who ruled over some 10 million subjects.

With over 500,000 inhabitants Tenochtitlán by this period was larger than any contemporary European city. Aztec society was based on a hierarchy of classes. The highest class was the aristocracy, which was made up of relatives of the king. The largest class was the commoners who were divided into 20 clans, each with its own quarter of Tenochtitlán, own schools, temples and communal farms. The lowest classes were the slaves and the conquered peoples, who served the aristocracy as labourers.

Enormous quantities of tribute poured into Tenochtitlán from the empire's provinces every year, including 7000 tons of maize, 4000 tons of beans, two million cotton cloaks and a huge range of exotic luxuries unavailable in the valley, such as cocoa, the feathers of tropical birds and amber. Many areas, such as the kingdom of Tlaxcala, were deliberately left unconquered. The Aztecs believed that their god Huitzilopochtli needed to be supplied with the hearts of enemy warriors or the sun would cease to rise and all life would come to an end. To this end the Aztecs began the 'Flowery Wars' with Tlaxcala and other states with the sole

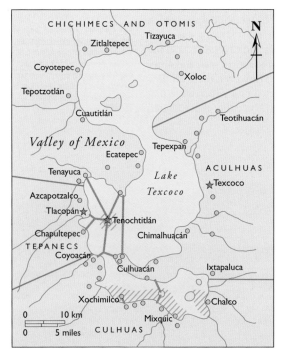

The Valley of Mexico

★ members of the Triple Alliance

○ other Aztec sites

▨ *chinampas* (floating gardens)

▬ causeways

— tribal boundaries

purpose of capturing prisoners for sacrifice. Decisive victory and annihilation of the enemy was never an aim, indeed it would have been counterproductive.

Fall of the Aztecs

The Aztec empire collapsed quickly following the invasion of the Spanish conquistador Hernan Cortés in 1519. The superiority of Spanish weapons and armour was only a minor factor in the Aztecs' defeat. Moctezuma reacted indecisively to the invasion, fearing that Cortés might be Quetzalcóatl returning as Toltec legend had foretold. Their custom of fighting with the objective of taking prisoners in battle also set the Aztecs at a significant disadvantage against the Spanish soldiers, who fought to kill. Most importantly, Cortés discovered many allies – especially the Tlaxcallans – who were only too eager to take revenge on the Aztecs for the cruelty and humiliations suffered at their hands. The Aztecs' destruction was completed by diseases introduced by the Spanish, like smallpox, to which they had no resistance.

A scene of ritual sacrifice from the Codex Magliabechiano manuscript. The Aztecs believed that the power of the gods had to be maintained by a constant supply of human sacrificial victims.

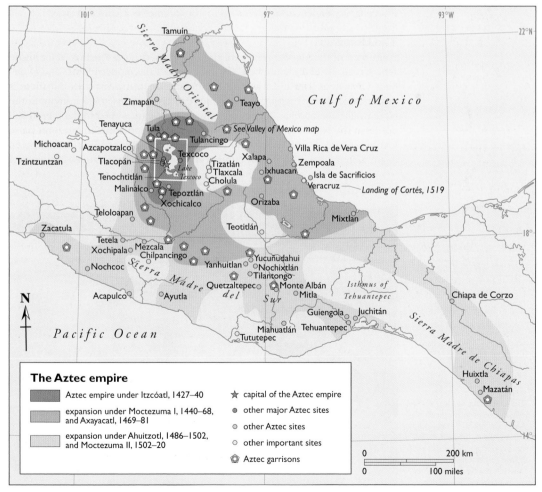

The Aztec empire

- Aztec empire under Itzcóatl, 1427–40
- expansion under Moctezuma I, 1440–68, and Axayacatl, 1469–81
- expansion under Ahuitzotl, 1486–1502, and Moctezuma II, 1502–20
- ★ capital of the Aztec empire
- ● other major Aztec sites
- ○ other Aztec sites
- ○ other important sites
- ⬡ Aztec garrisons

0   200 km
0   100 miles

Farmers of the Southwestern Deserts

The deserts of the southwest saw the development of the first complex societies of North America after the introduction of maize farming in the 1st millennium AD. Archaeologists recognize three main cultural traditions, the Hohokam, the Mogollon and the Anasazi or Ancestral Pueblo. All three lived in large permanent settlements or pueblos *(from the Spanish for 'town').*

The Anasazi developed on the Colorado plateau in the 8th century when local hunter-gatherers, known as Basketmakers, who had grown maize as a sideline, turned to full-time farming. The Anasazi built villages on mesas (flat-topped elevations with clifflike sides) or along the walls of canyons to take advantage of the shelter afforded by natural overhangs. Villages took the form of large multiroomed apartment blocks, sometimes several stories high, and underground circular chambers called *kivas*, which were used as communal rooms for social or religious gatherings. The largest of these complexes, Pueblo Bonito in Chaco Canyon, was five stories high and had 650 apartments and 32 *kivas*. Chaco was an important religious and trading centre with links to Mesoamerica and the Pacific. At its height in the 12th century Chaco was probably the capital of a chiefdom or state covering 65,000 square kilometres. A network or roads linked Chaco to dependent settlements up to 100 kilometres (62 miles) away.

The Hohokam

Southwest of the Anasazi area were the Hohokam (from a Pima word for 'those who have vanished'), who were the ancestors of the modern Pimas and O'Odham. Their economy and way of life were similar to the Anasazi's but there is evidence of contact with the Mesoamerican civilizations, most notably in the large oval-shaped arenas built at many sites, which are similar to the sacred ball courts of the Maya. Some experts, however, are more inclined to interpret these features as ceremonial dance courts. Mesoamerican influence is also to be seen in the neighbouring Mogollon cultural tradition. At Casas Grandes in northern

"The Pueblo communities are all well built with straight, well-squared walls. Their towns have no defined streets. Their houses are three, five, six and even seven stories high, with many windows and terraces. The men have as many wives as they can support. The men spin and weave and the women cook, build the houses, and keep them in repair. "

Gaspar Perez de Villagra, *History of New Mexico* (1610)

The Cliff Palace at Mesa Verde in Colorado is one of the best examples of Pueblo cliff dwellings. It had over 200 rooms housing 400 people and 23 *kivas* (ceremonial chambers) which can be recognized by their circular shape.

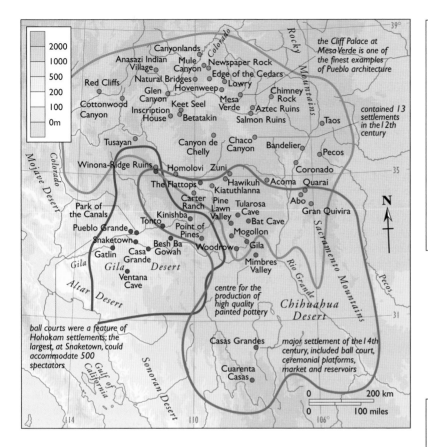

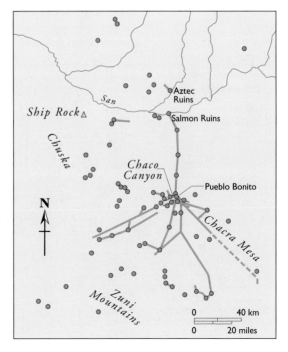

Mexico a thriving town developed in the 14th century, with many Mesoamerican features such as a ball court and ceremonial platforms. Specialized craft activities on the site, including the casting of copper axes using the lost-wax method, also show Mesoamerican influences. It has been claimed that the town was founded by Mesoamerican merchants as a trade outpost but there is no evidence that it was affiliated to any Mesoamerican state. A major regional variation of the Mogollon was the Mimbres tradition, noted for its fine geometrically patterned pottery. This centre also played a role in long-distance trade with Mesoamerica.

Decline of the Pueblos

The early pueblo cultures went into decline in the 14th and 15th centuries and towns like Pueblo Bonito and Casas Grandes were abandoned. Climatic data suggests that the early pueblo cultures developed at a time when droughts were less frequent and water tables were higher than they are today. With the onset of drier conditions from the 14th century on, it became impossible to support concentrated populations and the people dispersed across the countryside into smaller villages, and the development of these nascent civilizations came to an end.

The Mound Builders

In the 1st millennium BC hunter-gatherers in the eastern woodlands of North America began to build burial mounds and ritual earthworks. The mound-building tradition continued in the region, attaining monumental scale in the last centuries before the arrival of Europeans.

"The Natchez temple, the front of which looks toward the rising sun, is placed on a mound of earth ... which rises about eight feet above the natural level of the ground.... This temple measures about thirty feet wide on each side. "

Antoine-Simon Le Page du Pratz, *History of Louisiana* (1758)

The earliest earthwork in North America was built by hunter-gatherers at Poverty Point, Louisiana, *c.* 1300 BC. About 1800 metres (5900 feet) across, it consisted of concentric ridges built around a central plaza. The site is presumed to have been a ceremonial centre. Poverty Point appears to have been an isolated development. Around 500 BC the people of the Adena culture in the Ohio River valley began to bury their dead under small conical mounds. Although they were hunter-gatherers, the Adena people cultivated some native plants, like sunflowers, for their seeds, and used pottery. Over time, the Adena burials became more elaborate, with wooden burial chambers and large mounds. One, at Grave Creek, was about 19 metres (62 feet) high and 73 metres (240 feet) across and was surrounded by a moat. The appearance of such burials is probably a sign of the development of a more hierarchical social structure.

The Hopewell

Around 100 BC, the Adena culture was replaced by the Hopewell culture, which was characterized by a long-distance exchange network extending to Canada and the Gulf of Mexico. The Hopewell buried their dead under mounds but also built them for other, presumably, ceremonial purposes, sometimes linking them together with embankments. Some mounds appear to have had symbolic importance, such as the Serpent Mound in Ohio. The Hopewell cultivated maize, beans and squash but still relied primarily on hunting and gathering.

The transition from hunting and gathering to farming was made by the Mississippians, beginning *c.* AD 800. The Mississippian was a complex of cultures which developed in the region around the confluence of the Ohio with the Mississippi river and spread out over most of the eastern woodlands area. The transition was probably made possible by the introduction of new strains of maize that were better suited to a temperate climate. The Mississippian cultures saw the development of social hierarchy, centralized power and towns. The Mississippians built large, flat-topped mounds which had wooden buildings on top, some of which were temples, others residences of high status individuals.

Cahokia

The largest Mississippian settlement was at Cahokia, which, at its peak in the 13th century was an important city with 30,000 inhabitants that displays most of the signs of having been organized at the level of a state. The largest mound at Cahokia, Monk's Mound, is a terraced structure over 30 metres (98 feet) high. The summit platform was occupied by a large wooden palace that was the residence of the city's ruler. High-status individuals were buried in mound-top mortuaries accompanied by grave goods and human sacrifices. In one a

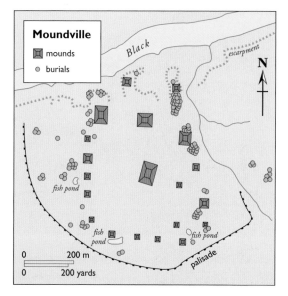

Moundville
- mounds
- burials

Black
escarpment
N
fish pond
fish pond
fish pond
palisade

0   200 m
0   200 yards

male was buried on a platform of 20,000 shell beads with 800 arrowheads and other artefacts and nearly 80 humans, most of them young females aged 18–23, sacrificed to join with him in death. Another significant site is at Moundville in Alabama, the centre for the 'Southern Cult' which was not so much an organized religion as a complex of beliefs and motifs which were shared over much of southeast North America.

The Mississippian cultures went into decline in the 15th century. Their heartland became a depopulated 'vacant quarter' and Cahokia was abandoned. Elsewhere, the mound-building traditions continued among peoples such as the Natchez up to the arrival of Europeans in the late 17th century and beyond.

This copper-embossed face, possibly that of a distinguished warrior, has the facial decorations typical of the Southern Cult of Mound Builders. It dates to around AD 1000.

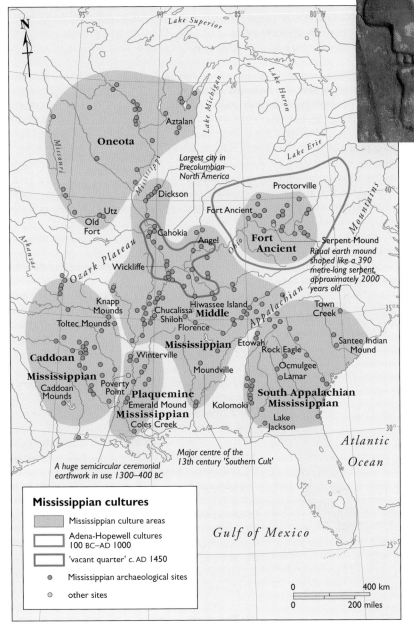

Lake Superior

Lake Michigan

Lake Huron

Lake Erie

Oneota

Aztalan

Largest city in Precolumbian North America

Dickson

Proctorville

Fort Ancient

Utz

Old Fort

Cahokia

Angel

Fort Ancient

Serpent Mound
Ritual earth mound shaped like a 390 metre-long serpent, approximately 2000 years old

Wickliffe

Knapp Mounds

Chucalissa

Hiwassee Island

Middle

Town Creek

Toltec Mounds

Shiloh

Florence

Santee Indian Mound

Mississippian

Etowah

Rock Eagle

Winterville

Caddoan

Mississippian

Moundville

Ocmulgee

Lamar

Caddoan Mounds

Poverty Point

Plaquemine

Emerald Mound

Kolomoki

South Appalachian Mississippian

Mississippian

Coles Creek

Lake Jackson

Atlantic

Ocean

Major centre of the 13th century 'Southern Cult'

A huge semicircular ceremonial earthwork in use 1300–400 BC

Gulf of Mexico

Mississippian cultures

- Mississippian culture areas
- Adena-Hopewell cultures 100 BC–AD 1000
- 'vacant quarter' c. AD 1450
- Mississippian archaeological sites
- other sites

0   400 km
0   200 miles

Missouri

Mississippi

Arkansas

Ozark Plateau

Ohio

Appalachian Mountains

The Origins of the Andean Civilizations

The earliest complex cultures of South America developed in two contrasting regions of Peru, in the valleys and plateaus of the high Andes and in the narrow strip of desert lowlands sandwiched between the mountains and the Pacific Ocean.

"Ancient Viracocha, skilful creator, who makes and establishes.... May food be plentiful for those you have created, those you have made. You say 'Potatoes, maize, may there be all kinds of food'."

Zithuwa Indian ritual

In most parts of the world, the development of social complexity was dependent on the adoption of the farming way of life. South America was unusual in that the first complex societies arose in fishing communities, on the Pacific coast of Peru, that had not even adopted the use of pottery. Although the Peruvian coast is extremely arid, the marine resources of this area are so rich that settled communities developed and some of these had labour to spare for ambitious construction projects such as ceremonial centres and temples.

Aspero

Perhaps the earliest of these centres was built at Aspero c. 2600 BC. Six platform mounds, the largest of which was 10 metres (33 feet) high, were built using a mixture of adobe (mud brick) and stone rubble. Masonry shrines or temples were built on the summits of the mounds. The Aspero people did not cultivate plants for food but they did grow cotton for textiles and gourds which were used to make floats for fishing nets. At about the same time that the Aspero mounds were being built, communities in the Andes Mountains were making the transition from hunting and gathering to farming based on growing potatoes and other root crops, quinoa (a native Andean cereal) and herds of domesticated llamas and alpacas. Permanent villages and monumental ceremonial centres had appeared by c. 2000 BC.

Pottery

None of these early Andean communities used pottery. Pottery first came into use in the Americas in Colombia and Guyana c. 3500 BC and spread south only slowly, reaching Peru by c. 1800 BC. The adoption of pottery marks the beginning of the Initial Period (1800–800 BC), the period in which agriculture became the normal basis of subsistence throughout the Andean region. The adoption of farming in the coastal lowlands was the result of the development of irrigation techniques, which greatly increased the area of cultivable land by diverting water from the rivers that ran through the desert from the mountains to the sea.

Huge U-shaped ceremonial centres were built; one of the largest, at Garagay required an estimated 3.2 million working days to complete. A frieze at Cerro Sechin, showing executed and dismembered prisoners, provides evidence for organized warfare. Long-distance trade routes developed linking the fishing communities on the coast and the farming communities in the desert river valleys with the mountains and the upper Amazon basin. This interaction between the inhabitants of different environmental zones became an important factor in the later cultural and political development of the Andean civilizations.

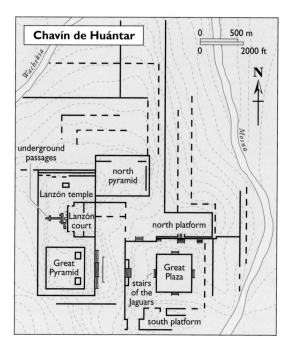

Chavín de Huántar

underground passages

north pyramid

Lanzón temple

Lanzón court

Great Pyramid

north platform

Great Plaza

stairs of the Jaguars

south platform

In the Early Horizon Period (800–200 BC) sophisticated monumental architecture first became widespread. The dominant culture of this period was the Chavín style which originated at Chavín de Huántar, a large complex of masonry temples, underground passages and ceremonial courts with monolithic carvings of deities and supernatural figures, in a high valley in the eastern Andes. At its peak around 400 BC Chavín had a population of about 3000 but it went into decline soon after and was eventually abandoned. Chavín is thought to have been a pilgrimage centre for a religious cult which eventually spread over much of the central Andes, taking its iconography with it. Complex societies with shared religious beliefs also developed around Lake Titicaca during the Early Horizon Period. The Early Horizon saw major technological changes in metal-working and textiles. The most accomplished textiles of the time were produced by the Paracas culture. Chavín designs were painted onto cotton fabric and tapestries embroidered with depictions of supernatural creatures were used as mummy wrappings.

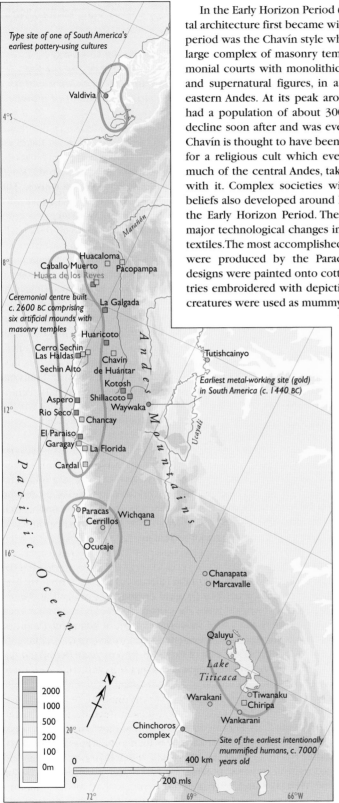

Type site of one of South America's earliest pottery-using cultures

Valdivia

4°S

Marañón

8°

Huacaloma
Caballo Muerto Pacopampa
Huaca de los Reyes

Ceremonial centre built c. 2600 BC comprising six artificial mounds with masonry temples
La Galgada

Huaricoto

Cerro Sechin
Las Haldas
Sechin Alto   Chavín
de Huántar
Kotosh
Aspero   Shillacoto
Rio Seco   Waywaka
Chancay
El Paraiso
Garagay   La Florida
Cardal

Tutishcainyo

Earliest metal-working site (gold) in South America (c. 1440 BC)

Andes Mountains

Ucayali

Paracas Wichqana
Cerrillos

Ocucaje

12°

16°

Chanapata
Marcavalle

Pacific Ocean

Qaluyu

Lake Titicaca

Warakani   Tiwanaku
Chiripa
Wankarani

Chinchoros complex

Site of the earliest intentionally mummified humans, c. 7000 years old

20°

N

2000
1000
500
200
100
0m

0   400 km
0   200 mls

72°   69°   66°W

This colourful Paracas textile, embroidered from alpaca wool, is typical of the linear style. The textile features complex mythological creatures.

First Andean civilizations

- Valdivia tradition 3800–1700 BC
- El Paraiso culture 1800–850 BC
- Chavín culture 900–200 BC
- Paracas culture 650–150 BC
- early South-Central Andean traditions
- ▣ sites with monumental buildings before c. 1800 BC
- ● other important sites before c. 1800 BC
- ▢ sites with monumental buildings c. 1800 BC– c. AD 100
- ○ other important sites c. 1800 BC– c. AD 100

The First Andean Empires

The first states in South America developed during the Early Intermediate Period (200 BC–AD 750). The beginning of the period was marked by the decline of the widespread Chavín culture and its replacement by several local cultures, the most significant of which were the Moche and the Nazca.

The earliest South American state developed in the Moche valley on the coast of northern Peru *c.*100 BC. The centre of the Moche state was at two vast adobe pyramids, the Huaca del Sol and the Huaca de la Luna ('huaca' is a word denoting a variety of sacred sites). The largest of the two pyramids, the Huaca del Sol was a stepped structure over 40 metres (130 feet) tall, built of 143 million adobe bricks. Each brick has its maker's mark on it suggesting that the Moche state had a labour tax similar to that known to have existed in the later Inca empire. The objects in these burials reveal Moche craftsmen to have been highly skilled, full-time specialists in textiles, pottery and gold, silver and copper metalwork.

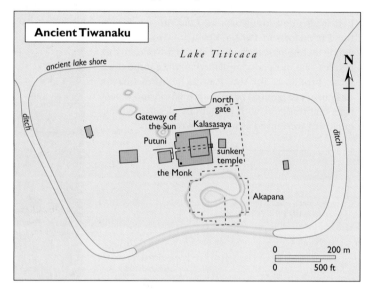

The Moche did not use writing but conveyed messages using beans that were painted or marked with patterns of dots and lines. By AD 200 the Moche had conquered the neighbouring valleys where provincial capitals and fortresses were built. Around AD 500 massive flooding forced the relocation of the Moche capital to Pampa Grande. At nearby Sipán a cemetery contained incredibly rich royal burials including that of the 'Lord of Sipán' which comprised spectacular gold artefacts and a sacrificed dog and five humans.

Nazca Geoglyphs

The Nazca culture was a development of the Paracas culture. The Nazca are best known for their enormous geoglyphs (ground drawings) of animals and birds and intriguing patterns of straight lines. The purpose of the geoglyphs has been the cause of an enormous amount of speculation, most of it fanciful. The most credible explanations are that they represented ritual walkways and alignments on sacred sites. Not until after the end of the Early Intermediate Period did the Nazca begin to develop a complex political organization and even then there was probably never anything resembling a Nazca state.

Tiwanaku

Towards the end of the Early Intermediate Period new states were emerging in the highlands, where the use of terracing was increasing the cultivable area. During the Middle Horizon Period (AD 750–1000) which followed, two highland states emerged as rival imperial powers, Tiwanaku and Wari (or Huari). The motive for the Tiwanaku and Wari imperial expansion, as for later Andean empires, was to achieve control over a broad range of highland, lowland and

"Viracocha went to a place now called Tiwanaku in the province of Collasuyu, and in this place he sculptured and designed on a great piece of stone, all the nations he intended to create."

Pedro Sarmiento de Gamboa, *History of the Incas* (1572)

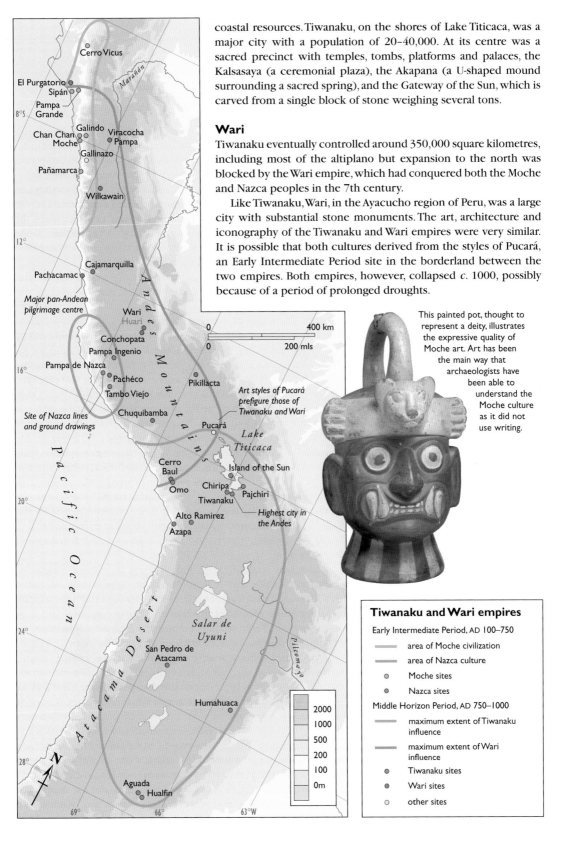

coastal resources. Tiwanaku, on the shores of Lake Titicaca, was a major city with a population of 20–40,000. At its centre was a sacred precinct with temples, tombs, platforms and palaces, the Kalsasaya (a ceremonial plaza), the Akapana (a U-shaped mound surrounding a sacred spring), and the Gateway of the Sun, which is carved from a single block of stone weighing several tons.

Wari

Tiwanaku eventually controlled around 350,000 square kilometres, including most of the altiplano but expansion to the north was blocked by the Wari empire, which had conquered both the Moche and Nazca peoples in the 7th century.

Like Tiwanaku, Wari, in the Ayacucho region of Peru, was a large city with substantial stone monuments. The art, architecture and iconography of the Tiwanaku and Wari empires were very similar. It is possible that both cultures derived from the styles of Pucará, an Early Intermediate Period site in the borderland between the two empires. Both empires, however, collapsed *c.* 1000, possibly because of a period of prolonged droughts.

This painted pot, thought to represent a deity, illustrates the expressive quality of Moche art. Art has been the main way that archaeologists have been able to understand the Moche culture as it did not use writing.

Tiwanaku and Wari empires

Early Intermediate Period, AD 100–750

— area of Moche civilization
— area of Nazca culture
◦ Moche sites
◦ Nazca sites

Middle Horizon Period, AD 750–1000

— maximum extent of Tiwanaku influence
— maximum extent of Wari influence
◦ Tiwanaku sites
◦ Wari sites
◦ other sites

The Inca Empire

The last and greatest of the civilizations of ancient South America was the Inca empire, a formidably well-organized state which united almost the entire Andean region under its rule.

The Inca state emerged in the long period of political fragmentation which followed the fall of the Tiwanaku and Wari empires known as the Late Intermediate Period (1000–1470). In the power vacuum created by the fall of these empires, dozens of small states emerged, most of them controlling no more than a single valley. The first regional power to emerge was the Chimú empire, which controlled around 1000 kilometres of the Peruvian coast between the 13th and 15th centuries. The Chimú capital at Chan Chan in the Moche valley had at its heart ten compounds or *ciudadelas* ('little cities'), containing palaces, administrative buildings, stores, wells and burial platforms. Each compound was the residence, and after death the mausoleum, of an individual Chimú ruler.

Empire Emerges at Cuzco

The Chimú empire survived until 1470 when it was conquered by the Incas. According to tradition, the Inca state was founded by Manco Capac, a semi-legendary figure, at Cuzco sometime around 1200. The Incas regarded Cuzco as the centre of the universe (the name means 'navel' in the Incas' Quechua language), from which the Four Quarters of the world radiated. The Inca name for their empire was Tawatinsuyu, the 'Land of the Four Quarters'. Inca imperial expansion took place almost entirely in the reigns of Pachacutec (1438–71) and Tupac Yupanqui (1471–93). By the end of Tupac's reign the empire was reaching its effective limits. It made little sense for the Incas to try to conquer the Amazonian rainforest or the southern Andes as these sparsely populated areas were environmentally unsuited to intensive agriculture. After the death of Huayna Capac (r. 1493–1525) the empire was fatally weakened by civil war and it was easily conquered by the Spanish in 1532–36, who plundered and destroyed most of its cultural heritage.

Secrets of Success

One factor in Inca success was their skill in maximizing agricultural productivity, building irrigation canals and transforming the appearance of entire mountainsides with stone-faced terraces, still used by farmers today. Inca architecture utilized huge stone blocks, each shaped to fit its neighbours exactly without the use of mortar. To unite their empire, the Inca built a network of roads and paths estimated at around 40,000 kilometres (25,000 miles) in length.

The main secret of Inca success was, however, their administrative system, which allowed them to exploit the human and material resources of the empire very efficiently. Inca society was highly centralized and rigidly hierarchical. At the head of society was the semi-divine emperor, whose power, in theory at least, was absolute. Below the emperor were the prefects of the Four Quarters and below them the provincial governors, district officers, local chiefs and at the bottom foremen, each responsible for supervising groups of ten families. It has been estimated that there were around 1331 officials per 10,000 head of the population, a number unparalleled in any other known ancient society.

All agricultural land in the empire was divided into thirds, for the support of the people, the gods and the state respectively. All Inca men and women paid tax in the form of labour on the land allocated to the gods and the state.

"If there came a lean year, the Incas opened the storehouses and the provinces were lent what supplies they needed; then, in a year of abundance, they paid back all they had received. No one who was lazy or tried to live by the work of others was tolerated; everyone had to work."

Pedro Cieza de Leon
(1540)

Able-bodied men also had to perform *mit'a*, a draft which could range from military service to labouring on civil engineering projects. This complex system was run without any form of writing. The Incas used instead a complex system of knotted cords called *quipus* for record-keeping.

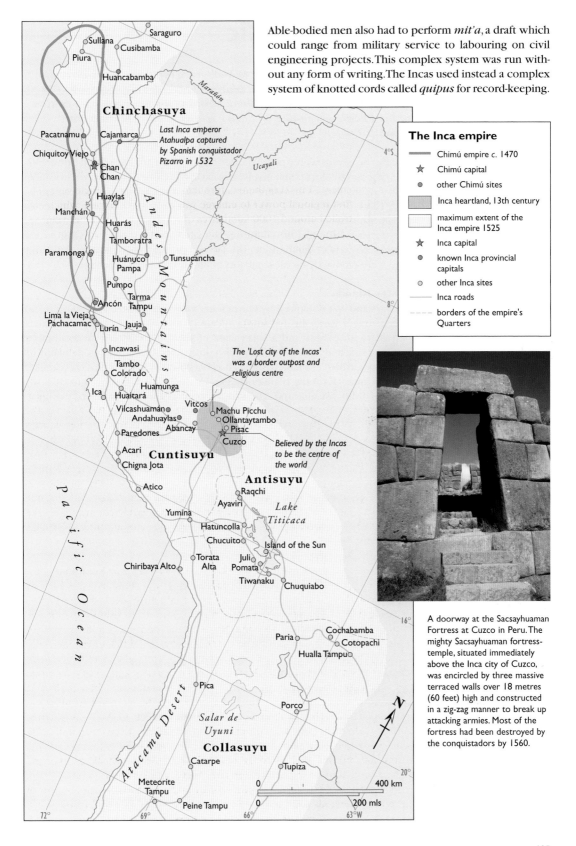

Chinchasuya

Sullana
Saraguro
Cusibamba
Piura
Huancabamba

Marañón

Pacatnamu
Cajamarca

Last Inca emperor Atahualpa captured by Spanish conquistador Pizarro in 1532

Chiquitoy Viejo
Chan Chan

Ucayali

Huaylas
Manchán
Huarás
Tamboratra
Paramonga
Huánuco Pampa
Tunsucancha
Pumpo
Tarma
Ancón Tampu
Lima la Vieja
Pachacamac
Lurín
Jauja
Incawasi
Tambo Colorado
Huamunga
Ica
Huaitará
Vilcashuamán
Vitcos
Andahuaylas
Machu Picchu
Ollantaytambo
Abancay
Pisac
Paredones
Cuzco
Acari
Chigna Jota
Atico

The 'Lost city of the Incas' was a border outpost and religious centre

Believed by the Incas to be the centre of the world

Cuntisuyu

Antisuyu
Raqchi
Yumina
Ayaviri
Lake Titicaca
Hatuncolla
Chucuito
Island of the Sun
Chiribaya Alto
Torata Alta
Juli
Pomata
Tiwanaku
Chuquiabo

Pacific Ocean

Andes Mountains

Cochabamba
Paria
Cotopachi
Hualla Tampu

Pica
Porco

Atacama Desert

Salar de Uyuni

Collasuyu
Catarpe
Tupiza
Meteorite Tampu
Peine Tampu

N

0   400 km
0   200 mls

72° 69° 66° 63°W
4°S
8°
16°
20°

The Inca empire

— Chimú empire *c.* 1470

★ Chimú capital

● other Chimú sites

▨ Inca heartland, 13th century

☐ maximum extent of the Inca empire 1525

★ Inca capital

● known Inca provincial capitals

○ other Inca sites

— Inca roads

--- borders of the empire's Quarters

A doorway at the Sacsayhuaman Fortress at Cuzco in Peru. The mighty Sacsayhuaman fortress-temple, situated immediately above the Inca city of Cuzco, was encircled by three massive terraced walls over 18 metres (60 feet) high and constructed in a zig-zag manner to break up attacking armies. Most of the fortress had been destroyed by the conquistadors by 1560.

135

Chiefdoms of the Pacific

Although most of the Pacific islands were too poor in resources for complex societies to develop, powerful chiefdoms did arise in Fiji, Tahiti, Hawaii and New Zealand. Perhaps the most complex culture of the Pacific developed on Easter Island, the world's remotest inhabited place.

The Pacific islands were among the last places on earth to be settled by humans. The process of colonization involved incredible transoceanic voyages in double-hulled sailing canoes that were unparalleled before the age of European expansion. Three distinct Pacific ethnic-cultural groups had evolved by 300 BC: the Melanesians, who were closely related to the peoples of New Guinea, the Micronesians, who had mixed Melanesian and South East Asian origins, and the Polynesians, whose cultural identity formed in the Tonga and Fiji islands but who were ultimately the descendants of South East Asian peoples.

Easter Island

Easter Island was colonized by Polynesians sometime between AD 400 and 700. The islanders were divided into a hierarchical society of clans, with chiefs, hereditary aristocrats and a small class of specialist workers, for example in stone carving and fishing. The islanders constructed ceremonial stone platforms called *ahu*, which contained burial chambers used by members of the same kin group. Around 1000 the islanders began carving stone ancestor figures known as *moai* from volcanic tuff. The statues were a source of spiritual power, or

> *"The gigantic statues are built with hewn stones of a very large size and the workmanship is not inferior to the best plain piece of masonry we have in England.... We could hardly conceive how a nation like these, wholly unacquainted with any mechanical power, could raise such stupendous figures."*
>
> Captain James Cook
> (1774)

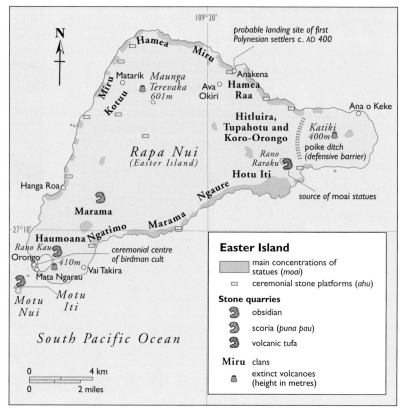

mana, and chiefs began to compete to erect even bigger *moai,* consuming more and more resources in the process. Working with simple stone picks it took 20 workers a year to make one statue and the efforts of hundreds to move it and erect it on an *ahu.* The statues helped assert each clan's claim to its territory, an important matter in such a confined environment. At some point the islanders devised a so-far undeciphered form of hieroglyphic script called *rongorongo,* which was the only indigenous writing system developed in the Pacific.

About 1000 *moai* had been carved by the time the tradition came to an end in a sudden spasm of violence around 1500. Vast quantities of obsidian spear points and daggers were manufactured, the Poike defensive ditch was dug, and the *moai* were overthrown in inter-village raids and a new birdman cult replaced the traditional ancestor cult. The cause of the catastrophe was the islanders' own reckless destruction of the environment. At the time of its settlement Easter Island was densely forested. Over the centuries the forests were felled to make fields, for fuel, building and for rope, rollers and levers to erect the *moai* until by the 16th century the island was completely treeless. Deforestation led to soil erosion, the collapse of agriculture and the decline of fishing as boats could no longer be built. The islanders could not even leave. Famine led to the dissolution of the social order and endemic warfare and the population decreased from around 7000 in the 15th century to only 2000 at the time of the first European landing on Easter Island in 1722.

A large platform, or *ahu,* with seven *moai* statues on Easter Island. The statues originally had eyes of white coral with pupils of black obsidian. Some were fitted with topknots made from red scoria. The Easter Island statues are thought to have been part of an ancestor cult.

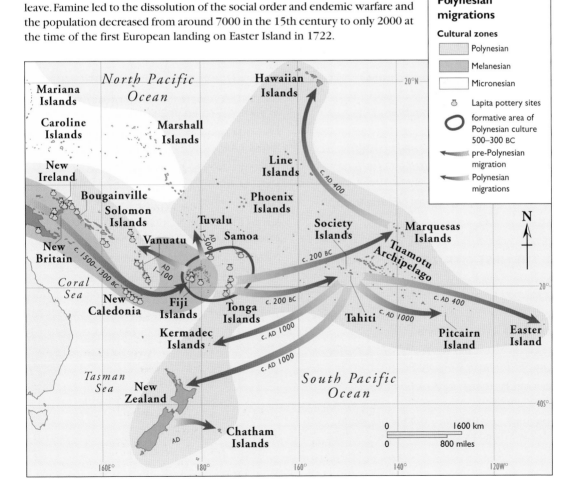

Polynesian migrations

Cultural zones
- Polynesian
- Melanesian
- Micronesian

- Lapita pottery sites
- formative area of Polynesian culture 500–300 BC
- pre-Polynesian migration
- Polynesian migrations

Further reading

I. THE ANCIENT NEAR EAST

Cook, J. M., *The Persian Empire* (London, 1983)

Crawford, H., *Sumer and the Sumerians* (Cambridge, 2004)

Gurney, O. R., *The Hittites* (revised edn, Harmondsworth, 1990)

Leick, G., *Mesopotamia: the Invention of the City* (London, 2002)

Roaf, M., *Cultural Atlas of Mesopotamia and the Ancient Near East* (Oxford and New York, 1990)

Roux, G., *Ancient Iraq* (revised edn, London, 1990)

Saggs, H. W. F., *The Might that was Assyria* (London, 1984)

Saggs, H. W. F., *Babylonians* (London, 2000)

2. THE AFRICAN CIVILIZATIONS

Clayton, P., *Chronicle of the Pharaohs* (London, 1994)

Connah, G., *African Civilizations* (Cambridge, 1987)

Kemp, B., *Ancient Egypt* (London, 1989)

Manley, B., *The Penguin Historical Atlas of Ancient Egypt* (Harmondsworth, 1996)

Shaw, I., *The Oxford History of Ancient Egypt* (Oxford, 2003)

3. THE FIRST CIVILIZATIONS OF ASIA

Jun, L. X., *Chinese Civilization in the Making 1766–221 BC* (New York, 1996)

Kenoyer, J. M., *Ancient Cities of the Indus Valley Civilization* (Oxford, 1998)

Lindesay, W. & Baofu, G., *The Terracotta Army of Qin Shi Huangdi* (London, 1999)

Rawson, J., *Mysteries of Ancient China* (London, 1996)

Thapar, R,. *Early India: from the origins to AD 1300* (London, 2002)

4. THE FIRST EUROPEAN CIVILIZATIONS

Cunliffe, B. (ed.), *The Oxford Illustrated Prehistory of Europe* (Oxford, 1994)

Cunliffe, B., *The Ancient Celts* (Oxford, 1997)

Fitton, J. L., *Minoans* (London, 2003)

Morkot, R., *The Penguin Historical Atlas of Ancient Greece* (Harmondsworth, 1996)

Price, T. D. (ed.), *Europe's First Farmers* (Cambridge, 2000)

Scarre, C., *The Penguin Historical Atlas of Ancient Rome* (Harmondsworth, 1995)

Taylour, L. W., *The Mycenaeans* (London, 1990)

5. THE ANCIENT AMERICAS

Bahn, P. & Florey, J., *Easter Island, Earth Island* (London, 1992)

Bawden, G., *The Moche* (Oxford, 2003)

Coe, M. D. & Koontz, R., *Mexico: from the Olmecs to the Aztecs* (London, 2002)

Coe, M. D., Snow, D. & Benson, E., *Atlas of the Ancient Americas* (Oxford, 1986)

D'Altroy, T. N., *The Incas* (Oxford, 2003)

Fagan, B. M., *Ancient North America* (London, 1991)

Martin, S. & Grube, N., *Chronicle of the Maya Kings and Queens* (London, 2000)

Nietzel, J., *Pueblo Bonito* (Washington DC, 2004)

Pauketat, T. R., *Ancient Cahokia and the Mississippians* (Cambridge, 2004)

Townsend, R. F., *The Aztecs* (London, 2000)

Index

Acknowledgements

PICTURE CREDITS

Pages: 8 Scala, Florence/Iraq Museum, Baghdad; 9 Scala, Florence/British Museum, London; 10 The Bridgeman Art Library, London; 11 The Bridgeman Art Library, London/Ashmolean Museum, Oxford; 12 Scala, Florence; 13 Werner Forman Archives; 18 Scala, Florence/Iraq Museum, Baghdad; 19 The Bridgeman Art Library, London/Louvre, Paris; 20 The Bridgeman Art Library, London/Louvre, Paris; 21 The Bridgeman Art Library, London/British Museum, London; 22 Scala, Florence/Archeological Museum, Amman; 24 Scala, Florence/British Museum, London; 26 The Bridgeman Art Library, London/Iraq Museum, Baghdad; 28 Scala, Florence/Iraq Museum, Baghdad; 32 The Bridgeman Art Library/Louvre, Paris; 35 AKG, London/Louvre, Paris; 37 The Art Archive/ Museum of Anatolian Civilizations, Ankara; 39 The Bridgeman Art Library, London/Louvre, Paris; 41 Scala, Florence/Museo Preistorico ed Ethnografico Pigorini, Rome; 42 The Bridgeman Art Library, London/British Museum, London; 45 Scala, Florence/British Museum, London; 47 The Bridgeman Art Library, London; 49 The Bridgeman Art Library, London/Iraq Museum, Baghdad; 52 Scala, Florence/Museo Archeologico, Forence; 54 Werner Forman Archives/British Museum, London; 55-6 Scala, Florence/Egyptian Museum, Cairo; 57 The Art Archive/Egyptian Museum, Cairo; 58 Werner Forman Archives/Egyptian Museum, Cairo; 62-4 The Bridgeman Art Library, London/ Egyptian Museum, Cairo; 66 Werner Forman Archives; 68 Werner Forman Archives; 71 Werner Forman Archives/British Museum, London; 72 Scala, Florence/National Museum, Karachi; 73 The Bridgeman Art Library; 74 Scala, Florence/British Museum, London; 75 The Bridgeman Art Library, London/British Museum, London; 76 The Bridgeman Art Library, London/National Museum, Karachi; 78 Corbis/Burstein Collection; 80 Scala, Florence; 82 The Bridgeman Art Library, London/ Museum of Art and Far Eastern Antiquities, Ulricehamn; 84 The Bridgeman Art Library, London; 86 Scala, Florence/British Museum, London; 88 The Bridgeman Art Library; 90 Scala, Florence; 91-6 John Haywood; 98 Scala, Florence; 99 Simon Hall; 100-6 John Haywood; 109 Scala, Florence/ Musei Capitolini, Rome; 110 John Haywood; 113 Scala, Florence/National Archeological Museum, Madrid; 114 Werner Forman Archives; 115 AKG, London; 116 The Art Archive/Museo Ethnografico Pigorini, Rome; 117 The Art Archive; 118-20 Scala, Florence/British Museum, London; 123 Werner Forman Archives; 125 Scala, Florence/ National Library, Florence; 127 Werner Forman Archives; 129 Werner Forman Archives/Museum of the American Indian, Heye Foundation, New York; 131 Werner Forman Archives/David Bernstein Fine Art, New York; 133 Scala, Florence/Museo Preistorico ed Ethnografico Pigorini, Rome; 134 Corbis/Wolfgang Kaehler; 137 Werner Forman Archives.

Conceived and produced by John Haywood and Simon Hall
Designed by Darren Bennett
Edited by Fiona Plowman
Picture research by Veneta Bullen
Illustration by Roger Hutchins
Cartography by Tim Aspden and the University of Southampton Cartography Unit

... a Haywood & Hall production for Penguin Books